Counseling Troubled Teens and Their Families

Counseling Troubled Teens and Their Families

A Handbook for Pastors and Youth Workers

Andrew J. Weaver, M.Th., Ph.D.
John D. Preston, Psy.D.
Leigh W. Jerome, Ph.D.

Abingdon Press
Nashville

COUNSELING TROUBLED TEENS AND THEIR FAMILIES
A HANDBOOK FOR PASTORS AND YOUTH WORKERS

This book is printed on elemental-chlorine—free paper.

Library of Congress Cataloging-in-Publication Data

Weaver, Andrew J., 1947–
    Counseling troubled teens and their families : a handbook for pastors and youthworkers / Andrew J. Weaver, John D. Preston, Leigh W. Jerome.
        p. cm.
    Includes bibliographical references and index.
    ISBN 0-687-08236-6
    1. Problem youth—Pastoral counseling of.   2. Church work with problem families.
I. Preston, John, 1950– II. Jerome, Leigh W., 1958– III. Title.
    BV4464.5 .W43 1999
259' .23—ddc21

                                                                                98-53614
                                                                                CIP

Scripture quotations, unless otherwise noted, are from the New Revised Standard Version of the Bible. Copyright © 1989 by the Division of Christian Education of the National Council of the Churches of Christ in the United States of America. All rights reserved.

Scripture quotations noted TEV are from Today's English Version—Old Testament: Copyright © American Bible Society 1976; New Testament: Copyright © American Bible Society 1966, 1971, 1976, 1992.

99 00 01 02 03 04 05 06 07 08—10 9 8 7 6 5 4 3 2

MANUFACTURED IN THE UNITED STATES OF AMERICA

To John and Hattie Tulloch with gratitude
—AJW

To the Reverend Larry George—JDP

To Stephen M. Korow—LWJ

Acknowledgments

We are very grateful to the Reverend Carolyn L. Stapleton for her invaluable help. Her exceptional editing and research skills added immeasurably to the quality and usefulness of the text. We are thankful for her ministry.

Thanks to Carrie O'Connor and Michelle Riekstins for their excellent help with the manuscript preparation.

Even youths will faint and be weary, and the young will fall exhausted;
but those who wait for the LORD shall renew their strength,
they shall mount up with wings like eagles,
they shall run and not be weary, they shall walk and not faint.

—Isaiah 40:30-31

Contents

Preface *by James M. Wall*   11

How to Use This Book   13

PART I: INTRODUCTION

Religion, Clergy, and the Mental Health Care of Adolescents   17
Adolescent Development   27
    Growing Up Healthy
    Unavoidable Obstacles
    Nurture or Harm
    Normal or Not

PART II: CASE STUDIES

Addictions
    Case   1: Alcohol and Drugs   47
    Case   2: Tobacco   59
    Case   3: Gambling   67

Violence
    Case   4: Abuse   73
    Case   5: Incest   81
    Case   6: Date Rape   89
    Case   7: Violence and Post-Traumatic Stress   97

Family Crises
    Case   8: Divorce   105
    Case   9: Stepparenting   115
    Case 10: Pregnancy   121
    Case 11: Runaways   131
    Case 12: AIDS/Sexually Transmitted Diseases   137
    Case 13: Chronic Medical Problems   147

Grief and Depression
    Case 14: Bereavement   155
    Case 15: Depression   163
    Case 16: Suicide   171

Other Disorders and Problems Facing Teens
Case 17: Eating Disorders   177
Case 18: Attention Deficit Disorder   185
Case 19: Conduct Disorder/Delinquency   193
Case 20: Anxiety Disorders   201
Case 21: Learning Disabilities   209
Case 22: Schizophrenia   217

PART III: COLLABORATION WITH MENTAL HEALTH SPECIALISTS:
    YOU ARE NOT ALONE

Collaboration with Mental Health Specialists   227
Glossary of Terms   233
Summary and Conclusions   239
Index   241

Preface

In her novel *The Good Mother*, Sue Miller writes one line that has stuck with me ever since I first read her heartrending story of a divorced mother who must decide how to react to an incident that occurred between her lover and her young daughter. In making that decision, the mother says, "Above all, we must keep the children safe." The incident between an adult and a child involved what may or may not have been an inappropriate sexual contact. Miller does not let the reader have an easy time of it. Is the man guilty of abuse? Or is it all a misunderstanding? Her conclusion is not simple, but her priorities are clear: keep the children safe.

The absolute importance of a child's emotional and physical safety is at the heart of the book you hold in your hands. Read it and both rejoice and weep over the wide-ranging collection of material and resources that are designed to serve religious professionals who work with teenagers. You will weep because this book reveals, starkly, that we are raising children in a dangerous environment, both in society and within the families to whom children and teenagers are entrusted. But you rejoice because there is help available, a great deal of help if only we will look in the right places.

The breakdown of the family structure, the greater availability of illegal substances with which teens can retreat from reality, and a general decline in values and moral principles in a society that celebrates personal pleasure over responsible behavior all contribute to the unsettling environment in which we raise our children. It is, of course, also an environment with remarkable potential for growth for the young with an abundance of opportunities to experience beauty and joy. The task facing religious professionals and parents is to help children and young people through the pitfalls that block them from finding that beauty and joy.

The enormous gift this book brings to professionals and to parents who struggle to raise families is the combination of a wealth of resource information coupled with case studies to which professionals and parents can relate.

There is the example of the victim of a date rape, a young girl who was pushed into a sexual encounter she did not desire. Overnight her behavior shifted from normal—which for a teenager is a mixture of happiness and grumpiness, often in the same instant—to that of a haunted soul, her spirit troubled and her parents confused. An alert clergyperson, as so often happens, is the first line of support to whom the young girl can turn. In the case cited in this book, the girl tries to deny the cause of her confusion and pain. She made a "mistake," but surely this "normal" behavior, as her peers might describe it, would not be enough to send her into such a tailspin. But it was, and it did. And here it is that the religious professional is so essential in responding to the clues that are not always so easy to read, especially by indifferent or unfeeling adults. Changed, erratic, or unruly behavior is a signal that the safe harbor of a child has been violated; such signals must not be ignored.

What the reader will find here are specific cases in which teens are seen struggling against a series of frightening attacks, sometimes from within their own families, as in the case of abuse or incest, and sometimes from outside the family, in the form of drug dealers or peers who persuade them that happiness is to be found in a bottle or in reckless behavior. There are also case studies of teens burdened with chemical imbalance or genetic malfunctions that lead to antisocial or dysfunctional behavior.

The journey from birth to adulthood takes one through a series of treacherous paths filled with emotional valleys and across experimental mountain peaks. This journey needs loving assistance from family and religious support groups. In this book you will discover not only examples of what to look for in dealing with troubled teens but also, in each section, a list of specific resources (complete with up-to-date Internet addresses) where assistance can be found.

Before I went to graduate school to study how to relate theology to psychology, I served as pastor of two small Methodist churches in Georgia. As I recall my daily visiting rounds with parishioners in those rural communities, I think back on how valuable this book would have been to me. The pastorate and, indeed, parenthood are lonely endeavors. We need as much help as we can find in our assignment to keep the children safe. This book will be indispensable in carrying out that task.

James M. Wall
Christian Century magazine
Chicago, Illinois

How to Use This Book

Counseling Troubled Teens and Their Families is designed to be a text for those in training for pastoral ministry and youth work, as well as a practical resource casebook for women and men involved in ministry with teens and their families. The book addresses mental health issues commonly found among young people. Part I offers information about the important role clergy serve in the mental health care of families with teens. This section spells out the need for special expertise of pastors and youth workers to recognize and address many of the problems teenagers and their families face. We also summarize the scientific evidence that nonpunitive, nurturing religious beliefs and practices serve both preventive and healing functions for teens and their families. Last, the section reviews some of the normal developmental issues teens and their families can expect to encounter as well as barriers to normal emotional development.

Part II is the heart of the book and is presented in a case study format using real-life situations while highlighting practical implications for pastoral care. The case studies reflect the current research on issues relevant to teens and their families. They are multidisciplinary in approach, integrating clinical knowledge in pastoral care, psychology, medicine, psychiatry, family therapy, nursing, and social work along with current scientific findings on the role of religion in mental health care. The book recognizes that the difficulties troubled teens and their families face do not stand in isolation from one another but are interrelated. For example, the case study on alcohol and drugs will also refer you to those on depression, suicide risk, violence, and delinquency.

The book is designed so that the reader may quickly and easily locate information about mental health issues for which young people and their families seek counsel. It is a practical, easy-to-use guide on how to assess problems and what to do about them. The table of contents lists twenty-two cases that exemplify common mental health issues experienced by teens and their families. Each case provides an example of a teenager who needs help with a specific problem. Included in each chapter is information about how a pastor or youth worker would assess the problem, what aspects of the case are most important, how to identify the major issues, specific directions about what the pastor and congregation can do, when to refer for professional assistance, and specific information about national resources that can provide help. National self-help organizations (often with toll-free numbers and Internet addresses) that provide information and support for teens and their families facing mental and emotional problems are identified for each issue addressed. Cross-cultural issues are identified and discussed as well. Technical terms that may be unfamiliar to the reader are defined in the Glossary.

The text is written for people of all faiths, with an appreciation for the richness of multicultural diversity in the religious community. The authors are people of faith with specialties in mental health. Dr. Weaver is a clinical psychologist, licensed marriage and family therapist, and ordained United Methodist minister who has served rural and urban parishes. Dr. Preston is a professor in clinical psychology and layman in The United Methodist Church. Dr. Jerome is a clinical psychologist, specializing in working with teenage girls and their families, who is interested in the intersection of religion and mental health.

PART ONE

Introduction

Religion, Clergy, and the Mental Health Care of Adolescents

Research over the last three decades has demonstrated that religious commitment has a positive influence on several key adolescent mental health problems. Pastors, priests, and rabbis work on the front lines of mental health care—especially among families with children. Clergy need to be informed about the ways religion is both preventive and healing for troubled teens and their families. This chapter reviews research showing that nurturing, nonpunitive religion has positive mental health benefits. We will recommend ways that clergy and the faith community can improve their ministry to youth.

The Adolescent Mental Health Crisis

U.S. News and World Report compared the top discipline problems reported by public school teachers in 1940 with those in 1990. The teachers in 1940 disciplined students for talking out of turn, chewing gum, making noise, running in the halls, cutting in line, dress-code violations, and littering. A mere two-and-a-half generations later, teachers listed the following problems: drug abuse, alcohol abuse, pregnancy, suicide, rape, robbery, and assault. Clergy and youth workers, like teachers, are now confronted by a set of issues dramatically different from those of past generations. Contemporary American teens live in a society with epidemic levels of alcohol and drug abuse, suicide, violence, pregnancy, child abuse, and destabilized families. Underlying these problems is an unconscionable rate of poverty. American youth are by far the poorest age-group, with 1 in 4 impoverished, double that of adults (U.S. Bureau of the Census 1994). The rate of youth poverty in the United States is higher than that of any other industrialized country (Males 1996).

Growing numbers of families with teenagers will be asking the clergy for counseling in the early part of the twenty-first century. Influenced primarily by the rising number of annual births since 1977 (sometimes called the baby-boom echo), the number of teenagers in the United States is increasing markedly. Student enrollment in grades 7–12 in 1990 was 15.3 million. That number increased to 17 million in 1995 and will further increase to 20 million by 2007, a rise of 17 percent from 1995 (National Center for Educational Statistics 1997).

Teens and Their Families Seek Pastoral Help

Clergy are a primary mental health resource for American families. In thirteen separate studies representing a diverse group of urban and rural clergy between 1979 and 1992, we found that those who seek pastoral counsel bring problems predominantly related to marriage, family, and parenting issues (Weaver, Koenig and Larson 1997). Wasman, Corradi, and Clemens (1979) report that 85 percent of parish-based clergy indicated that family problems were the most frequent and difficult counseling issues they were asked to address. Especially noted were marital conflict and problems with adolescent children. In a survey of 405 pastors in ten geographic regions of the United States, Benner (1992) found that 84 percent of the clergy acknowledged marriage and divorce as the most frequently presented problems, and about 1 in 3 pastoral counseling sessions involved problems with children.

Unfortunately, most surveyed pastors reported feeling inadequately prepared to address basic parent-child counseling issues (Virkler 1979). When experienced clergy were asked to suggest training areas in which they could use help, most of the topics involved marriage and parenting issues—alcohol and drug problems, divorce and separation, parenting problems, marital counseling, child or spouse abuse, remarriage/stepfamily issues, and premarital counseling (Ingram and Lowe 1989; Lowe 1986).

Teens rarely seek out a mental health specialist or pastoral help on their own. Most adolescents receive assistance from mental health professionals or clergy through their families' initiative. Only 1 percent of teenagers indicated they would find a pastor when faced with a serious personal problem, even though 4 out of 10 teens stated that their religious beliefs are very important to them. Teens report holding high regard for pastors, and more than 8 out of 10 teens give clergy high marks for service to the community (Gallup and Bezilla 1992). One of the primary reasons for writing this book is to give clergy and other religious workers information about mental health issues that will assist them in becoming more effective helpers for troubled teens and their families.

Although some congregations already reach out to troubled youth, there is an urgent need for additional efforts. In a study of 637 black churches in the northern United States, a full two-thirds offered some type of family-oriented community outreach program, although only about one-fourth of the churches had programs directed toward adolescents. Few churches addressed the most critical issues that concern teens and their families. A mere 4 percent of churches (27 of 637) had programs addressing youth substance abuse or human sexuality and teen pregnancy, while only 1 percent had programs addressing AIDS or other youth health-related issues. The researchers noted, "Generally, it was found that some of the most prominent issues facing black adolescents are not being adequately addressed by the black church." The churches that showed the most interest in youth groups were Methodist, middle-class, and more than 400 in membership (Rubin, Billingsley and Caldwell 1994).

Teens and Religion

Americans are a highly religious people, and based on the findings of a 1992 national Gallup poll, this will continue to be the case for the next generation. Large numbers of American teenagers continue to believe in God (95 percent), pray alone frequently (42 percent), read scriptures weekly (36 percent), belong to a church-sponsored youth group, and attend worship services weekly (45 percent). About half of all teens name a Protestant denomination as their religious preference, 3 out of 10 indicate the Roman Catholic Church by preference, and 2 percent identify with the Jewish or Mormon faiths. In a surprising finding, 27 percent of teens consider religious faith to be more important to them than it is to their parents, indicating that they are slightly more likely to attend church than adults (Gallup and Bezilla 1992).

Studies link religious involvement to many positive social benefits. Youth who practice their faith have more prosocial values and caring behaviors than those without religious involvement. Among the 3 teens in 4 who are members of a religious group, 62 percent are volunteers and 56 percent make charitable contributions. Among those who have no religious affiliation, just 44 percent are volunteers and only 25 percent are contributors (Gallup and Bezilla 1992). Other researchers have found that the importance of religion and church attendance is associated with concern for the poor and helping behaviors (Benson, Williams, and Johnson 1987).

Religious involvement also helps teens reduce "at-risk" behaviors such as alcohol and drug use, antisocial behavior, premature sexual involvement, unsafe sexual behaviors, and suicide (Donahue and Benson 1995)—many of the negative behaviors about which adolescents express the greatest concern. When teens are asked "What is the biggest problem facing people your age?" drug and alcohol use accounts for nearly half the responses (47 percent), followed by peer pressure (15 percent), AIDS (11 percent), teenage pregnancy (9 percent), sex (6 percent), crime and teen gangs (6 percent), and school problems (5 percent). Somewhat surprisingly, only 2 percent of the adolescents indicated that getting along with their parents was their biggest problem (Gallup and Bezilla 1992).

Alcohol and Drug Use

Teens cite alcohol and drug use as their greatest problem. In spite of the illegality of selling alcoholic beverages to minors in all fifty states, it has become the drug of choice for most teenagers. In 1995 the National Institute on Drug Abuse found that 80 percent of high school seniors had tried alcohol and almost 30 percent had participated in binge drinking (having five or more drinks in a row) in the preceding 2 weeks. The rate of binge drinking among eighth graders was almost 15 percent. A large number of high school seniors had tried other illicit drugs: marijuana (42 percent), inhalants (17 percent), LSD (12 percent), and cocaine (6 percent). This is of particular concern when one realizes that the greatest risk of developing a long-term substance abuse problem occurs in the teenage years (Burke et al. 1990).

A troubling 3 in 10 adolescents indicate that alcohol is "a cause of trouble in their family," while about 1 in 10 reported a family troubled by drug use (Gallup and Bezilla 1992). Teen drinking may be related to school problems. Gallup found that those who feared they would not graduate from high school more frequently used alcohol than those confident of graduation. Gallup also found that teenage church attenders were about twice as unlikely to use alcohol as their peers who had not attended church recently. This survey supports the social benefits of religion in limiting and preventing drug use (Gallup and Bezilla 1992).

Numerous additional studies over the past three decades substantiate the Gallup Youth Survey results that found alcohol and drug use decreases among teens who have a religious commitment. These studies have found that high religious involvement is a powerful preventive of social problems among adolescents, including the use of alcohol and other substances. For example, among Caucasian high school students in Atlanta, Georgia, those who attend church frequently were less likely to drink alcohol (5 percent versus 21 percent) or use other drugs (12 percent versus 21 percent) than those who attended church infrequently. These statistical relationships remained after controlling for the effects of family factors such as closeness to mother, frequency of disagreements with parents, and use of drugs by friends (Haraway, Elifson and Petersen 1984). Canadian high school students not affiliated with a religious group were three to seven times more likely to be heavy drinkers than religious students who attended church at least five times a year. Again, the preventive value of religion persisted among the students even after considering parental control and support (Schlegel and Sanborn 1979). Arizona high school students who were not religious were almost twice as likely to use marijuana as were their religious counterparts (Hardert and Dowd 1994).

A study of 326 Mexican American youth in a drug abuse intervention program found that both family support and religious involvement were significantly related to reduction of problem behavior such as drug and alcohol use, school problems, and legal involvement (Barrett, Simpson and Lehman 1988). When considering the risk factors for crack cocaine use among Miami, Florida, adolescents, researchers found that religious involvement was a strong predictor of lowered crack cocaine use after controlling for ten separate factors, including family background, structure, and relationships; peer associations and influences; and school history (Yarnold and Patterson 1995). In Great Britain, a study involving 4,753 adolescents found that religious belief and practice had a strong association with a young person's attitudes toward the impropriety of substance abuse, including the use of marijuana, alcohol, glue, heroin, butane gas, and tobacco (Francis and Mullen 1993).

Sex, Religion, and Teens

In 1983 when teens were asked, "What do you feel is the biggest problem facing people your age?" no teenagers answered either AIDS or teenage pregnancy and less than 0.5 percent answered sex. One decade later, 11 percent of adolescents answered AIDS, 9 percent answered teenage pregnancy, and 6 percent gave sex as the problem—indicating that 1 in 4 teens think these sex-related issues are the biggest difficulties they face (Gallup and Bezilla 1992). This shift in teen problems to sexual issues is highlighted by the fact that several hundred thousand girls under the age of 18 give birth each year in the United States.

Several negative consequences are associated with adolescent sexual intercourse and teen pregnancy. Early sexual intercourse predisposes youth to subsequent sexual behavior with a large number of partners and sexual partners older than themselves (Koyle et al. 1989). Sexually active teens are more likely to be involved in delinquent behavior and to use drugs and alcohol (Elliott and Morse 1989). Teenage parents are more likely to drop out of school, creating long-term educational and economic disadvantages. A high number of teen pregnancies end in abortion, which may lead to psychological consequences, especially for younger teens (White and DeBlassie 1992).

Research has consistently shown the constraining effects of religious involvement on premature sexual behavior among adolescents. Lower rates of sexual intercourse, fewer sexual partners, and more negative attitudes toward premarital sexual activity have been found in teens who regularly attend church and believe religion is important in their lives than in those who do not. It has been estimated that adolescents involved in religious life may be 50 percent less likely to engage in sexual intercourse than their nonreligious peers (Spilka, Hood, and Gorsuch 1985). However, one study indicated that sexually active churchgoing teenage girls are less likely to use contraceptives than those who do not attend church, presenting greater risk of unsafe sexual behavior (Studer and Thornton 1987). When teens are asked if their church or synagogue is doing a good job fighting AIDS, about half say "good" or "excellent" and the other half say "fair" or "poor" (Gallup and Bezilla 1992).

Delinquency and Teen Violence

In the 1992 Gallup Youth Survey, 1 in 4 students indicated that they feared for their physical safety while at school. Seven percent of teens reported having been physically assaulted at school, 15 percent of students had money stolen, and 14 percent had personal property vandalized on campus. An alarming 28 percent of the polled students indicated that peers bringing guns and knives to school is a serious problem.

Teen fears about violence and crime are supported by the facts. Homicide is the third leading cause of death among children and youth under the age of 21 (National Center for Health Statistics 1993). The Centers for Disease Control reported that in 1991, 4 percent of all high school students and 21 percent of African American teenagers had carried a firearm in the past month (O'Donnell 1995). About 17 percent of arrests for violent crimes are of individuals age 18 or younger (Federal Bureau of Investigation 1992). In an inner-city population of primarily African American children (ages 7–18), researchers found an alarmingly high 85 percent had witnessed and 7 out of 10 had been victims of a violent act. Not surprisingly, almost 1 out of 3 of the inner-city children were found to be suffering the symptoms of severe psychological trauma similar to those found in combat veterans (Fitzpatrick and Boldizar 1993).

Teen delinquency is multifaceted. Many factors have been examined in research to predict the risk of antisocial behavior among youth, including family stability, peer relationships, school environment, and religious involvement. There is mounting evidence to support the case that religious practice and strength of religion in the family are inversely associated with antisocial behavior in teens (Evans et al. 1996). Tittle and Welch (1983) reviewed sixty-five studies on the relationship between religion and delinquency and found that in 85 percent of the studies, religious youth were less likely to have antisocial behaviors than their nonreligious counterparts. For example, teens in Atlanta who attended church were found to be less likely to engage in delinquent behaviors such as skipping school, using force to obtain money from others, car theft, driving without a license, coming home after midnight, running away from home, carrying a weapon, fighting, or destroying property (Higgins and Albrecht 1977). In a more recent national study, religious involvement among youth was associated with less likelihood of trouble with the police, fighting, vandalism, gang involvement, physically hurting someone, and use of a weapon to steal (Donahue and Benson 1995). There is some evidence that in regions of the United States where religion is the most widespread, the positive effects of religion on delinquent behavior is greatest (Stark 1996).

Suicide and Teens

Suicide is the second leading cause of death among children and youth under the age of 21, and 73 percent of all suicides of persons ages 15 to 24 are of white males. For 15- to 19-year-olds, the rate of suicide in 1950 was only 2.7 per 100,000. A mere two generations later, in 1990, the rate had grown to 11.1, an increase of more than 400 percent (National Center for Health Statistics 1993). Experts estimate that for each completed suicide there are 50 to 100 adolescent suicide attempts. The Gallup Youth Survey found that an alarming 6 teenagers in 10 knew someone who had taken his or her life.

Research indicates that the risk of taking one's life is lowered for frequent church attendees across the life span (Lester 1991; Weaver and Koenig 1996). Nurturing religion provides a buffer against hardships and losses, diminishes isolation, and encourages hopefulness while offering an active support system. In a study of 437 high school students, those who did not attend church were at a greater risk of self-harm (Conrad 1991).

Adolescent suicide has been linked to three key factors: depression, substance abuse, and antisocial behavior (Brent et al. 1988). Religion lowers the risk of all three factors. Among high school students of both sexes in Texas, infrequent church attenders with low spiritual support had the highest rates of depression; and these rates were often measured at clinically significant levels (Wright, Frost and Wisecarver 1993).

Suicide prevention appears to be an area where faith communities have been involved, according to teens. In the Gallup Youth Survey, more than 1 teen in 4 (28 percent) indicated that their local religious group had suicide prevention services they could use, such as discussion groups on the topic and counseling services. Most surveyed youth felt that the religious community could do more by providing increased family counseling services (79 percent), offering hot-line phone services to those contemplating suicide (77 percent), or having more qualified adults with whom troubled teens could discuss their problems (84 percent).

Summary

If commitment to nonpunitive, nurturing religious beliefs and activities reduces alcohol and drug use, premature sexual behavior, depression, suicide, and antisocial behavior—as well as increasing prosocial behaviors and enhancing positive coping strategies among teens—then religious communities are crucial resources to help meet emotional needs of adolescents and their families. Whether churches, synagogues, and mosques will be prepared to meet the increasing psychological needs of teens and their families in the twenty-first century remains an unanswered question. The facts underscore the need for clergy and other religious workers to learn how to competently recognize mental health problems in teenagers, to train members in their faith community to provide emotional support to adolescents and their families, to find what community resources are available to assist teens, and to identify when to make referrals for them to professional mental health help. Greater cooperation between secular and religious groups working with teens and increased research to further understanding of the role of religion and spirituality in adolescent mental health care is a necessity.

References

Barrett, M.E., Simpson, D.D. and Lehman, W.E.K. (1988). Behavioral changes of adolescents in drug abuse intervention programs. *Journal of Clinical Psychology, 44(3).* 461-473.

Benner, D.G. (1992). *Strategic Pastoral Counseling: A Short-Term Structure Model.* Grand Rapids, MI: Baker Press.

Benson, P.L., Williams, D. and Johnson A. (1987). *The Quicksilver Years: The Hopes and Fears of Early Adolescence.* San Francisco: Harper and Row.

Brent, D.A., Perper, J.A., Goldstein, C.E., Kolko, D.J., Allan, M.J., Allman, C.J. and Zelenak, J.P. (1988). Risk factors for adolescent suicide: a comparison of adolescent suicide victims with suicide inpatients. *Archives of General Psychiatry, 45.* 581-588.

Burke, K.E., Burke, J.D., Regier D.A. and Rea, D.S. (1990). Age at onset of selected mental disorders in five community populations. *Archives of General Psychiatry, 47.* 511-518.

Conrad, N. (1991). Where do they turn: Social support systems of suicidal high school adolescents. *Journal of Psychosocial Nursing, 29(3).* 14-20.

Donahue, M.J. and Benson, P.L. (1995). Religion and the well-being of adolescents. *Journal of Social Issues, 51(2).* 145-160.

Elliott, D.S. and Morse, B.J. (1989). Delinquency and drug use as risk factors in teenage sexual activity. *Youth and Society, 21(1).* 32-57.

Evans, T.D., Cullen, F.T., Burton, V.S., Dunaway, R.G., Payne, G.L. and Kethineni, S.R. (1996). Religion, social bonds, and delinquency. *Deviant Behavior, 17.* 43-70.

Federal Bureau of Investigation. (1992). *Uniform Crime Reports for the United States, 1991.* Washington, DC: U.S. Department of Justice.

Fitzpatrick, K.M. and Boldizar, J.P. (1993). The prevalence and consequences of exposure to violence among African American youth. *The Journal of the American Academy of Child and Adolescent Psychiatry, 32.* 424-430.

Francis, L.J. and Mullen, K. (1993). Religiosity and attitudes toward drug use among 13–15-year-olds in England. *Addiction, 88.* 665-672.

Gallup, G.H. and Bezilla, R. (1992). *The Religious Life of Young Americans.* Princeton, NJ: The George Gallup International Institute.

Haraway, C.K., Elifson, K.W. and Petersen, D.M.M. (1984). Religious involvement and drug use among urban adolescents. *Journal for the Scientific Study of Religion, 23(2).* 109-128.

Hardert, R.A. and Dowd, T.J. (1994). Alcohol and marijuana use among high school and college students in Phoenix, Arizona: A test of Kandel's socialization theory. *The International Journal of Addictions, 29(7).* 887-912.

Higgins, P.L. and Albrecht, G.L. (1977). Hellfire and delinquency revisited. *Social Forces, 55.* 952-957.

Hohmann, A.A. and Larson, D.B. (1993). Psychiatric factors predicting use of clergy. In E.L. Worthington Jr. (Ed.). *Psychotherapy and Religious Values* (pp.71-84). Grand Rapids, MI: Baker Book House.

Ingram, B.L. and Lowe, D. (1989). Counseling activities and referral practices of rabbis. *Journal of Psychology and Judaism, 13.* 133-148.

Koyle, P., Jensen, L., Olsen, J. and Cundick, B. (1989). Comparison of sexual behavior among adolescents having an early, middle, and late first intercourse experience. *Youth and Society, 20(4).* 461-475.

Lester, D. (1991). Social correlates of youth suicide rates in the United States. *Adolescence, 26(101).* 55-58.

Lowe, D.W. (1986). Counseling activities, and referral practices of ministers. *Journal of Psychology and Christianity, 5.* 22-29.

Males, M.A. (1996). *The Scapegoat Generation.* Monroe, ME: Common Courage Press.

National Center for Educational Statistics. (1997). *Projections of Educational Statistics to 2007.* (NCES97-382). Washington, DC: NCES.

National Center for Health Statistics. (1993). *Vital statistics report.* Hyattsville, MD: NCHS.

O'Donnell, C.R. (1995). Firearm deaths among children and youth. *American Psychologist, 50.* 771-776.

Rubin, R.H., Billingsley, A. and Caldwell, C.H. (1994). The role of the black church in working with black adolescents. *Adolescence, 29(114).* 251-266.

Schlegel, R.P. and Sanborn, M.D. (1979). Religious affiliation and adolescent drinking. *Journal of Studies on Alcohol, 40(7).* 693-703.

Spilka, B., Hood, R.W. and Gorsuch, R.L. (1985). *The Psychology of Religion: An Empirical Approach.* Englewood, NJ: Prentice-Hall.

Stark, R. (1996). Religion as context: Hellfire and delinquency one more time. *Sociology of Religion, 57(2).* 163-173.

Studer, M. and Thornton, A. (1987). Adolescent religiosity and contraceptive usage. *Journal of Marriage and the Family, 49.* 117-128.

Tittle, C.R. and Welch, M.R. (1983). Religiosity and delinquency: Toward a contingent theory of constraining effects. *Social Forces, 61.* 653-683.

U.S. Bureau of the Census. (1994). *Poverty in the United States, 1992.* Washington, DC: U.S. Department of Commerce.

Virkler, H.A. (1979). Counseling demands, procedures, and preparation of parish ministers: A descriptive study. *Journal of Psychology and Theology, 7.* 271-280.

Wasman, M., Corradi, R.B. and Clemens, N.A. (1979). In-depth continuing education for clergy in mental health: Ten years of a large scale program. *Pastoral Psychology, 27.* 251-259.

Weaver, A.J. and Koenig, H.G. (1996). Elderly suicide, mental health professionals and the clergy: a need for clinical collaboration, training and research. *Death Studies, 20(5).* 495-508.

Weaver, A.J., Koenig, H.G. and Larson, D.B. (1997). Marital and family therapists and the clergy: a need for clinical collaboration, training and research. *Journal of Marital and Family Therapy, 23(1).* 13-25.

White, S.D. and DeBlassie, R.R. (1992). Adolescent sexual behavior. *Adolescence, 27(105).* 183-191.

Wright, L.S., Frost, C.J. and Wisecarver, S.J. (1993). Church attendance, meaningfulness of religion, and depression symptomatology among adolescents. *Journal of Youth and Adolescence, 22(5).* 559-568.

Yarnold, B.M. and Patterson, V. (1995). Factors correlated with adolescents' use of crack in public schools. *Psychological Reports, 76.* 467-474.

Growing Up Healthy

By the middle of the twentieth century, a good deal of writing and research in psychology and child development had begun to point a finger of blame toward bad parenting as the cause of mental illness, substance abuse, violence, and any number of social and emotional problems. Certainly, emotionally toxic interactions with parents can cause harm to developing children. However, this early literature did not fully understand the wide spectrum of factors that could contribute to emotional disturbances in young people. Also, the dominant perspective of research focused on illness, with little attention paid to healthy factors. Only recently have mental health professionals taken a closer look at those conditions and factors that play a role in healthy emotional development.

Of course mental health professionals are parents too, and we suspect that many breathed a personal sigh of relief when noted child developmental specialist D. W. Winnicott proclaimed in 1965 that good emotional health could be promoted in children by simply being a "good enough" parent. Not a super parent, but a good enough parent.

Today, most experts acknowledge that for almost all families, life is often a challenge. No one lives in a stress-free or idyllic environment. All parents have human limitations and make mistakes. A bumper sticker says, "I'm dysfunctional... You're dysfunctional." To a degree this seems to be the case. Maybe a corollary should be, "I'm human... You're human."

It is clear that certain kinds of early life experiences are important for healthy emotional development. Conversely, particular kinds of experiences and environments can be harmful. In this section we will touch briefly on those factors that are generally agreed upon to be important elements in a positive, growth-promoting family atmosphere. The next two sections will examine particular elements in families that *may* contribute to emotional problems in children and adolescents.

The Basic Ingredients

We human beings share a set of common fundamental needs. These include the following: needs for basic physical survival (warmth, food, adequate sleep, etc.); the need to feel reasonably safe and secure; the need to feel valued and loved by others; the need for making and maintaining positive connections with others, including the need to belong and to feel attached; the need for some degree of predictability in life (a common source of considerable stress is life circumstances that are either chronically chaotic and unpredictable or events that suddenly catch people off guard and unprepared); and the need to feel a sense of self-worth (that you are a decent person and acceptable in the eyes of others and God). Beyond these *basic needs* are what are often referred to as *higher needs*, which may include: the need to make a difference in the world, the need to pursue a meaningful calling or mission, the need for a personal relationship with God, and the development of one's spiritual self.

A family that responds to fundamental needs stands the best chance of contributing to positive emotional development in children. First and foremost, such an environment provides an atmosphere of deep love and respect for the child. Not that children are continuously showered with love and affection, but rather that the overall day-in, day-out experience is that of feeling valued and cherished. Youngsters growing up in these families come to believe that they matter.

A second characteristic is that children in healthy family environments experience the acknowledgment of their feelings and needs. "Good enough" parents naturally sense when youngsters are in distress; take their feelings seriously; and try to intervene by talking to their children, holding them, listening, and helping them to find ways to cope or to solve problems.

Children have varying abilities to take on tasks, depending on their age, their past experiences, strengths, and their level of emotional maturity. Good parents are able to give their children age-appropriate tasks while being sensitive to their realistic limits. The message transmitted is, "I believe in you....I trust that you will find ways to handle certain life demands and to continually grow. I also know that youngsters have limits too, and I'll make sure that expectations are reasonable and realistic." This represents an important balancing act between encouraging growth, on the one hand, while at the same time being sensitive to the fact that children do have limits, that there simply are things they are not yet ready to handle.

Good parents are able to appreciate, encourage, and support the emergence and growth of the child's unique *self*. This may be manifest in the child's developing abilities, special interests, and talents. Almost inevitably, it will show itself as youngsters speak out, sometimes in ways that parents do not welcome with joy, saying "No!" or "I don't want to do what you say" or "I disagree." Again this requires a balancing act for parents—trying to foster the development of appropriate and socially approved behavior while also helping the child to find his or her own voice and unique identity.

Good parents not only teach, but more important, model positive values and beliefs. Such values vary from one culture to another, but generally are defined by the desire to avoid harming others and to work for goodness in the world.

Good parents help children to develop effective coping skills so that they can make it in the real world—such skills include, among others, how to get along with people and how to resolve conflicts. In the words of child development specialist Margaret Mahler, good parents provide "roots and wings" by offering a base of love, acceptance, nurturing, and encouragement to grow and to become who one is. Youngsters blessed with this kind of upbringing know they have a "home" (an emotional place of belonging, even after they move out on their own) and a solid enough sense of self to enable them to leave the nest and venture out into the world.

A number of factors can, however, set the stage for developmental problems. These can best be seen as coming from three sources: *nature, nurture,* and *unavoidable circumstances.*

Unavoidable Obstacles

Many young people experience significant emotional and behavioral problems caused by abnormalities of biology. We would like to address this issue briefly in this section and focus on some specific problems in later sections of the book.

President George Bush rightly declared that the 1990s would be known as the "decade of the brain." Recent years have witnessed an explosion of new technologies and new discoveries in the neurosciences.

It is now abundantly clear that a number of emotional and psychological problems can be traced to disorders of brain functioning. A classic example is that of schizophrenia. In the 1950s and 1960s a popular theory that attempted to explain the causes of schizophrenia focused on the role of disturbed, chaotic parenting. It was popular then to refer to "schizophreni-genic mothers." These were seen as emotionally toxic parents who, over a period of years, raised children in a certain way that predisposed them to developing a severe psychotic illness.

Schizophrenia affects 1 percent of the population, and during the baby boomer years many thousands of parents of psychotic children and adolescents felt guilty for causing the terrible suffering seen in schizophrenia. Thirty years later, it is widely understood that schizophrenia is a neurological disease. Some parents of schizophrenic people may have emotional problems, but any *blame* should be aimed at disordered brain chemistry, not at these unfortunate parents.

Likewise, a number of emotional problems are now understood to be caused either by brain dysfunction or at least partly attributed to biological causes. The list includes: attention deficit disorder (ADD or hyperactivity), severe mood disorders (such as depression and bipolar/manic-depressive illness), some forms of substance abuse, obsessive-compulsive disorder, and some types of anxiety disorders.

Beyond these specific problems, it is likely that some variations in temperament and personality can be traced to subtle differences in brain chemistry, for example, emotional sensitivity, impulsivity, irritability, and the tendency for moodiness.

Many children who come into the world with biologically based emotional problems or tendencies are born into healthy, loving families. Yet, despite very good care and ample doses of nurturing, the children develop psychological or behavioral problems ranging from subtle to severe. All pastors will encounter situations where a youngster is clearly suffering from an emotional disorder, yet when meeting with the parents it becomes obvious that it is *not* a disturbed or dysfunctional family. All good parents care deeply about their children, and many are prone to blame themselves. When emotional problems are caused by biological factors, it is very important to help educate the parents (and sometimes the teenagers, too) so that they have a more realistic understanding of the causes, thereby reducing or eliminating unnecessary guilt.

A number of common problems seen in children and teens also can be traced to biologic roots. These include: chronic physical illness (such as asthma or epilepsy); learning disabilities; mental retardation; physical handicaps; sensory impairment; deformities; and other physical features such as obesity, severe dermatological conditions, and unattractiveness—all of which have significant social and emotional consequences. Growing up is hard under normal conditions, and teens with these limitations face special challenges. School failure and social rejection are common experiences for such youngsters, even for those who grow up in loving homes.

Unavoidable Circumstances

This list is also long and includes: the death of a loved one; parental divorce or separation; parents who suffer from major physical or mental illness; severe financial strain or abject poverty; social conditions, such as racial or ethnic discrimination; natural disasters; and random violence. Obviously, children do not have control over such conditions. These terrible events can pierce into the heart of any family. Bad things do happen to good people.

One reason for discussing the role of nature and unavoidable life events is because of the widespread tendency of people to engage in judgment and blame. Troubled families, regardless of the source of stress, are often looked down upon by others. Even today there are those who assume that if bad events occur to people, somehow they must have deserved them. People who are the target of blame often sense this. They see it in others' eyes; they feel it as people back away and manage to avoid them. It becomes fuel for gossip fires. The experience of feeling judged never promotes healing.

Many people also engage in ruthless self-criticism. When facing difficult times, one of the single most destructive forces interfering with coping and emotional healing is harsh self-blame and criticism. A part of what must be done to help people during times of crisis is to reduce self-blame and promote a sense of self-compassion.

Nurture or Harm

Later chapters will focus on specific emotional problems and stressful life circumstances. Here, however, we will examine a number of unfortunately common, painful childhood experiences that in a general way characterize the day-to-day atmosphere in a family. These circumstances may develop in the wake of tremendous family stress. Sometimes they can be understood as stemming from emotional problems in one or both parents. Many times the conditions outlined below become fixed, persistent styles of interaction that may become extraordinarily difficult to change.

As pastors or religious workers, you look into the most personal corners of your parishioners' lives. Occasionally you will see interactions and events that will be personally disturbing, tragic, or shocking. At times, such circumstances can only be seen as manifestations of *people's inhumanity to others* or even as expressions of evil. However, in most situations if one looks closely, listens carefully, and is open to understanding (rather than judging), it becomes clear that people are simply doing their best to survive. What at first glance may look like cruelty, harshness, or insensitivity often can be seen from a different perspective once one knows the context. Many parents are under incredible stress; sometimes they are suffering from chemical addictions or serious mental illnesses themselves.

When medical and mental health professionals witness child abuse or neglect they are required to take action to stop such abuse (in most states this includes the mandate to report it to appropriate authorities). In a concrete way these professionals are saying, "This must stop!" However, there are ways to do this that are based in anger and disgust, and there are ways this can be done in the service of love, caring, and concern.

Let's begin by taking a look at the nature of stress and a handful of common situations that you are certain to encounter.

When It Hurts to Grow Up

In 1989, according to estimates by the National Association for Prevention of Child Abuse, 2.4 million children were referred to child protective services agencies in the United States (49 percent for neglect,

27 percent for physical abuse, 16 percent for sexual abuse, and 8 percent for emotional abuse). The 2.4 million are only those cases reported. Importantly, the available evidence suggests that false allegations of child abuse/neglect are infrequent—only 8 percent according to one major study. Clearly many children are abused and/or neglected and never come to the attention of authorities. A number of studies estimate that as many as 33 percent of all women and 1 of every 6 or 7 men were sexually molested in some manner as children or adolescents. Some authorities claim these staggering figures represent an underestimate of the actual incidence of child abuse/neglect.[1]

How Harmful Is Childhood Trauma?

Emotionally damaging experiences take a heavy toll on a child. The amount of harm depends on a number of factors. We would like to briefly highlight the most important of these conditions by posing the following four questions:

Is the painful event a single blow or a recurring/pervasive experience? Unless extremely severe, single-blow traumas generally do not change the course of a person's emotional life. In contrast, recurring or pervasive experiences gradually shape a child's emerging personality. If day-in, day-out experiences are negative, the painful effects can be deeply etched into a child's view of the world, her attitudes toward others, and enduring beliefs about herself.

Does the painful event also undercut or destroy a child's primary support network? For example, sexual abuse by a neighborhood boy, although traumatizing to a child, is probably less damaging than molestation by a parent. In the latter case, in addition to the severe emotional injury of the molestation, the child also is faced with a situation in which the primary giver of care and protection has now become a victimizer. The youngster's most natural source of safety and nurturance is no longer available and is indeed the *cause* of extreme emotional distress.

How traumatic is the painful event? It would be convenient to be able to rate severity of events in a clear, quantifiable manner such as is done in rating the intensity of earthquakes. However, what matters most is not the event itself but how the child perceives the event. A 7.0 earthquake centered in downtown San Francisco is surely more destructive than another 7.0 earthquake occurring in a remote wilderness area. To use an example offered by child therapist and author James Garbarino, children seriously hurt in auto accidents or sporting events experience much less emotional trauma than if the same degree of physical injury were inflicted by an abusing parent (1986).

---

1. This section has been adapted from *Growing Beyond Emotional Pain: Action Plans for Healing* (1993) by John Preston, reproduced by permission of Impact Publishers, Inc., P.O. Box 1094. San Luis Obispo, CA 93406. Further reproduction is prohibited.

When we examine types of emotional pain later in this chapter, bear in mind that there are varying degrees of severity associated with painful life events and that determining severity is often incredibly difficult. There are undoubtedly some rare children who live through hellish experiences and bear few scars. At the same time, some more sensitive youngsters will experience fairly mild levels of neglect as being overwhelmingly traumatic. The magnitude and meaning of emotional stress are *always* based on the child's perception.

What resources does the child have to turn to in times of distress? Intact families, the provision of open expression of feelings and nurturance, and appropriate role models of healthy emotional functioning can make a crucial difference as a child attempts to heal and recover following major stressful events.

Traumas That Derail Human Attachment

Some types of emotional trauma have an impact on the human tendency to seek out connections with others. The desire to bond with others—to reach out for support, help, and companionship—is part of our emotional hardware, our "psychological makeup." Psychiatrist Karen Horney called it the tendency to "move toward others." It takes something powerful and devastating to extinguish this human tendency, but *extremely* traumatic experiences early in life will sometimes derail the natural tendency for attachment. Horney described two outcomes of such painful experiences: the first is "moving away from others." There are people who, at a deep level, may want contact with others, but are extremely afraid of intimacy, openness, or attachment. The psychological literature describes them as "avoidant personalities." Even more severely damaged people are "schizoid personalities" who may have had even the tiniest flicker of need for human connections totally extinguished.

Unfortunately, some of the same kinds of horrible experiences early in life that lead to individuals who are emotionally detached from others may, in some cases, provoke the development of a style Horney calls "moving against." These people have decided at a deep level that "people are no good and can only serve one purpose: to meet my needs." Narcissistic individuals, as they are called, treat others like a can of soda—they suck them dry and, without a second thought, cast them aside. Psychopaths are the most malignant version of this style. These people thrive on creating pain, and they derive enjoyment from hurting others. Such individuals in relatively benign forms are con artists; in the extreme, they commit violent rape, murder, and sadistic torture. It should be noted that, although these types of personality disorders can develop as a result of extremely painful life experiences, some theorists suggest that these behavior patterns may be due to inherent temperamental and/or biochemical factors.

Here is a final question to add to the list of four above: *To what extent have childhood traumas extinguished the desire to move toward others?* During very stressful times, meaningful contact with another human being can be a major component of successful coping and emotional healing. In a trusting and supportive human encounter—with a relative, a friend, a pastor, or a therapist—people can find their best chance of movement toward emotional health. When the desire to connect has been totally lost, the prospects for emotional healing are extremely poor.

Is It Abuse . . . or Not?

A multitude of potentially damaging events befall children. Distinctions among blatant child abuse, mental injury, and neglect are often blurry and poorly defined. Child protective agencies may be at a loss to clearly identify cases of emotional abuse that leave invisible injuries to the heart and the spirit of a child with no physical bruises. Garbarino and his colleagues have suggested the term "psychological maltreatment" to describe a wide array of experiences that damage youngsters. Some types of psychological maltreatment are of an active nature—willful, intentional abuse of children. Others are more passive (for example, a child is ignored) or quite unintentional (for example, a child is emotionally neglected because her mother is bedridden with a severe illness). This discussion will focus on the nature and meaning of the events, rather than attempting to blame or judge, although some types of abuse clearly are the result of cruel, intentional brutality. It should be borne in mind that, although certain factors (such as a parent's mental illness or alcoholism) may play a role in contributing to child abuse and may be at least partial *explanations*, they do not in any way constitute *excuses* for such mistreatment of children.

The following section presents ten categories of psychological maltreatment, the first five of which have been suggested by Garbarino and his colleagues. It is important to emphasize that in all families, even those considered to be healthy and growth-promoting, occasional emotional distress is the rule. Even the best of parents are from time to time preoccupied—ignoring their children's needs, stressed-out, irritable, and prone to making blunders in dealing with the difficult job of raising children. Occasional times of emotional upset do not constitute maltreatment or abuse. Youngsters must grow up knowing that life is not always rosy, and learning how to live through stressful times is an essential experience as a child comes to develop coping skills and emotional resilience. Maltreatment occurs when one of two conditions are met. First, it is "a concerted attack by an adult on a child's development of self and social competence, a *pattern* of psychologically destructive behavior" (Garbarino, Guttman and Seeley 1986). The key word is *pattern*. It is typically ongoing mistreatment; if a single blow, it is a tremendously intense or severe event. Second, there is a significant lack of essential nurturing, support, respect, guidance, and protection provided by a parent.

Types of Psychological Maltreatment

Rejecting: The youngster is actively shunned. The parent refuses to acknowledge the child's worth and the legitimacy of the child's needs. Parents may refuse to touch or hold their offspring; they may exclude children from family activities or fail to acknowledge accomplishments. In more severe instances, there can be clear-cut emotional abandonment or a strong message given to the child, "I hate you."

Seventeen-year-old Gretchen was at a loss to understand why she felt so terribly depressed throughout her childhood. She searched her memories and was totally unable to recall any episodes of physical abuse, sexual molestation, or severe loss. However, very gradually she realized that in her apparently normal, happy, conventional family, she had continuously felt left out. During talks with her youth minister, she gradually came to understand that, in a very deep way, her parents hated her. They took no interest in her schoolwork, they belittled her art, and they repeatedly told her she was "too sensitive" and "too emotional." Gretchen developed a pervasive sense of worthlessness and unlovability. Until she put the pieces together, she could not understand the nature of her despair.

People often think they must be able to point toward very clear and concrete signs of abuse (for example, physical bruises or sexual violation) to legitimate feeling bad. Profound rejection, belittling, and harsh criticism can be tremendously painful experiences for a young child. The poet Robert Bly has said:

> Verbal batterings are injuries. Blows that lacerate self-esteem, puncture our sense of grandeur, pollute enthusiasm, poison and desolate confidence, give the soul black-and-blue marks, undermining and degrading...these all make a defilement. They damage and do harm.

Ignoring: Rather than an active process, as is the case with rejecting, ignoring has more to do with unavailability; it is passive and neglectful. Ignoring can occur for a number of reasons. In some instances, a child may be temperamentally quiet, passive, and nondemanding. Such children have the same inner needs for love and closeness as do others, but their needs are less evident—they are less inclined to demand attention. They may seem relatively content and thus can fairly easily fade into the background, becoming increasingly less a part of the parents' lives.

Sharon explains, "My mother often says, 'In a minute.' I'll go to her, she'll wave me off...the minute never comes. She is just so busy. I think sometimes she feels guilty. She'll say, 'I'm sorry...I know I need to spend more time with you.' But she doesn't. It's just incredibly lonely."

At times, significant physical or mental illness can result in a parent being unavailable emotionally for prolonged periods of time. Some families are so stressed by life events (for example, extreme poverty) that parents expend all their energy simply coping with day-to-day survival. Children are told to stay in their rooms or are left for hours sitting before a television set. Ignoring is also seen in homes where parents are primarily occupied with their careers or other life interests, taking little time for their children. Youngsters in these families often grow up feeling worthless—"worth less" than their parents' careers, according to therapist/author John Bradshaw.

Ignoring also occurs if a parent simply fails to notice when a child needs help. The child may have academic problems, may be hurt or abused by a sibling, or may be in a state of depression—it all goes unnoticed. In many homes where one parent is abusive toward the child, the other parent may be either uninvolved or oblivious to the abuse and unwilling to take a stand to stop it. At times, a sibling sexually molests a brother or sister, unnoticed by parents. In this case, *two* children are being ignored: the violated child and the one doing the molesting. These children often aren't simply "bad" or "perverted," but suffer severe emotional pain of their own—the sexual acting out is but one symptom of that youngster's psychological distress. Even in the absence of more active abuse, significant ignoring can transform a child's life into an emotional wasteland.

Isolating: "The adult cuts the child off from normal social experiences, prevents the child from forming friendships and makes the child believe that he or she is alone in the world" (Garbarino 1986). Isolating can lead to tremendous loneliness, and over time the youngster fails to be a part of normal social life. He doesn't learn how to make friends or to develop normal social skills.

Terrorizing: This involves threatening a child in extreme ways, and it can lead to a pervasive sense of fear. "In its 'mild' form, it suggests an arbitrariness and the use of scare tactics to discipline" (Garbarino, Guttman and Seeley 1986). Verbal threats, bullying, intimidation, brutal criticism, and humiliation characterize this form of maltreatment. In the extreme, children are physically abused, sadistically tortured, or subjected to horrific forms of brainwashing. Terrorizing abuse is often unpredictable, making it impossible for a child to anticipate when the abuse will occur or to take action to avoid it. Such youngsters are often plagued with a continuous sense of incredible fear.

In many cases of sexual molestation, threats generate feelings of terror: "If you tell, I will kill you" or "If you tell, I will kill your mother" or "If your mother finds out, she will commit suicide." Sometimes abusers will kill small animals in front of a child and say, "I'll do this to you if you tell."

Children need a certain degree of safety in their world in order to feel secure and to grow. Early experiences of terrorism can plant seeds of tremendous fear and mistrust that can last a lifetime.

It should be noted that sometimes parents who genuinely love their children periodically become enraged. They lose control of their anger and explode. They may hit or shake their children, call them names, or say "I'm going to kill you," only to later experience a tremendous sense of guilt and regret. These parents may not intend to damage their children, but such episodic rages can be devastating to youngsters. This pattern of maltreatment is often seen in parents who are under tremendous stress, who have impulse control problems, and/or are abusing alcohol or drugs.

Corrupting: Some parents, intentionally or inadvertently, actually train their children in antisocial or deviant behaviors. Aggression, sexuality, and substance abuse are common areas of such unfortunate misguided parenting. The broad category of maltreatment includes sexual abuse in all of its subtle and blatant forms; encouraging the use of alcohol or other drugs of abuse; involving children in criminal acts (including prostitution); modeling and reinforcing hostile, aggressive behavior; and exposing children to pornography.

Sally was a lonely child whose mother was a tense and cold woman. She and Sally's father had divorced when Sally was two. Because there was very little open affection or nurturing in the family, Sally was emotionally starving to death. When Sally was six, her uncle Bob moved in with the family and spent a lot of time holding her on his lap. It felt warm and good. However, within a few weeks, Uncle Bob's hugs turned into sexual caresses and eventually led to stimulation of Sally's genitals. He told her that he loved her, but if she told anybody about their "cuddling," he would leave her forever. Sally developed a facial tic, chewed her fingernails, and developed strong feelings of potential abandonment—all direct results of the sexual assault by her uncle.

These kinds of intense feelings and resulting strong emotional conflicts take a tremendous toll on children. To the extent that use of addictive substances or illegal behaviors are encouraged, moral development can also get off track. The long-term consequences may be the development of severe personality disorders, repeated encounters with the law, and/or a lifetime of drug or alcohol abuse.

Intrusiveness: Although parents must spend time with their children and provide oversight and guidance, youngsters must also have some time alone—privacy and space to be on their own. At times, however, parents can become so overinvolved with their offspring that they go beyond certain limits, and children experience a sense of intrusion. In its milder form, this may involve overmonitoring of children's behavior. In more extreme cases, the youngster may have little or no sense of privacy.

All people need times of solitude when they can be alone with their thoughts and feelings. These times give children the sense of a boundary between self and others and contribute to the development of a unique, individual identity separate from that of their parents.

Overprotection: Protecting a child from undue distress and danger is an important part of parenting. Infants and young children are vulnerable and helpless. The urge to reach out and catch a toddler as he starts to fall is etched in parental instincts. Yet in some families, protection is taken to inappropriate extremes. All children must be kept safe and at the same time gradually exposed to age-appropriate challenges. Parents must at some point back off and let a child explore the world. This is how youngsters eventually begin to learn to stand on their own two feet and deal with the demands of life. A child develops ever-increasing skills that help her cope and master the tasks of growing up. When the exposure to new challenges happens in appropriate ways, the youngster not only acquires skills, she also develops an inner sense of mastery and competency. As most parents have observed, when a child first walks on his own or successfully stacks several blocks, a large grin comes to his face, as if he's saying, "Wow! Look at me! I did it!"

Overprotective parents usually have good intentions, but many inadvertently stifle a youngster's development by "smothering" and "infantilizing." In the name of providing protection, unfortunately they send the child a message, "I don't think you have what it takes to cope with the world." Most youngsters growing up under these circumstances do not develop a solid inner sense of esteem and competency.

Sometimes parents react with overprotection because they have come to see the world as a very dangerous place. Many of these adults encountered frightening situations when they were young and are now trying to weave a protective web around their own children. Their offspring may begin to view the world as being a dangerous place to live. This fear thus becomes a multigenerational problem. In other instances, parents may have felt little involvement from their own mothers and fathers. The current overprotective atmosphere is a sort of compensation; they are attempting to provide their children with what they missed, but are overdoing it. Many parents, if not most, feel a sense of loss as babies become young children and eventually teenagers. Holding and hugging your child feels good. But sooner or later, most pull away and it is a loss. With growth and maturation, youngsters naturally move toward increasing independence. All parents must come to terms with this change, but for some it is very difficult. The response may be to continue babying a child, hoping somehow that he will stay young and remain close.

Adolescents who have the good fortune to receive the right amount of protection *and* encouragement to grow up find leaving home and moving into adulthood easier. They can separate and individuate yet retain a positive connection with their parents.

Inappropriate Discipline: Three broad types of faulty discipline can occur: discipline that is *too harsh,* discipline that is *too lax,* and discipline that is *inconsistent.* What is considered to be "appropriate" discipline has been a controversial issue for many years. Older notions of "spare the rod, spoil the child" gave way to ultrapermissive, lax approaches to child rearing. It is far beyond our own wisdom to know what is *the* right type and amount of discipline. Although it is hard to know what's "right," it is clear both from anecdotal findings and well-controlled research studies that *extreme harshness damages children and so does excessive permissiveness.*

Very *harsh discipline,* especially when combined with verbal attacks directed toward the worth of the child, scares children. It dampens or destroys spontaneity and aliveness. It can lead to an inner hatred of the punishing parent. It can provide a model for aggressive-critical behavior. And often it simply does not work, since it is not a very effective method for *teaching* youngsters. Children subjected to harsh punishment tend to develop in one of two directions: either as overly repressed, submissive, compliant, and fearful, or seriously aggressive—many delinquents and criminals were raised by exceedingly harsh parents.

Overpermissiveness, on the other hand, often results in children who are selfish, demanding, and inconsiderate—in a word, *spoiled.* These youngsters, raised with little or no parental discipline, often fail to develop a true appreciation for social norms and are at high risk for entering into relationships where they exploit others. They grow up expecting others to cater to their whims—after all, Mom and Dad did!

Markedly *inconsistent* discipline can make it difficult for the child to establish stable values for guiding behavior. These youngsters often grow up feeling confused and afraid. Parents' behavior is hard to predict—one time they fly into a rage, another time they ignore the child. Unpredictability almost always leaves children with a sense of uncertainty and fear. Don't misunderstand here: *absolute* consistency in discipline is not possible. Parents often disagree with one another about certain disciplinary issues, and follow-through and consistency simply take a lot of energy. Mild levels of inconsistency don't damage youngsters. But when the parent's reaction is *grossly* inconsistent or extreme and/or highly unpredictable, the stage is set for developmental problems.

Unrealistic Demands: Some parents place excessive demands upon children to do things that they cannot reasonably do. We are not talking here about appropriately encouraging or challenging a child, but instead demanding the youngster perform in ways that are inappropriate for his age. Such demands are often unrelenting standards for accomplishment and perfection. "These parents," says psychologist Jeffrey Young, "place a higher priority on achievement than on happiness." Under such pressures, a child may be able to stretch himself and achieve at a high level, but often at great costs emotionally. These children often feel incredibly tense and worried. They become adults at a very early age and sacrifice their sense of playfulness and aliveness. In many instances the demands take on an all-or-none quality: "You either get an A+ or you are a failure." From this perfectionist view, if the youngster falls 1 percent below the mark, he's worthless. So even if maintaining a 100 percent performance, the child feels an ever-present, impending sense of worthlessness should he not live up to expectations. Young people growing up under these conditions incorporate the unrealistic, demanding parent into their own conscience, so that years after leaving home they hear parental voices echoing in their minds: "You either do it perfectly or you are a failure."

Unrealistic demands not only pertain to achievement, but also to moral issues. This emphasis can be seen in families that state, "You are *never* to get angry in this family" or "All sexual feelings are sinful." Personal opinions may not be allowed, "Children should be seen and not heard!" Such demands can lead to a severe constriction of normal human feelings, the development of excessively harsh or unrealistic guilt feelings, and the stifling of autonomy. When teenagers in these families invariably confront issues of morality and sexuality, it is *very* unlikely that the teen will talk openly with his or her parent. Fearing criticism, lines of communication shut down.

Too few demands can result in serious developmental problems, too. There is, of course, an important place for parental expectations. These are the only way to help children internalize values and develop inner guides for appropriate behavior. The key is to communicate to youngsters reasonable expectations, which can be characterized by the following: they are age-appropriate, are not extreme or rigid, and do not attack the basic worth of the child. All parents get irritated with their offspring and have frustrating moments of disappointment. It's not only OK but also necessary to give children feedback on their behavior. However, attacking the *person* of the child is damaging: "You are worthless," "You're a total failure," "You are just a good-for-nothing little brat." This kind of name-calling is maltreatment. When a teenager makes a serious error or really disappoints her parents, it is natural for the parents to feel upset; but *there are ways to discipline without attacking the child.* Transmitting reasonable expectations to a youngster might take this form, "I really want you to do well in school. I expect you to do your best, but you need to know you don't have to be 100 percent perfect. And even if you don't do well, know that I'll still love you."

Invalidation: Jennifer, a 16-year-old sophomore, told her pastor that when she had her first menstrual period, she experienced tremendously painful cramping. She complained to her mother, who responded, "You are too young to have a period. Quit faking it and leave me alone." This is but one example of a very common type of maltreatment in childhood. The youngster is simply expressing the truth: an emotion, a physical sensation, an opinion, or idea. The parent responds that it should not or does not exist: "It doesn't hurt," "You aren't afraid," "We don't say that kind of thing in this family!"

What is a child to do in such a situation? Some fight back and insist it *is* true. But for many, if not most children, fighting back is very hard to do. Parents are seen as being extremely powerful. Most commonly young people manage in some way or another to suppress the pain, ignore it, banish the thoughts from their minds, or change the subject. Children also may start to *feel* crazy. Their natural experience is directly denied and invalidated, one of the most devastating experiences a child can endure. The youngster not only fails to receive much-needed support and caring but is left doubting her own perceptions.

Invalidation is such a common experience that it deserves extra attention here. To explore this form of emotional maltreatment in childhood, we would like to propose an analogy: the evolution and growth of an individual self is somewhat like the creation of fine pottery.

In the beginning stages of making pottery, the clay is molded and takes on its own unique shape and form. However, once formed, it is crucial that the pot (bowl, plate, vase) be fired in a kiln for a particular period of time and at a certain temperature. The process of firing allows the piece to develop tremendous added strength and durability. Unfired, the clay either stays soft and very malleable or it dries out, cracks, and falls apart. The firing is necessary, but something already within the clay, the inherent makeup of the clay, allows its transformation into an object of greater solidity and strength.

Like clay, the stuff that is fashioned into an expression of the self is initially quite fragile. Certain experiences in life either can transform the emerging self into a more solid form or can cause it to fall apart. The real self is made up of the physical sensations, perceptions, emotions, thoughts, hunches, images, beliefs, values, needs, and hopes that naturally arise out of a person's inner being. These experiences of the self can be registered only at an unconscious level and are barred from conscious awareness. They may be noticed inwardly but without outward expression or can be revealed to others by expressing your feelings, stating an opinion, or taking action.

The process of validation is one of the primary life experiences that can turn a *potential* personal quality into an *actual* one. It is like the heat that fires the pottery. When a young child cuts his finger and cries, if his parent acknowledges his pain, the experience is validated. When the teenage girl breaks up with her boyfriend and tells her mother, "I feel devastated," and the mother says, "I believe you, honey," the experience is validated. Validation does not mean passing judgment, such as *good, bad, right,* or *wrong.* It simply involves a verbal or nonverbal message that conveys, "I believe you." It is as if the parent shines a light on the reality of the daughter's feeling and says, "This is real ... You *are* hurting, and I accept that it's the truth." The girl's expression of pain is a brief demonstration of one part of herself. When someone else, particularly someone as powerful as a parent, recognizes and believes a feeling, that show of emotional support influences both the development of the child's self at the moment and in a more profound and lasting way.

An important message shines through when a parent validates a child, "You are worth listening to and worth believing." Children need to know that they matter. This is the message that is registered in the heart of the young person when an adult acknowledges her pain or experience. In a powerful way the acknowledgment shows a deep sense of respect for the experiences of that youngster. And each time she expresses something, whether joy, pain, or an idea, and it is treated with respect, the adult encourages further self-expression and strengthens the child's self.

Some early painful events, unfortunately, may be unavoidable. If a child is emotionally hurt, to be with the youngster, hear the pain, and say, "I believe you" are probably the most important and compassionate things an adult can do to help. This basic statement of belief in the child is like water for a young plant. It nourishes the growth of the self.

References

Daro, D. (1989). The most frequently "asked about" issues regarding child abuse and neglect. Toledo, OH: N.C.E. Foundation for the Prevention of Child Abuse.

Garbarino, J., Guttman, E. and Seeley. J. W. (1986). *The Psychologically Battered Child.* San Francisco: Jossey-Bass Publishers.

Preston, J. (1993). *Growing Beyond Emotional Pain.* San Luis Obispo, CA: Impact Publishers.

Normal or Not?

*Teenagers are sometimes like two-year-olds,
but with active hormones and wheels.* —Frank Seitz

Adolescence has long been recognized as a time of transition and emotional upheaval. It's a time of new challenges, raging hormones, separation, and moodiness. Often parents, teachers, and pastors alike are confronted with what appear to be troublesome behaviors in teenagers and are left with the question, Is this normal or not? Distinguishing transient age-appropriate behavior problems from more serious signs of emotional distress is often difficult.

Before launching into a discussion of common teenage problems, it is appropriate to sketch out what appear to be the most common markers of adolescent emotional adjustment—those likely to occur, probably quite normal, and often fairly temporary characteristics.

First and foremost, this is a time for separation. Teenagers almost invariably show signs of their emerging autonomy and separateness from their family and parents. Often, behaviors signaling separation will be troublesome to parents, but they must be seen as important and healthy developmental thrusts as the teen spreads his or her wings and carves out a unique sense of self. Even in the context of healthy, loving families we will see a multitude of separation-driven behaviors, including some of the following:

- Wanting to be with friends and withdrawing from family and family activities.
- Adopting values that are at odds with parental values. This may include the desire to attend a different church or expressing beliefs that run contrary to long-held family beliefs.
- Being very influenced by peer pressures.
- Heightened sensitivity to the opinions of peers.
- Comments such as "You don't understand!" or "My parents are unreasonable."
- Teenagers often seem to need to feel persecuted by their parents and will struggle over even trivial issues with their folks.
- Testing the limits (for example, coming home past a particular curfew time).

A second common characteristic of adolescents is a shift into significant egocentricity. This may take the form of obliviousness to others' feelings, a lack of compassion, and wanting their needs always to be placed before the needs of others. We must underscore that this apparent *regression* to a more childish, selfish way of interacting occurs even in teens who have in the past been very compassionate. Adolescents typically get caught up in their own needs or emotions of the moment, and this is one symptom.

Teenagers are often preoccupied with their looks and other outward manifestations that may relate to social desirability and acceptance. Thus a pimple is a tragedy, and it really does take an hour and a half to fix your hair.

Regardless of upbringing, in one way or another, age, peer pressure, and erupting hormones in collusion will spark interest in sexuality. The question is not, Will this issue surface? The question is, How will it come up, and how will parents address sexuality with their adolescents?

Adolescence is like a ride on an emotional roller coaster; many teenagers experience a good deal of emotional sensitivity—ups and downs. Small things upset them, moodiness is not uncommon, and often strong emotions lead them to act in impulsive ways. It's human for people, in the wake of very strong feelings, to lose perspective; and sometimes this results in incredibly poor judgments. Some exasperated parents remark, "How can he be so stupid?" Many times poor judgments are best seen not as problems of impaired intellect, but as the consequence of two factors: intense emotion and loss of perspective. Caught up in the intensity of the moment, rational thinking is temporarily suspended.

Yet another factor that may contribute to poor judgment and impulsive behavior stems from a sort of adolescent feeling of omnipotence. Many teenagers *know* that it is dangerous to drink and drive; they *know* drug use is potentially quite risky or that unsafe sex can result in grave consequences. Yet these otherwise bright teens experience feelings of a sort of invulnerability or omnipotence. "Oh, I can handle it." "I won't get addicted." "I won't get AIDS." We want to underscore that such risky behavior may occur in the context of families and children who do, in fact, have solidly developed morals and values. The combination of peer pressure, impulsivity, and teenage feelings of omnipotence can set the stage for poor judgments.

Some of the issues mentioned above can be seen within the realm of "normal" adolescent behavior, in that they may not be a sign of serious psychopathology or family dysfunction. But this is not to imply that they are necessarily OK. Teenagers, of course, need to be encouraged to think carefully about the consequences of their behavior and should be given appropriate limits by their parents. And what has been understood by many child therapists is that although teens may struggle against limits, on an inner (possibly unconscious) level, they want and need reasonable limits.

As a pastor or religious worker, you will be confronted time and time again with the question, Is this normal or not? Many of the problems addressed in this book involve life events or psychological disorders that are clearly beyond the realm of "minor and normal." But many teenagers or their parents who approach you will have adjustment difficulties that fall into gray areas. Be assured that the Is this normal? question is often difficult for mental health professionals to answer with assurance. The conservative guideline is that if you are not sure, err in the direction of caution, provide help, and do not hesitate to make a referral to a mental health professional.

PART TWO

Case Studies

Case 1

Alcohol and Drugs

"He Didn't Have Fun Unless He Was High"

Jason's family had been involved in the church for years. They became especially active after the sudden and unexpected death of the oldest daughter in an automobile crash one year before. The family asked to have a visit with Pastor King at the church because they were very concerned about Jason, age 15. He had been noticeably withdrawn from both family and friends for several months and had become less interested in his appearance. Jason had stopped participating in the youth group, and his grades had dropped at school. His teachers told the family that Jason had fallen asleep in classes and had had several absences in recent weeks. He was moody and had become pessimistic in his outlook toward life. Recently, friends had reported that they had seen Jason drinking with a group of older boys after school. When confronted by his parents, he denied drinking or using drugs. The family explained that Jason had been very close to his older sister and appeared to have been the most affected and least accepting of her accidental death. They asked Pastor King for assistance.

It is helpful that several people are actively interested in Jason's life situation: his family, Pastor King, teachers, and the youth director. To have a team of caring and concerned adults working together as helpers with Jason increases the likelihood of finding solutions. Studies indicate that early and continued family involvement increases the success of helping teens with alcohol and drug problems.

It is important to begin with an accurate picture of his possible alcohol and drug use. Some experimentation is to be expected in young people. Is this the case for Jason? The rapid and negative changes in his life suggest something more serious has developed. Are the symptoms the result of a

Pastoral Assessment

physical illness? Consulting a physician is a good early step. Is he using alcohol in an attempt to cope with unresolved grief related to the sudden death of his sister? It is not uncommon for alcohol and drug abuse to mask grief, depression, anxiety, or psychological trauma (Case 7). The use of alcohol and drugs for self-medication is often the pattern of people with poor coping skills and high addictive potential. How much is Jason in denial about his substance abuse problem? Does he minimize his drug and alcohol abuse? How much insight does Jason have into his problem? Does Jason understand the negative consequences of substance abuse? Is Jason having suicidal thoughts (Case 16)? It is important that teens abusing substances be assessed for suicide risk (Crumley 1990).

Relevant History

Jason's paternal grandfather had an alcohol dependence problem. Jason is a somewhat shy personality in a gregarious family.

Diagnostic Criteria

Substance abuse has as its basic feature a pattern of substance use characterized by negative, recurrent, and significant consequences related to repeated use. This diagnosis needs only one of the following criteria in the past twelve months (APA 1994):

1. Recurrent substance use results in a failure to fulfill major obligations at home or work (such as repeated neglect of school responsibilities).
2. Repeated use of substance in situations in which use is known to be physically hazardous.
3. Recurrent substance-related legal problems.
4. Continued use despite having persistent or recurrent social or interpersonal problems resulting from the effects of the substance (such as arguments with friends or family members about the consequences of using the substance).

Substance dependence is a more serious diagnosis that is characterized by a group of symptoms indicating that an individual continues to use a substance despite significant resulting problems. Persons suffering substance dependence have a pattern of compulsive substance use usually leading to tolerance and withdrawal. A "craving" to use a substance is present. According to the *Diagnostic and Statistical Manual of Mental Disorders, Fourth Edition* (DSM-IV) criteria, at least three of the following symptoms are present at the same time over a twelve-month period:

1. *Tolerance* has developed, which is a need for increased amounts of a substance to achieve the desired effect or markedly diminished effects with continued use of the same amount of substance.
2. *Withdrawal* symptoms, such as physical discomfort, illness, or severe complications, are experienced by the person when the substance is not available.

3. The substance is frequently consumed in larger amounts or over longer periods of time than intended.
4. There is a persistent desire or unsuccessful attempts to control or cut down on substance use.
5. A lot of time is devoted to activities related to obtaining the substance, using it, or recovering from its effects.
6. Important social, occupational, or recreational activities are reduced or stopped as a result of substance consumption.
7. The substance is used in spite of persistent or recurrent psychological or physical problems caused or exacerbated by its use.

Jason has many of the classic signs of a teen who is having an alcohol or drug problem. He is withdrawing from family and friends and has stopped activities he had enjoyed at church. He has serious school problems, and his falling asleep at school may be a sign of daytime fatigue. Jason has had a significant and sudden change in mood and has become negative in his thinking. His family reports Jason is less interested in his physical appearance. He may have developed peer relationships with youth who are using alcohol and other substances.

Pastor King and the family decided to confront Jason with his behavior. Pastor King has had some relationship with Jason through the youth group, so the pastor will first try to talk to him alone. If that intervention is insufficient, the whole family and the youth director will confront him as a group.

The pastor used his active listening skills while assessing Jason's situation. He sat, listened, and emphatically responded to Jason at the family home. When he talked with Jason, the teen confessed increasing use of alcohol and experimentation with marijuana. When Pastor King reminded Jason of how much his family and older sister loved him, he broke down and sobbed. He was in deep grief over the tragic death of his sister. He said, "It has become hard for me to have a good time without alcohol."

After the pastor had spoken with him, Jason was willing to talk to his family and the youth director. Jason agreed to see a psychologist who specialized in teenage substance abuse problems. Over the next several months of therapy, it became clear that Jason had begun to rely on alcohol and had experiences with marijuana, inhalants, cocaine, and LSD. Jason was successfully treated as an outpatient for alcohol dependence and drug abuse because he had strong family and church support and was motivated to change.

This situation was an instance where a crisis became an opportunity. Jason's family had to address their lack of communication and isolation after the death of a family member. They came to see that Jason had poor skills to cope with loss and needed special attention. Jason's substance abuse was a symptom of their pain as a family and his inability to express

Response to Vignette

himself. The family was able to develop a deeper bonding and a renewed faith as they worked together through the crisis.

Treatment Within the Faith Community

Substance abuse is the number one teenage mental health problem. According to the U.S. Department of Health and Human Services, about half of high school seniors have tried an illicit substance. Alcohol is the most commonly misused drug. An estimated three million Americans under 18 years of age have an alcohol problem (Brown 1990). Young people between 18 and 24 spend $2 billion annually on beer alone. By the time the average teen is 18 years old, he or she has been exposed to 100,000 television beer commercials (Parrott 1993). The National Highway Traffic Safety Administration's statistics highlight the danger of alcohol abuse for teens—they show that more than 1 out of 5 youths (22 percent) between the ages of 15 and 20 who were killed in automobile accidents were seriously impaired by alcohol. The faith community must work cooperatively with those seeking to decrease teen alcohol and drug abuse. One valuable organization that provides such education and advocacy is Mothers Against Drunk Driving (see MADD under Resources).

Pastors indicate that teen alcohol and drug use is a great concern. In a national survey of clergy, a majority (55 percent) indicated that alcohol and drug use was the greatest teen pastoral care concern in their congregation. In the same survey, only 1 in 4 (26 percent) of the pastors felt their church's ministry to teens with alcohol or drug problems was good. Twenty-eight percent said that ministry to adolescents with alcohol and drug problems was nonexistent or poor in their parish (Rowatt 1989). Clearly, religious communities need to develop a more effective ministry to teens with alcohol and drug problems.

Research indicates that stable families lower the risk of alcohol and drug abuse, so programs that focus on strengthening the family can be a preventive strategy (Johnson et al. 1996). A strong youth program that promotes good communication and social skills is a valuable preventive measure. Teen alcohol and drug abusers tend to have poor assertion skills, high social anxiety, and low self-worth. Social skills training can enhance coping, self-control, social problem solving, social awareness, negotiation skills, and assertiveness skills, as well as increasing the ability to resist peer pressure (Haggerty et al. 1989).

Encouraging teens and their families to be active in the life of the community of faith is in itself a powerful preventive strategy when addressing substance abuse. Studies find that adolescent regular church attenders are half as likely to use alcohol (Gallup and Bezilla 1992) or marijuana (Hardert and Dowd 1994) as teens who do not attend church regularly. These surveys add to the extensive evidence supporting the social benefit of nurturing, nonpunitive religious practice in limiting and preventing alcohol and drug use (Gorsuch 1995).

Indications for Referral

An assessment will need to be made as to whether or not inpatient care is required. If substance dependency is associated with danger to self (such as an overdose) or another, other antisocial behavior (such as truancy), or severe mental illness (such as major depression); if previous attempts in outpatient treatment have failed; or if no support system is available, inpatient care may be required for adequate treatment. Involuntary hospitalization is a last resort since it reduces the chance of future treatment compliance, but it may be necessary in some cases.

Treatment by Mental Health Specialist

When considering referring a teen to a mental health professional, it is important to ask what plan of action the specialist will use. A pastor needs some knowledge of standard treatment protocols to assess whether a mental health professional is knowledgeable and experienced in treating teens. Here is an example of the sort of treatment considerations one would make in a treatment plan for an adolescent suffering from alcohol abuse.

Early Stage: The therapist would encourage Jason to tell his story and empathize with his viewpoint to foster a therapeutic alliance. The mental health specialist would ask Jason to discuss his understanding of the negative consequences of alcohol and drug abuse and to assess his level of insight into his situation and whether he is in denial. It would be valuable to provide reassurance that help is available and that change happens with commitment. The family would be involved early and often in treatment to lend support and insight, because treatment without their involvement has little hope of success. In Jason's case, the family could be an important part in healing unresolved grief. It would also be helpful to develop a substance abuse history of the extended family because relatives with abuse issues increase the risk of addiction.

A referral to Alcoholics Anonymous for teens (Alateen) can provide Jason with education and continued support for abstinence. The early stages of abstinence require considerable support, and the therapist will make clear that occasional relapses are possible and need to be seen as "human slips" not "failures" that confirm Jason's low self-worth.

Later Stages: The therapist would continue to work with Jason and his family to prevent relapse and work through temporary relapses if they occur. Sessions would continually review the reasons for the recovery process; provide support, reassurance, encouragement, and praise for ongoing work; and explore for insight into the roots of the addiction. The therapist would encourage Jason to become involved in extracurricular social, athletic, or artistic activities with positive peer groups and to expand his interests.

Research indicates that cognitive therapy can help negative, distorted thinking and irrational beliefs present in many individuals who abuse alcohol and drugs. Typically, a teen substance abuser will say things like,

"The only way I can have fun is to get drunk with my friends" or "I am only creative when I am stoned." Cognitive therapy involves a systematic training in self-observation to improve a person's awareness of the connection between thoughts and emotions.

It would be important to identify and address family problems that may be complicating Jason's alcohol and drug abuse. Family sessions could be used to teach communication skills and explore underlying family dysfunctions (such as an inability to express feelings) that may be related to the addictive behavior.

Cross-Cultural Issues

Researchers found that African Americans aged 13 through 18 who use crack cocaine were more isolated, more likely to recall unpleasant childhood memories, and more likely to have begun sexual behavior with casual partners than nonuser peers. African American adolescents who did not use crack cocaine had a history of quality family, peer, and community relationships (Bowser and Word 1993).

Resources

National Resources

National Center on Addiction and Substance Abuse at Columbia University, 152 West 57th St., 12th floor, New York, NY 10019; (212) 841-5200; www.casacolumbia.org.

National Clearinghouse for Alcohol and Drug Information (NCADI), P.O. Box 2345, Rockville, MD 20847; (800) 729-6686; TDD: (800) 487-4899; www.health.org, provides free, useful materials about the many aspects of adolescent alcohol and drug abuse treatment and prevention. Several of these publications are designed for the faith community.

American Council for Drug Education, 164 West 74th St., New York, NY 10023; (800) 883-DRUG; www.acde.org; privera@phoenixhouse.org.

The National Council on Alcoholism and Drug Dependence (NCADD) is a nonprofit organization that offers information and referral services through 200 state and local affiliates. It provides preventive educational programs for community organizations such as churches and temples. Persons seeking assistance can contact their area affiliate or call a national toll-free help line: (800) 622-2255; 12 West 21st Street, New York, NY 10010; www.ncadd.org; national@ncadd.org.

Another Empty Bottle, www.alcoholismhelp.com, is a Web site for the friends and families of alcoholics.

Mothers Against Drunk Driving (MADD) is an educational and advocacy organization with 400 chapters. MADD is devoted to heightening awareness of the dangers of impaired driving. It has programs designed to address underage drinking and driving, 511 E. John Carpenter Frwy, #700, Irving, TX 75062; (800) GET-MADD; www.madd.org; info@madd.org.

New Life Clinics, (800) NEW-LIFE, www.newlife.com, and Rapha Treatment Centers, (800) 383-HOPE, offer professional inpatient chemical dependency programs for youth from an evangelical Christian orientation.

The American Academy of Child and Adolescent Psychiatry has a web site with information on teen problems including alcohol and drug abuse, www.aacap.com/factsfam/teendrug.htm.

Jewish Alcoholics, Chemically dependent people and their Significant others (JACS), 426 West 58th St., New York, NY 10019; (212) 397-4197; www.jacsweb.org; jacs@jacsweb.org.

Self-Help Resources

Family members and friends of alcohol abusers can find help through Al-Anon. This organization sponsors about 18,000 self-help groups in the United States for persons affected by someone else's drinking. Local Alateen groups can be found in most phone directories. Al-Anon groups follow the traditional twelve-step approach, and members participate anonymously. The organization has books, videos, and cassettes for teens and their families that focus on understanding and coping with problems that result from alcoholism. Al-Anon Family Group Headquarters, Inc., 1600 Corporate Landing Parkway, Virginia Beach, VA 23454; (800) 344-2666; www.Al-Anon-Alateen.org; info@Al-Anon-Alateen.org.

Center for Substance Abuse Information, Treatment and Treatment Referral Hotline, (800) 622-HELP.

Narcotics Anonymous, P.O. Box 9999, Van Nuys, CA 91409; (818) 773-9999; www.na.org; info@na.org.

800-COCAINE is a twenty-four-hour hotline that can help in locating professionals in your area who specialize in substance abuse treatment, 164 W. 74th St., NY, NY 10023; www.drughelp.org.

Cocaine Anonymous, P.O. Box 2000, Los Angeles, CA 90049; (310) 559-5833; www.ca.org; cawso@ca.org.

Overcomers Outreach is a Christian oriented twelve-step support group for teens, found in most states, 520 N. Brookhurst, Suite 121, Anaheim, CA 92801; (800) 310-3001; crc.iugm.org/oo.html; info@oo.shepard.com.

National Families in Action, Century Plaza II, 2957 Clairmont Rd., Suite 150, Atlanta, GA 30329; (404) 248-9676; www.emory.edu/NFIA; nfia@mindspring.com.

United Methodists in Recovery is an anonymous mailing list to share experience, strength, and hope; umrlist@aol.com; www.winternet.com-webpage/UMR.html.

References

American Psychiatric Association (1994). *Diagnostic and Statistical Manual of Mental Disorders-Fourth Edition*. Washington, DC: APA.

Bowser, B.P. and Word, C.O. (1993). Comparisons of African American adolescent crack cocaine users and nonusers. *Psychology of Addictive Behaviors* 7(3). 155-161.

Brown, S.A. (1990). Adolescent alcohol expectancies and risk for alcohol abuse. *Addict Recovery, 10.* 16-19.

Crumley, F.E. (1990). Substance abuse and adolescent suicidal behavior. *Journal of the American Medical Association, 263(22).* 3051-65.

Gallup, G.H. and Bezilla, R. (1992). *The Religious Life of Young Americans.* Princeton, NJ: The George Gallup International Institute.

Gorsuch, R.L. (1995). Religious aspects of substance abuse and recovery. *Journal of Social Issues, 51(2).* 65-83.

Haggerty, K.P., Wells, E.A., Jenson, J.M., Catalano, R.F. and Hawkins, J.D. (1989). Delinquents and drug abuse: A model program for community reintegration. *Adolescence, 24.* 439-456.

Hardert, R.A. and Dowd, T.J. (1994). Alcohol and marijuana use among high school and college students in Phoenix, Arizona. *The International Journal of the Addictions, 29(7).* 887-912.

Johnson, K., Strader, T., Berbaum, M., Bryant, D., Bucholtz, G., Collins, D. and Noe, T. (1996). Reducing alcohol and other drug use by strengthening community, family, and youth resiliency. *Journal of Adolescent Research, 11(1).* 36-67.

Parrott, L. (1993). *Helping the Struggling Adolescent.* Grand Rapids, MI: Zondervan.

Rowatt, G.W. (1989). *Pastoral Care with Adolescents in Crisis.* Louisville: Westminster John Knox Press.

Illicit Substances Commonly Used by Teenagers

Marijuana—pot, grass, reefer, ganja, joint, weed, mary jane, roach, pakalolo, Thai sticks, dope

Marijuana is the most commonly used illicit drug in the United States. In 1995 the Monitoring the Future Study found that 15.8 percent of eighth graders and 34.7 percent of high school seniors had used marijuana at least once in the past year.

This drug is made from the leaves and flowers of the hemp plant. It is usually smoked, but can be eaten. The main mind-altering ingredient in marijuana is THC (dela-9-tetrahydrocannabinol), which determines the strength of its effect. Today marijuana is much stronger than in the 1970s. This more potent marijuana increases physical and mental effects and the possible health problems for the user. Hashish, or hash, is made by taking the resin from the leaves of the marijuana plant and pressing them into cakes, which can be five to ten times as strong as marijuana.

A teen who is "high" on marijuana tends to have poor judgment and make unnecessary mistakes. It can interfere with learning by impairing thinking and short-term memory as well as reducing comprehension. A person who uses a lot of marijuana can start to lose energy and motivation. Long-term regular users may become psychologically dependent and can even have panic reactions. Smoking marijuana can damage the lungs, and its use in conjunction with driving can be the cause of car crashes.

Inhalants—glue, bolt, bullet, locker room, rush, whippets, Texas shoe shine

Inhalants are breathable chemicals that produce psychoactive (mind-altering) vapors. Inhalants are generally not thought of as drugs because most of them were never meant to be used that way—examples are model airplane glue, nail polish remover, gasoline, and lighter and cleaning fluids. Aerosols that are used as inhalants include paints, cooking coating agents, and hair sprays, as well as nitrous oxide in a metal cylinder or in whipped cream spray cans (whippets). Amyl nitrite and butyl nitrite are chemicals that can be abused. Amyl nitrite is a clear, yellowish liquid sold in cloth-covered, sealed bulbs. When the bulb is broken, it makes a snapping sound—thus the nicknames "snappers" and "poppers." Butyl nitrite is packaged in small bottles and sold under a variety of names, such as "locker room" and "rush."

The typical inhalant user is an adolescent male. The Monitoring the Future Study on drug abuse found in 1995 that 11.7 percent of eighth graders and 9.1 percent of tenth graders had tried an inhalant in the past year. Inhalants are widely used because they are legal, inexpensive, and found in every household. The immediate negative effects of inhalants include nausea, sneezing, coughing, nosebleeds, fatigue, lack of coordination, slurred speech, and loss of appetite. Solvents and aerosol sprays also decrease heart and respiratory rates and impair judgment. Deep breathing of the vapors or high doses over a short period of time can result in loss of reality-based thinking, violent behavior, unconsciousness, or death. Sniffing or "huffing" highly concentrated amounts of solvents or aerosol sprays can produce heart failure and instant death. Sniffing can cause death the first time or any subsequent time of use. Deliberately inhaling from a paper or plastic bag brings the added risk of suffocation. Repeatedly sniffing concentrated vapors over a number of years can cause permanent damage to the nervous system and body organs. As in all drug use, taking more than one drug at a time multiplies the risks.

Hallucinogens—acid, blotter acid, windowpane, microdots

Hallucinogens, or psychedelics, are drugs that distort an individual's sensations, perceptions of time and space, thinking, and emotions.

Hallucinogens include such drugs as LSD, mescaline, and psilocybin. LSD is manufactured from lysergic acid, found in a fungus that grows in some grains. LSD is an odorless, colorless, and tasteless substance that has potent mood-changing chemicals. It is sold on the street in tablet, capsule, or liquid form. Most often LSD is added to absorbent paper, such as blotter paper, and sold in single square doses. The user starts feeling the effect within thirty to ninety minutes and the "trip" can last up to twelve hours. The effects of LSD depend on the amount taken, the user's personality, and the surroundings. A "bad trip" can be terrifying and dangerous. The user may experience panic, confusion, fearfulness, and loss of control. Chronic users may become psychologically dependent on the drug. In 1995, the Monitoring the Future Survey found that 11.7 percent of high school seniors had tried LSD.

Mescaline comes from the peyote cactus; and although it is not as strong as LSD, its effects are similar. Mescaline is usually smoked or swallowed in the form of capsules or tablets. Psilocybin comes from certain mushrooms. It is sold in tablet or capsule form. The mushrooms themselves may be eaten.

Cocaine—coke, dust, toot, line, nose candy, snow, sneeze powder, girl, white pony, flake, the lady, cain, rock, crack, C

Cocaine, a very addictive drug, is white and looks like a crystalline powder. Crack cocaine looks like small white rocks. "Crack" is a slang term for smokable cocaine and refers to the cracking sound it makes when it burns. Cocaine comes from the leaves of the South American coca plant. It can be injected, smoked, sniffed, or snorted. Snorting is the process of inhaling cocaine powder through a nostril, where it is absorbed into the bloodstream through the nasal tissue. Cocaine can also be heated into a liquid and its fumes inhaled through a pipe in a method called "freebasing," which is especially dangerous because of the high concentrations of the drug that enter the bloodstream. Cocaine is an "upper" or stimulant that gives the user a false sense of power and energy. When users "come down," they are usually depressed, edgy, and crave more. Cocaine users may have angry, hostile, and anxious feelings. Long-term use can cause addiction, loss of appetite, sleeplessness, irregular heartbeat, paranoia, and confusion. In 1995, the Monitoring the Future Study found that about 4 percent of high school seniors had tried cocaine in the past year. The data also show that cocaine use among eighth graders rose from 2.3 percent in 1991 to 4.2 percent in 1995.

Amphetamine—speed, cross-tops, whites, black beauties, bennies, uppers (Brand names: Ritalin, Preludin, Dexedrine)

Amphetamines are prescribed by a physician or obtained through forged prescriptions. These drugs are usually reduced to yellow crystals that are sniffed or injected. Amphetamine use results in mood elevation and increased energy. High doses can produce a toxic syndrome that is marked by visual and auditory hallucinations, paranoia, and distorted thinking. Amphetamines are psychologically addictive. Users become dependent on the drug to avoid the "down" feelings they often experience when the drug's effect wears off. Drug cravings increase with continued use. Drug withdrawal after long use is marked by prolonged sleep, depression, irritability, low energy, and cravings for the substance.

Methamphetamine—speed, meth, chalk, ice, crystal, glass

Methamphetamine is a drug that strongly activates part of the brain. The drug is chemically related to the stimulant amphetamine but is more potent. It is made in illegal laboratories and is addictive. It is taken orally, snorted, injected, or smoked. The user gets an immediate "rush" or "flash." Because the drug elevates mood, many experimenters increase their use, especially depressed young people. In small amounts methamphetamine increases wakefulness and euphoria while decreasing appetite. Continued use can cause insomnia, confusion, convulsions, paranoia, aggressiveness, heart damage, brain damage, stroke, and death. In 1995, the Monitoring the Future Study found that 3.4 percent of high school seniors had used crystal methamphetamine at least once in their lifetime, an increase from 2.7 percent in 1990.

Heroin—a bag (single dose of heroin), sugar hill, smack, dope, gumball, harry, horse, junk, scag, tootsie roll, black tar, H

Heroin is a very dangerous drug, and recent years have seen its increased use among teens. According to the Federal Center for Substance Abuse Prevention, in 1995 about 35,000 adolescents tried heroin for the first time. Young and new users tend to smoke or snort it, but longtime users often inject heroin into their veins because it is the fastest way to get a "fix" from the drug.

Heroin is produced from morphine, which comes from the opium poppy plant. Pure heroin is a white powder, though that sold on the street varies in color from black to white. Black tar is a type of heroin from Mexico that is either sticky or hard and looks like roofing tar. It is mixed into liquids before being injected into a user's vein. Heroin is highly addictive—users find they need repeated doses, and attempts to stop using the drug lead to painful withdrawal symptoms. It is so addictive because it activates many regions of the brain, particularly those responsible for producing pleasure and physical dependence.

Symptoms of heroin use can include watery eyes, runny nose, shallow breathing, nausea, panic, insomnia, shakes, tremors, and convulsions. An overdose causes stupor and sometimes death. Because the potency of street heroin is unknown, overdoses are a significant danger. "Speedballing," an extremely dangerous practice, occurs when heroin and cocaine are injected into the body together.

PCP—angel dust, crystal supergrass, killer joint, ozone, whack, rocket fuel

PCP (Phencyclidine) is unique among abused drugs. It was developed as a powerful tranquilizer for veterinary medicine. PCP is a white crystalline powder with a bitter chemical taste. It is readily soluble in water or alcohol; and it can be snorted, smoked, or eaten.

PCP has stimulant, depressant, or hallucinogenic effects on human beings. Which of these will be most pronounced depends on the user's personality, psychological state, and environment at the time. In small doses PCP produces euphoria; feelings of unreality; distorted thinking; and distortions of time, space, and body image. In higher doses it produces restlessness, panic, disorientation, paranoia, delusions, mental turmoil, and fear of death. People who use PCP for long periods of time report memory loss, speech problems, depression, and weight loss. In 1995, the Monitoring the Future Study found that 1.8 percent of high school seniors had used PCP at least once in the preceding year, an increase from 1.4 percent in 1993.

MDMA—ecstasy, adam, X-TC

MDMA (methylene-dioxymethamphetamine) is a synthetic, mind-altering drug with hallucinogenic and amphetamine-like properties. Taken by mouth, ecstasy makes people feel lively, alert, sociable, and happy. Ecstasy is widely sold in clubs and discos, and many young people use it regularly on weekends at dance club events known as "raves."

Users can experience serious physical and psychological problems, including confusion, depression, sleep problems, and severe anxiety. Physical symptoms include nausea, blurred vision, muscle tension, faintness, chills, and sweating. Increased heart rate and high blood pressure are risks to people with heart problems, and frequent use may cause liver damage. Some have died from the effects of this drug.

Tobacco

"He Tried to Stop Several Times"

Sixteen-year-old Brad, a member of the church youth group, recently attended a citywide youth rally where he rededicated his life to Christ. He asked to meet with Bill Clark, the church youth director. Brad told Bill of his new commitment to Christ and the joy of being "born again." He confessed that he was struggling with a sin that was hard to break—smoking tobacco. He had begun experimenting with chewing tobacco with his buddies at age 13, and within the next few months they were buying and smoking cigarettes on a regular basis. Brad said that before his recent rededication he had tried to stop smoking several times without success. Brad described that after a day or two without cigarettes he felt "bummed," irritable, restless, and had trouble sleeping. Brad believes that smoking helps him calm down and relax. Several members of his youth group and his new girlfriend were praying that God would help him overcome the habit. He asked for Bill's support and prayer. He also wanted advice on how to stop smoking.

Pastoral Assessment

Brad needs to understand that among those who successfully quit smoking, less than 25 percent quit on their first attempt; and most people have three or four failures before they stop smoking for good (APA 1994). With the support of his family, pastor, new girlfriend, and other youth group members and with their prayers, Brad should have a good chance of being able to stop smoking altogether. His religious commitment and peer support are strong incentives for a change in behavior.

Like most smokers, Brad began using tobacco products in his early teens. He wants to quit but finds it difficult to do so. Many young people use tobacco as an experiment during their adventurous years, and it turns into an addiction that can be hard to overcome because of nicotine cravings and the discomfort of withdrawal. Brad had experienced several withdrawal symptoms of nicotine dependence when he tried to stop smoking, including depressed mood, irritability, restlessness, and insomnia. It would be helpful to find out how many indicators of strong dependence on tobacco Brad has, such as: smoking soon after waking, smoking when ill, chain-smoking, using high-nicotine-yielding cigarettes, smoking more in the morning than the afternoon, and finding the first cigarette of the day the most difficult to give up. These signs are associated with people who are heavily dependent on nicotine and may need a great deal of assistance in overcoming the addiction.

Tobacco is associated with the increased likelihood of use of other substances and can act as a "gateway drug." It is generally the first drug used by teens who later use alcohol and illicit drugs. The surgeon general found that 12- to 17-year-olds who said they had smoked in the past thirty days were three times more likely to use alcohol, eight times more likely to smoke marijuana, and twenty-two times more likely to use cocaine within the past thirty days than those teens who had not smoked (Elders et al. 1994). Fortunately, Brad has not experimented with other substances.

Relevant History

Both his parents are heavy smokers but are encouraging Brad to stop smoking "before it is too late for him."

Diagnostic Criteria

Nicotine dependence is a pattern of compulsive use of nicotine-containing products (cigarettes, chewing tobacco, snuff, pipes, and cigars) that results in nicotine tolerance and withdrawal. As a person attempts to quit smoking or reduce the amount of nicotine used, several signs of withdrawal can begin within twenty-four hours including: depressed mood, insomnia, irritability, frustration, anger, problems with concentration, anxiety, restlessness, and weight gain. Cigarette smoking has the most intense habit-creating pattern among tobacco products and is the most difficult to quit. There is usually a craving to use cigarettes. Many individuals who become nicotine-dependent continue to smoke despite knowledge that they have a medical condition related to the smoking (such as bronchitis).

Cigarette smoking is the chief preventable cause of premature disease and death in the United States. About 1 out of every 6 deaths is due to tobacco use. Each year more than 400,000 Americans die from smoking-related illnesses. Smoking annually kills more Americans than AIDS, auto accidents, suicides, murders, fires, alcohol, and illegal drugs combined (CDC 1994). The early adolescent years (ages 11 through 15) are the crucial life stage for preventing tobacco use. After high school it is uncommon for tobacco use to begin (Johnston, O'Malley and Bachman 1995).

Tobacco use among teens is high and rising. From 1991 to 1994, smoking among eighth graders increased from 14 percent to 18 percent, among tenth graders from 20 percent to 25 percent, and among high school seniors from 27 percent to 31 percent (Johnston, O'Malley, and Bachman 1995). It is estimated that between one-third and one-half of adolescents who try only a few cigarettes become regular smokers, a process that takes an average of two to three years (Henningfield, Cohen and Slade 1991).

One key factor in the increased use of tobacco among youth is the rapid growth in the use of smokeless tobacco (chewing tobacco, snuff) among young Americans. In the 1970s most smokeless tobacco users were men over the age of 50. This changed in the 1980s as the tobacco industry marketed to a younger generation of American men. At present young males are the most common users of smokeless tobacco, with about 11 percent of male high school seniors using it (Johnston et al. 1995). Rather than decreasing the use of cigarettes, smokeless tobacco frequently becomes the introduction to tobacco use and regular cigarette smoking.

Response to Vignette

Helping teens stop smoking is an area where pastors and youth workers can offer significant help. The assistance that Brad needs will most likely not require a mental health specialist. The keys to quitting smoking are motivation, which it appears Brad has, and preparation, which a pastor or youth worker can help him develop. Brad needs to look closely at why he wants to stop smoking and how best to prepare to do so to foster success.

As a beginning it would be good to help Brad prepare a list of the reasons he wants to stop smoking that he can carry in his pocket and use to remind himself why he is quitting. It would also be important to help Brad create a list of places and times that it was difficult not to light up. What was he doing, how did he feel, and who was he with when he felt like smoking? This increased self-awareness could help him anticipate difficult situations and avoid them as he starts to become a nonsmoker. After a brief period of preparation, Brad could set a date to stop smoking and ask his youth group and family for support. The youth group and concerned adults in the congregation could lend help by being daily contacts over the phone or in person to encourage Brad with prayer and counsel. Ex-smokers are often motivated to help.

Family support would be particularly important for Brad because both of his parents are smokers. The risk for smoking increases threefold if one parent smokes (APA 1994), and children of smokers are at greater risk of becoming ill and dying from exposure to smoke-related illnesses. According to the Centers for Disease Control and Prevention, smoke from other people's cigarettes kills an estimated 50,000 Americans each year (CDC 1994). It would be helpful if Brad's parents could become non-smokers with him or at least make their home a smoke-free zone as long as Brad lives with them.

Most people have success with stopping "cold turkey," or all at once.

People who are very dependent on tobacco may try to cut down several cigarettes a day until they no longer are smoking. Many people find nicotine replacement devices like gum and skin patches useful to gradually wean them off nicotine. However, these devices usually do not work without counseling and a change of lifestyle, and it is best to speak to a nurse or physician about when to use them.

Like Brad, most teens say they smoke to relax and reduce stress (Gallup and Bezilla 1992). It is important that Brad find alternate ways to relax and self-soothe. These could include such activities as going for a walk, stretching, deep breathing, listening to music, and participating in youth group activities. As a Christian, Brad could also find prayer, scripture reading, fellowship, and worship helpful ways to cope with stress. Research has found that many traditional Christian practices enhance stress reduction and healthy living (Koenig 1997).

It is important to remember that nicotine is a powerfully addictive drug, and it can be very difficult to quit. It takes a lot of work. If Brad has a slip-up and smokes a cigarette, it is important that he not panic. He should be reminded that we all need second chances to start over and not to become discouraged.

Treatment Within the Faith Community

Church involvement has an effect on the attitudes and behavior of teens toward smoking cigarettes. Adolescents who attend church regularly are less likely to have smoked in the past thirty days than nonattendees (10 percent versus 17 percent) (Gallup and Bezilla 1992). Encouraging Brad in his connection to the youth group and the church can help reinforce social norms and provide peer support that can help him quit smoking.

In 1993, the tobacco industry spent $6 billion on advertising and promotion. Hundreds of millions of dollars were spent on promotional items such as T-shirts, hats, and catalog products that have a direct appeal to young people. Research has shown that teens who are exposed to these promotions are more likely to be smokers (Altman et al. 1996). In the United States, annual illegal sales of tobacco products to minors total 950 million packs of cigarettes and 26 million containers of smokeless tobacco (Heishman, Kozlowski and Henningfield 1997). About one-half of minors who attempt to purchase tobacco products report never being asked for proof of age (CDC 1996). It is interesting to note that states with the highest cigarette taxes have the lowest rates of smokers.

Tobacco use prevention programs for teens would be a valuable ministry of the church, especially since the Gallup Youth Survey indicates that 1 in 10 teenagers who regularly attend church report smoking (Gallup and Bezilla 1992). Intervention programs need to help teens recognize social and advertising pressures to use tobacco as well as develop skills to resist pressures. Increased self-reliance and self-esteem with decreased social alienation appear to be important factors in resisting the pressure to smoke. Public commitment not to use tobacco also increases the likelihood that a teen will stop smoking (Bruvold 1993).

Repeated attempts to quit smoking without results call for referral to a specialist. Heavily addicted smokers with poor health and limited social support are more likely to require intensive, professionally-designed smoking cessation programs.

Most intensive smoking cessation interventions are a combination of psychological and pharmacological approaches. The psychological interventions can be broadly grouped as self-management and aversive techniques. Several of the self-management techniques were previously mentioned, including: setting a time to quit smoking, making plans for coping with the temptation to smoke, and seeking support during periods of high relapse potential. The aversion techniques include such strategies as smoke-holding and rapid smoking. Rapid smoking is designed to make persons aware of the negative effects of smoking so that they no longer feel the cravings. This entails rapidly smoking several cigarettes and feeling the ill effects. Formal smoking cessation clinics where these techniques are used are often found in university medical centers and psychology departments.

The pharmacological interventions are nicotine replacement therapy, which is used as an adjunct to psychological interventions. It is either in the form of gum or a patch designed to deliver nicotine into the body via the skin. The basic idea behind these is to slowly taper the smoker off the nicotine in the cigarettes by replacing it in a controlled manner and reducing the withdrawal symptoms. Once the ex-smokers have stabilized at the level of nicotine replacement, they can begin to bring their intake down in a controlled way. There is solid evidence that nicotine replacement *with counseling* helps smokers to become nonsmokers.

Although smoking rates have remained low among African American youth for many years, recent data indicates that the rate of tobacco use has begun to sharply increase among African American males in the 1990s (CDC 1996).

National Resources

INFACT's Tobacco Industry Campaign, 256 Hanover St., Boston, MA 02113; (617) 742-4583; www.infact.org; infact@igc.apc.org, is organized to stop the tobacco industry from addicting new customers, especially children and young people.

Nicotine Anonymous World Services (NAWS), P.O. Box 591777, San Francisco, CA 94159; nicotine-anonymous.org; info@nicotine-anonymous.org; (415) 750-0328. This is an international group, founded in 1985, with 500 affiliates. Based on a twelve-step model for people who want to recover from nicotine addiction in all forms, it has a newsletter and provides assistance in starting new groups.

Overcomers in Christ, P.O. Box 34460, Omaha, NE 68134; (402) 573-0966. This organization has 132 affiliated groups and was founded in 1987 as a Christ-centered recovery program that deals with every aspect of addiction, including the spiritual. It offers a newsletter, information, referrals, and assistance in starting new groups.

National Center for Tobacco-free Kids, 1707 L Street, NW, Suite 800, Washington, DC 20036; (800) 284-KIDS; www.tobaccofreekids.org; info@tobaccofreekids.org.

Foundation for a Smokefree America, P.O. Box 492028, Los Angeles, CA 90049; (310) 471-0303; www.tobaccofree.com; info@tobaccofree.org, was founded by R. J. Reynolds's grandson after he saw his father, brother, and other relatives die from cigarette-induced emphysema and cancer.

Action on Smoking and Health (ASH), 2013 H St., NW, Washington, DC 20006; (202) 659-4310; ash.org, has many resources, including a teen page on its Web site.

Kickbutt.org, P.O. Box 20065, Seattle, WA 98102; (206) 448-2949; kickbutt.org; washdoc@wln.com, is a Web site developed by Doctors Ought to Care on behalf of the tobacco control community. It has a set of youth pages.

Overcomers Outreach, 520 N. Brookhurst, Suite 121, Anaheim, CA 92801; (800) 310-3001; crc.iugm.org/oo.html; info@oo.sheperd.com. This is a national group with 1,000 affiliates, founded in 1985 as a Christ-centered twelve-step support group for individuals and families with any type of compulsive behavior, including smoking. It uses the twelve-step recovery model with Christian scriptures to support recovery. It has conferences and provides guidelines for new groups.

American Lung Association, www.lungusa.org, (800) 586-4872, provides information on the health effects of tobacco use and the latest information on efforts to combat tobacco use among teens.

Quitnet is an Internet site provided by the Massachusetts Tobacco Control Program at www.quitnet.org. It has very useful information for those seeking to stop smoking or those wanting to help others quit.

NicNet, The Nicotine and Tobacco Network, tobacco.arizona.edu, is an Internet resource for smoking and tobacco Internet links. It is sponsored by the Arizona Program for Nicotine and Tobacco Research.

Tobacco BBS, www.tobacco.org, geneb@tobacco.org, is a site with much information.

Self-Help Resources

American Cancer Society, (800) ACS-2345, www.cancer.org, annually sponsors the Great American Smokeout.

Growing Up Tobacco Free: Preventing Nicotine Addiction in Children and Youths, by Barbara S. Lynch and Richard J. Bonnie (NY: National Academy Press, 1994). This book addresses prevention programs for youth, explains nicotine's effects, describes the process of addiction, and provides guidelines for public action.

Teens and Tobacco: A Fatal Attraction, by Susan S. Lang and Beth H. Marks (NY: Twenty First Century Press, 1996) discusses the effects of smoking on teens and why they smoke.

Developing School-Based Tobacco Use Prevention and Cessation Programs, by Steve Sussman, Clyde W. Dent, Dee Burton and Alan W. Stacy (New Berry, CA: Sage Publications, 1995) offers a full picture of the key issues in designing and implementing a school-based prevention and cessation program. Many aspects of this program would be useful in congregational settings.

Quit for Teens/Read This Book and Stop Smoking, by Charles F. Wetherall (NY: Andrews and McMeel, 1995) gives reasons for teens to stop smoking, explains why teens smoke, and offers techniques to stop.

The report of the surgeon general: Preventing tobacco use among young people (1994) by M.J. Elders, C.L. Perry, M.P. Eriksen and G.A. Giovino (*American Journal of Public Health, 84(4). 543-547*) is a well written summary of the issue of teen tobacco use referenced to the current scientific findings.

References

Altman, D.G., Levine, D.W., Coeytano, R., Slade, J. and Jaffe, R. (1996). Tobacco promotion and susceptibility to tobacco use among adolescents aged 12 through 17 years in a nationally representative sample. *American Journal of Public Health, 86(11). 1590-1593.*

American Psychiatric Association. (1994). *Diagnostic and Statistical Manual of Mental Disorders-Fourth Edition.* Washington, DC: APA.

Bruvold, W.H. (1993). A meta-analysis of adolescent smoking prevention programs. *American Journal of Public Health, 83(6). 872-880.*

Centers for Disease Control and Prevention. (1994). Cigarette smoking among adults—United States, 1993. *Morbidity and Mortality Weekly Report, 43. 925-930.*

Centers for Disease Control and Prevention. (1996). Tobacco use and usual source of cigarettes among high school students—United States, 1995. *Morbidity and Mortality Weekly Report, 45. 413-418.*

Centers for Disease Control and Prevention. (1996, Feb. 16). Accessibility of tobacco products to youths aged 12–17 years old—United States, 1989 and 1993. *Morbidity and Mortality Weekly Report.*

Elders, M.J., Perry, C.L., Eriksen, M.P. and Giovino, G.A. (1994). The report of the surgeon general: Preventing tobacco use among young people. *American Journal of Public Health, 84(4).* 543-547.

Gallup, G.H. and Bezilla, R. (1992). *The Religious Life of Young Americans.* Princeton, NJ: The George Gallup International Institute.

Heishman, S.J., Kozlowski, L.T. and Henningfield, J.E. (1997). Nicotine addiction: implications for public health policy. *Journal of Social Issues, 53(1).* 13-33.

Henningfield, J.E., Cohen, C. and Slade, J.D. (1991). Is nicotine more addictive than cocaine? *British Journal of Addiction, 86.* 565-569.

Johnston, L.D., O'Malley, P.M. and Bachman, J.G. (1995). *National Survey Results on Drug Use from the Monitoring the Future Study, 1975-1994* (NIH Publication No. 95-4026). Washington, DC: U.S. Government Printing Office.

Koenig, H.G. (1997). *Is Religion Good for Your Health: The Effects of Religion on Physical and Mental Health.* NY: Haworth Press.

Pollay, R.W. (1997). Hacks, flacks and counter-attacks: Cigarettes, advertising, sponsored research, and controversies. *Journal of Social Issues. 53(1).* 53-74.

Gambling

"Winning Was a 'High' He Enjoyed"

The church youth worker, Gary Olson, came to Pastor Carter with a serious concern. Recently a teen in the youth group, Ken, confessed to the youth worker that he and several of his high school friends gambled on a regular basis. He asked for help. Ken was an athletic, good-looking, intelligent youngster from a loving, affluent family. The 15-year-old used a bookmaker to bet on sports, regularly played ten-dollar-a-hand blackjack with school chums, and routinely spent one hundred dollars a pop on a sports lottery. When he lost, Ken raided his savings account to pay off gambling debts. He and his friends had little problem finding gambling venues even though gambling is illegal for minors. Ken had friends who had stolen from their parents to cover their bets. Recently gambling began affecting Ken's schoolwork, leading to lower grades. Ken, an avid sports fan, began gambling when he was 13 years old. At first he bet only on baseball and basketball and did well. Winning was a "high" that he enjoyed. His friends came to him for advice on how to bet. Ken's parents were both social gamblers and regularly participated in parish bingo events.

Pastoral Assessment

This is the first generation of children who have grown up in a society in which gambling has been widely glamorized and legalized. Experts predict that gambling will be the fastest-growing addiction in the early twenty-first century (Freiberg 1995). The general public and churches are only beginning to understand the problems created by widespread gambling in society. Ken in many ways is typical of the type of young person who can become a compulsive or pathological gambler. Individuals with gambling problems are frequently highly energetic, industrious, and above-average in intelligence. The favorite gambling activities among youth are competitive in nature, such as card games, sports betting, and games of personal skill. Many adolescents with gambling problems report that their parents gamble, and most problem gamblers start betting early in life. In a study of adolescent gambling in Nova Scotia, Canada, the researchers found that youthful gamblers typically began at age 13 and developed problem gambler characteristics by age 15 (National Council of Welfare 1996).

Relevant History

A large number of adult pathological gamblers suffer from alcohol and other substance abuse problems, depression, and suicidal tendencies (Murray 1993) (see Cases 1, 15, 16).

Diagnostic Criteria

The essential feature of compulsive or pathological gambling is persistent and recurrent gambling behavior that disrupts personal, educational, or occupational life. The person is preoccupied with gambling, constantly thinking of the next gambling venture or ways to raise money to wager. Most pathological gamblers say that they seek the "high" of betting through wagering increasing amounts of money. They tend to "chase" the losses of one day with increased betting to cover their past losses. Pathological gamblers often continue to gamble despite repeated efforts to stop. They can be restless or irritable when they try to reduce or control their gambling. They may use gambling to escape problems or negative feelings like depression, guilt, or anxiety. Many pathological gamblers lie to family members, therapists, or others to hide their habit. Some commit illegal acts, like theft or fraud, to finance their gambling. Individuals damage or lose important relationships, jobs, or educational opportunities because of problem gambling.

Pathological gambling is most common among youth, the poor, and the poorly educated, who are constantly exposed to advertising's tempting visions of instant riches. Problems with gambling typically begin in adolescence in males and later in life in females. Males are three times more likely than females to have the problem (APA 1994). Because pathological gambling is a progressive condition, adolescent problem gamblers are a particularly vulnerable group in terms of the future development of the disorder.

Response to Vignette

It is a good sign that Ken is asking for help. Ken sees that he has a problem and has gone to a person he trusts for help. He will need the support of the youth worker, pastor, family, and friends to address his gambling. Ken met with Gary Olson and Pastor Carter and described how he began to realize that gambling was negatively impacting his life. He made a $500 bet on football to cover his losses of the past week and telephoned a sports hot line every five minutes all day for updated scores. At that point, it dawned on him that his gambling was out of control.

Ken, Gary Olson, and Pastor Carter researched the problem of youth gambling together on the Internet and found educational materials that informed them about the issue. They decided to have a family session with Ken's mother and father. Pastor Carter used the session to educate the family on the potentially addictive nature of gambling and the treatment options. He explained that compulsive gambling is a diagnosable malady, not a disgrace. Compulsive gambling is a disorder from which millions of North Americans suffer—this family is not alone. In the session it was learned that Ken's mother had a problem with slot-machine use. The family decided to enter treatment together and to see a psychologist who specialized in gambling addiction. As a result of this experience, Pastor Carter led a churchwide education group on the psychological and social effects of problem gambling. In a few months the congregation made the decision to stop sponsoring bingo as a way to raise church funds.

Gambling is a significant and rapidly growing social issue that needs to be addressed by the church. Researchers assert that gambling has the addictive quality of psychoactive drugs for some people (Shaffer and Hall 1996). Experts report that Americans now spend more than $500 billion annually in the United States on some form of gambling, spending more than on movies, sporting events, concerts, and the theater combined. In 1988, two states had large-scale casino gambling, now twenty-seven states have it. Thirty-seven states operate a lottery, and some form of gambling is legal in forty-eight states (Vogel 1997).

Treatment Within the Faith Community

Young people are particularly vulnerable to the get-rich-quick promotions of the gambling industry. Nine years after casino gambling was legalized in New Jersey, a survey of high school students in the Atlantic City area found that over 50 percent of the respondents had gambled in casinos (Arcuri, Lester, and Smith 1985). Studies involving more than 7,700 American and Canadian teens indicated that 4.4 to 7.4 percent of the adolescents meet the criteria for pathological gambling (Shaffer and Hall 1996). This figure is two to four times the current rate of pathological gamblers found among adults.

It is important for faith communities to be informed about the effects of gambling on individuals and their families. Symptoms of gambling-related problems are not well known nor does the general public understand that gambling can be addictive. Like alcohol, gambling is a social activity for most people, but for a minority it is a devastating addiction. The social impact of gambling must be understood and considered when the faith community uses gambling to raise money. For compulsive gamblers, consequences and behavior include financial and employment losses, family breakups, depression, substance abuse, and criminal activity (to raise money to gamble).

Hospitalization for pathological gambling is necessary when an individual is suicidal; violent; or suffers severe anxiety, panic attacks, substance

Indications for Referral

abuse, or severe depression. Legal referrals may be needed, given the high rates of illegal acts among compulsive gamblers.

Treatment by Mental Health Specialist

Treatment of pathological gambling is often patterned after the treatment used with alcohol and drug addiction. Like drug abusers, compulsive gamblers tend to deny the problem and avoid finding help. Gamblers Anonymous (GA) is a twelve-step group that encourages members to admit their problem and gives group support to help participants gain control over gambling. GA members recognize the denial and lies of the compulsive gambler and confront their distorted thinking. Family members may join Gam-Anon, which is modeled after Alanon, for group support. Compulsive gamblers must stop living in the fantasy world of the addiction and confront the reality of the consequences of their gambling.

Cognitive and behavioral therapies may be used to reframe thinking patterns and change habits that promote gambling behavior. Patients are taught to identify and record situations that bring on the compulsion to gamble and to recognize the distorted thinking that they can win against the odds. In a recent study of Canadian males who entered a course of treatment for pathological gambling using a cognitive-behavioral model that included relapse prevention training, a high 86 percent were no longer gambling a year after treatment (Sylvain, Ladouceur and Boisvert 1997).

Cross-Cultural Issues

Pathological gambling is an international problem. In Great Britain researchers found that 90 percent of adolescents had tried some form of gambling; in the United States the figure was 86 percent, and in Canada 76 percent (Bland et al. 1993). The Indian Gambling Regulatory Act of 1988 has led to the establishment of casino gambling on numerous reservations throughout the United States. This has fostered high rates of gambling problems among Native Americans in Minnesota where 1 in 10 was found to have a serious gambling problem (Zitlow 1992).

Resources

National Resources

Gam-Anon, founded in 1960, is an international organization with 380 groups. It is a fellowship of women and men who are family members and friends of compulsive gamblers and affected by the gambling problem. The aim of the program is to rebuild lives and give aid to gamblers and their families. There are Gam-a-teen groups for teens. Group guidelines and other literature is available; P.O. Box 157, Whitestone, NY 11357; (718) 352-1671; www.gamblersanonymous.org/gamanon.html.

Gamblers Anonymous (GA), P.O. Box 17173, Los Angeles, CA 90017; (213) 386-8789; www.gamblersanonymous.org; isomain@gamblersanonymous.org; is an international organization, founded in 1957, with 1,200 chapters. It is a fellowship of men and women who share experiences, strength, and hope with one another to recover from compulsive gambling, following a twelve-step program. GA publishes a monthly bulletin for members.

Overcomers Outreach is a Christian-oriented twelve-step program with 1,000 support groups for teens with any type of compulsive behavior, including gambling. 520 North Brookhurst, Suite 121, Anaheim, CA 92801; info@oo.shephard.com; (800) 310-3001; crc.iugm.org/oo.html.

National Coalition Against Legalized Gambling, 110 Maryland Ave., N.E., Washington, DC 20002; ncalg@ncalg.org; www.ncalg.org; (800) 664-2680; offers information on gambling and advocates against gambling expansion. The founder of the organization is a United Methodist minister, the Reverend Thomas Grey.

National Council on Problem Gambling, Inc., P.O. Box 9419, Washington, DC 20016; www.ncpgambling.org; (800) 522-4700; ncpg@erols.com; is a nonprofit health agency whose mission is to provide information about compulsive gambling and to promote the development of services for those suffering from pathological gambling.

Self-Help Resources

Gambling: A Challenge for Youth is a middle-school curriculum available from the Minnesota Extension Service, (612) 625-8173.

Improving Your Odds is a secondary-level curriculum and *Table Talk* is a program for families to discuss gambling issues. Both are available from Gambling Problems Resource Center, (800) 247-1303.

Wanna Bet? Everything You Wanted to Know about Teen Gambling But Never Thought to Ask is available from the Minnesota Council on Compulsive Gambling, (888) 991-1234, www.nati.org, info@nati.org.

What About Me, Too? was developed by Lutheran Social Services of North Dakota and is designed to help children of compulsive gamblers understand and cope with the addiction. This program is aimed at elementary-aged children and is available through Addiction Outreach for Recovery in North Dakota, (800) 950-2901. The American Psychological Association publication, *The Monitor*, reported in December 1995 that a study has found that 75 percent of children in the home of a problem gambler had gambled by age 11.

Healthy Youth and Families is a program designed to provide youth workers with information and activities to help Southeast Asian youth. Gambling concerns are addressed in their program. Contact Southeast Asian Community Coalition for Youth and Families, (612) 641-7290.

"Pathological Gambling and Pastoral Counseling" by Joseph W. Ciarrocchi, in the *Clinical Handbook of Pastoral Counseling, Volume 2*, edited by Robert J. Wicks and Richard D. Parsons (NY: Paulist Press, 1993) offers a helpful chapter from a pastoral care perspective.

References

American Psychiatric Association. (1994). *Diagnostic and Statistical Manual of Mental Disorders-IV*. Washington, DC: APA.

Arcuri, A.F., Lester, D. and Smith, F.O. (1985). Shaping Adolescent Gambling Behavior, *Adolescence, 20*. 935-938.

Bland, R.C., Newman, S.C., Orn, H. and Stebelsky, G. (1993). Epidemiology of pathological gambling in Edmonton. *Canadian Journal of Psychiatry, 38(2)*. 108-112.

Freiberg, P. (1995). Pathological gambling turning into epidemic. *American Psychological Association Monitor, December Issue*. Washington, DC: APA.

Murray, J. B. (1993). Review of Research on Pathological Gambling. *Psychological Reports, 72*. 791-810.

National Council of Welfare. (1996). *Gaming in Canada*. Ottawa, Ontario: National Council of Welfare.

Shaffer, H.J. and Hall, M.N. (1996). Estimating the prevalence of adolescent gambling disorders: A quantitative synthesis and guide toward standard gambling nomenclature. *Journal of Gambling Studies, 12*. 193-214.

Sylvain, C., Ladouceur, R. and Boisvert, J. (1997). Cognitive and behavioral treatment of pathological gambling: A controlled study. *Journal of Consulting and Clinical Psychology, 65(5)*. 727-732.

Vogel, J. (1997). *Crapped Out: How Gambling Ruins the Economy and Destroys Lives*. Monroe, ME: Common Courage Press.

Zitlow, D. (1992). *Incidence and Comparative Study of Compulsive Gambling Behaviors Between Indians and Non-Indians Within and Near a Northern Plains Reservation*. Bemidji, MN: Indian Health Service, Bemidji Area Office.

Case 4

Abuse

"Spare the Rod and Spoil the Child"

Mrs. Neal asked to see Reverend Elizabeth Lowe after worship. Mrs. Neal looked stressed and concerned. She had attended church a few times with her 13-year-old son, Richard, but his father had not joined them. The two adults met in the church office while Richard sat outside at the pastor's request. Reverend Lowe noticed that Richard appeared wary and withdrawn, and he had fresh bruises on his face. Mrs. Neal began by explaining that her husband had been out of work for several months, and the family had moved to the area seeking employment. She indicated that Mr. Neal has a drinking problem that has grown worse since he became unemployed. She and her husband did not agree on the disciplining of the teenager, who was having trouble in school. One of his teachers told Mrs. Neal that Richard is disruptive, hostile, and destructive and that he bullies other students.

Mr. Neal had always spanked the boy when he "needed it," but the corporal punishment was now out of control. Recently, Mr. Neal beat his son with a belt until he bled. In his uncontrolled anger, Mr. Neal had used the buckle end of his belt and had almost injured the teenager's eye when he hit Richard in the face. When Mrs. Neal confronted her husband, he justified his actions by quoting the Bible, "Spare the rod and spoil the child." Increasingly, he expected perfection of her and the child. In addition, Mr. Neal had become verbally abusive—belittling and threatening her and their son.

Mrs. Neal tells a story of physical and emotional child abuse. Striking a youngster until he bleeds is not discipline but abuse. It appears that Mr. Neal is out of control and the boy is in danger of permanent physical injury and lasting emotional trauma. Alcohol and drug use by parents is often a factor in severe child abuse cases.

Pastoral Assessment

Mrs. Neal is asking for help. You need to get a detailed account of the abuse and level of danger. How much danger is she in? Domestic violence and child abuse often go together. Many battered women in shelters indicate that the primary reason they fled their home was to protect their children from attack (New Beginnings 1990). Pastor Lowe needs to help Mrs. Neal develop a plan of action to get herself and her son through this crisis. Mrs. Neal has not remained isolated as most abusive families tend to do. She has brought her son to church, and she is asking the pastor questions. She has also shown a willingness to confront her husband about his behavior toward the boy. These are very positive factors in being able to receive help.

Parents like Mr. Neal who physically abuse children consider the use of force and physical punishment appropriate means to control a child. They often have strong opinions about the right to use physical punishment (Bavolek 1989). When a person says glibly, "Spare the rod and spoil the child," remember that most physical abuse of children comes as a result of severe corporal punishment and that about 1 in 8 cases of physical abuse result in major physical injury, such as fractured bones and skulls (American Humane Association 1984). Low self-esteem, extreme feelings of inadequacy, and insecurity with accompanying helplessness are often the reported feelings of abusive parents. They feel uncomfortable with problem behaviors in children. They tend to expect perfection of themselves and their children, and normal human failings are equated with worthlessness. These parents can be hypercritical of themselves and their children. Feelings of low self-regard are often passed from one generation to the next (Hamilton 1989).

Abusive parents also tend to be misinformed or uninformed regarding the normal needs and development of children and adolescents. These unrealistic, inappropriate, or rigid expectations of children and teens may make them ineffective at the basic tasks of parenting. During adolescence a youngster is gradually developing emotional and physical independence from parents and establishing an identity that is based on peer interactions as well as family relations. A teen's desire for autonomy and a decreased dependency on parents requires a shift in the authority structure of the family. Maltreatment of adolescents can be linked to the inability of parents to adjust to the changing needs of teens. Parents who become abusive are rarely evil or bad people. They are generally normal people with poor coping skills, rigid role expectations, and weak support systems. They often have more stress than they can manage and release their frustrations on their children in destructive acts of abuse.

Relevant History

If Reverend Lowe cannot obtain a clear picture of the situation after talking with the mother, Richard's teachers would be important persons with whom to consult, because his mother has reported that Richard is having trouble at school. What sort of trouble? When did it start? Teachers and school personnel are generally good resources for consultation if you suspect abuse or neglect. It is very important to understand that unless someone intervenes in the cycle of abuse in a family, it will continue.

Richard recently told a teacher that he felt like running away from home. Teens who run away are often victims of abuse. In 1990, Powers, Eckenrode, and Jaklitsch published research on 223 adolescents with a history of maltreatment who sought services from homeless or runaway youth programs. Sixty percent reported physical abuse, 42 percent emotional abuse, 48 percent neglect, and 21 percent sexual abuse. One-third of these children reported being "pushed out" of their homes (throwaways), rather than running away. The authors wrote, "We find this to be an alarming and dangerous statistic in view of the lethal risks these young people face on the street" (p. 96) (see Case 11).

Diagnostic Criteria

Mental health professionals divide child maltreatment into four areas: physical abuse, neglect, emotional maltreatment, and sexual abuse. Physical abuse is any act that results in a nonaccidental physical injury. Most often this occurs in the form of severe corporal punishment. Neglect arises from negligent treatment of a child in the forms of inadequate food, clothing, shelter, medical care, or supervision. Emotional maltreatment is behavior by a caretaker that is emotionally damaging or degrading to the child, usually in the form of severe belittling, screaming, threats, blaming, or continual family discord. Sexual abuse is any act of sexual assault or exploitation of a minor, which includes a range of actions from rape to handling of the genitals of a child to exposing a child to pornography (see Cases 5 and 6).

The primary target area for inflicting physical abuse is the back surface of the body from the neck to the knees. Unexplained injury may come in many forms. Bruises and welts in various stages of healing or clustered in regular patterns in the shape of an object are suspect. Burns with cigars and cigarettes, especially to the soles, palms, back, and buttocks, as well as immersion burns (for example, forcing a child into a bath of scalding water), are among burns most often noted in child abuse reports. Abused children also suffer unexplained fractures and lacerations, most commonly in the facial area (Office of the Attorney General of California 1985).

Response to Vignette

Prepare yourself before a crisis. Consult with the child protective services agency in your area regarding the procedures for reporting abuse in your jurisdiction. You can also consult mental health or medical professionals or educators who are required by law in most states to be trained in the family dynamics of child abuse and neglect. Be informed and prepared. In a crisis, have one or more mental health professionals available for support and assistance.

When dysfunctional families are under severe or multiple stressors, the risk of child maltreatment increases. Financial hardship, unemployment, marital strife, separation or divorce, a serious illness or death in the family, serious mental illness of a family member, a child in the family with special health needs (such as mental retardation), heavy continuous childcare responsibilities, and frequent changes of residence will put some families at risk of becoming abusive. When inadequate coping skills or a limited or nonexistent support system to manage the stress is added, the risk will further increase.

Among confirmed cases of child abuse and neglect, about 40 percent involve alcohol and other drugs (Wang and Daro 1997). Almost 14 million adult Americans abuse alcohol and 12 million use illicit drugs. It is estimated that 9 to 10 million children and teens live in homes affected by substance-abusing parents (Woodside 1988). Alcohol makes many people more impulsive, and they act out aggressive feelings. Treatment for alcohol or drug abuse is essential in stopping the pattern of abuse or neglect.

The abuse of children often takes the form of excessive verbal assaults. Children who have a regular diet of belittling, screaming, threats, blaming, sarcasm, continual family discord, and negative family moods experience degradation, becoming youngsters with low self-esteem. Emotional scarring from verbal abuse is no less injurious than physical assaults. Emotional maltreatment can cripple.

Being a parent is not easy. It is the responsibility of parents to teach a child discipline, which takes time and patience. Discipline involves helping a youngster develop self-control while setting limits and correcting undesirable behavior. Discipline includes encouraging children, guiding them, helping them feel good about themselves, and teaching them how to think independently. Punishing children with beatings and punitive language teaches children to be fearful of adults, rather than engendering respect. If parents want children to obey the rules and control their anger, they must set a good example. Richard's father is teaching his son to fear him, not to respect him.

Treatment Within the Faith Community

In 1996 there were almost 970,000 cases of confirmed child maltreatment reported—about 14 in every 1,000 children in the United States. Physical abuse represented 23 percent of the confirmed cases, neglect 60 percent, and sexual abuse 9 percent. About 1 in 5 victims of abuse are teenagers (Wang and Daro 1997). Given its extensiveness, clergy and congregations will inevitably come into contact with this issue.

Research has consistently pointed toward social isolation as a significant risk factor for child maltreatment (Moncher 1995). The family that becomes cut off from outside support systems, such as extended family, friends, and faith community, is less likely to cope adaptively with the stresses of family life and more apt to maltreat its children. The level of social isolation appears to increase as maltreatment in the family progresses. Child maltreatment is a community issue—no single group has the necessary knowledge or resources to address the problem alone.

Clergy are in a strategic position to intervene with these isolated families because they serve in one of the only helping professions in which home visits are a regular and even expected activity. Research indicates that the majority of pastoral crisis-counseling sessions take place during home visits, providing pastors with unusual access to people's lives (Mollica et al. 1986). Nearly 8 in 10 of those who sought help from clergy reported having preschool or school-age children in the home, and those who needed counsel tended to have low incomes and low educational achievement (Veroff, Kulka and Douvan 1981). If clergy and religious workers are alert to the risk factors of child abuse and neglect, they can greatly contribute to the critically needed effort to prevent and reduce abuse.

According to the 1997 National Clearinghouse on Child Abuse and Neglect Information Survey on Mandatory Reporting, most states require clergy to report child abuse and neglect. Pastors say that they are inadequately prepared for the task, viewing child abuse as a clinical arena in which they feel little competence. Most surveyed pastors indicated that they would like to have additional training in child abuse assessment and that the subject should be a required part of seminary education (Weaver 1995).

Indications for Referral

If you decide that a child abuse report is required to protect a young person in danger, you can probably do so by phone and anonymously. Your jurisdiction will probably protect you with immunity against civil liability for reporting if you act in good faith, that is, without malicious intent. The authorities will evaluate your report and are generally required to investigate within twenty-four hours. Contact your governmental authorities for specific details. There will be many different reactions from parents who are reported for child maltreatment. Some parents will deny what happened, others will be defensive and angry, and a few will be relieved someone intervened and stopped the abuse or neglect. Unless you are in an emergency situation, discuss your reporting strategy with an expert adviser to get a second opinion before taking action.

Reporting child maltreatment will not be an easy process. It may be even more difficult for clergy than other professionals who are not intimately connected in a community of faith that understands itself as an extended family. In some cases clergy may find themselves serving as pastor to families they have reported for abuse. It is important to educate the church or synagogue about your ethical and legal approach to this difficult issue so that the community will be prepared if you are faced with the responsibility of acting in the best interest of a child. A report of child maltreatment is the act of a responsible person trying to assist a family in crisis. It is important to inform your faith community that most abusive families repeat the abuse or neglect unless they receive treatment, which in many cases does not occur unless ordered and monitored by the court.

In what circumstance is a pastor ethically bound to report a case of child abuse or neglect? Is a clergyperson required to hold a secret even if it is harmful or life-threatening to a child in danger? Research indicates that although substantial numbers of child abuse cases come to the attention of clergy, few are reported to authorities (Johnson and Bondurant 1995). Some clergy use pastoral confidentiality to defend not reporting child abuse. One scholar in this area has noted that

> confidentiality is not intended to protect abusers from being held account-able for their actions or keep them from getting the help they need. Shielding them from the consequences of their behavior likely will further endanger their victims and will deny them the repentance they need. (Fortune 1987, 201)

Treatment by Mental Health Specialist

A mental health specialist would need to evaluate Richard for a variety of potential problems because child physical abuse has been strongly linked to many of the most troubling problems in our society. These would include severe emotional problems, aggressive and violent behavior, self-injurious behavior, suicide, psychological trauma, substance abuse, inter-personal problems, and academic difficulties (Malinosky-Rummell and Hansen 1993). Mr. Neal's treatment for alcohol abuse is essential to stop the pattern of abuse in this family.

Cross-Cultural Issues

In a study of American Indian families, 85 percent of the child neglect cases and 63 percent of the child abuse cases involved alcohol abuse (Lujan et al. 1989). Generally, being boys or children of color and having a male inflict the physical punishment increase the likelihood of a more serious injury to the young person (Hegar, Zuravin and Orme 1994).

Resources

National Resources

National Clearinghouse on Child Abuse and Neglect Information (NCCAN), 330 C Street, SW, Washington, DC 20447; (800) 394-3366; www.calib.com/nccanch; nccanch@calib.com. The NCCAN is a national resource for professionals and concerned citizens seeking information on the prevention, identification, and treatment of child maltreatment.

Childhelp USA/Forrester National Child Abuse Hotline, (800) 422-4453, provides a twenty-four-hour professional crisis counseling and referral service in all fifty states.

Family Violence Prevention Fund/Health Resource Center, 383 Rhode Island St., Suite 304, San Francisco, CA 94103; www.igc.org/fund; fund@igc.apc.org; (800) 313-1310; is a national nonprofit organization that focuses on domestic violence education, prevention, and public policy reform.

National Center for Missing and Exploited Children, 2101 Wilson Blvd., Suite 550, Arlington, VA 22201; (800) 843-5678; www.missingkids.org, serves as a national clearinghouse and resource center on issues relating to child victimization, specifically the abduction and sexual exploitation of youth. The twenty-four-hour toll-free hotline is for parents to report missing children and for citizens to gain free information on child protection.

National Committee to Prevent Child Abuse, 200 S. Michigan Ave., Seventeenth Floor, Chicago, IL 60604; (800) 55-NCPCA; www.childabuse.org; info@childabuse.org, will provide information on child abuse and prevention.

Canadian Society for the Prevention of Cruelty to Children, 356 First Street, Box 700, Midland, Ontario L4R 4P4 Canada; (cnet.unb.ca/orgs/prevention_cruelty/cspcc.htm); cc@bconnex.net.

National Council on Child Abuse and Family Violence, 1155 Connecticut Ave., NW, Suite 400, Washington, DC 20036; (800) 222-2000; NCCAFV@compuserve.com.

Center for the Prevention of Sexual and Domestic Violence, 936 N. 34th Street, Suite 200, Seattle, WA 98103; www.cpsdv.org; cpsdv@cpsdv.org; (206) 634-1903. The center offers training, consultation, videos, and publications to clergy, laity, seminary faculty, and students.

Self-Help Resources

Parents Anonymous, 675 West Foothill Blvd., Suite 220, Claremont, CA 91711; (909) 621-6184; www.parentsanonymous-natl.org; parentsanon@msn.com. This national organization, founded in 1970, is a professionally-facilitated peer-led group for those who are having difficulty and would like to learn more effective ways to parent. It provides group leaders, develops chapters, and has children's groups.

Violence in the Family: A Workshop Curriculum for Clergy and Other Helpers, by Marie M. Fortune (Cleveland, OH: The Pilgrim Press, 1996).

Treating Abused Adolescents, by Eliana Gil (NY: Guilford, 1996) provides a practical guide to treatment by a noted expert. It is a useful text for specialists in pastoral counseling.

Spare the Child: The Religious Roots of Punishment and the Psychological Impact of Physical Abuse, by Philip Greven (NY: Random House, 1992) is a superb analysis of the relationship between punitive religious beliefs and child abuse.

References

American Humane Association. (1984). *Trends in Child Abuse and Neglect: A National Perspective.* Denver, CO: AHA.

Bavolek, S.J. (1989). Assessing and treating high-risk parenting attitudes. In J.D. Pardeck (ed.) *Child Abuse and Neglect* (pp. 97-110). NY: Gordon and Breach Science Publishers.

Fortune, M.M. (1987). Confidentiality and mandatory reporting: A clergy dilemma? In M.D. Pellauer, B. Chester and J.A. Boyajian (eds.) *Sexual Assault and Abuse: A Handbook for Clergy and Religious Professionals* (pp. 198-205). San Francisco: Harper and Row.

Hamilton, L.R. (1989). Variables associated with child maltreatment and implications for prevention and treatment. In J.D. Pardeck (ed.) *Child Abuse and Neglect* (pp. 29-54). NY: Gordon and Breach Science Publishers.

Hegar, R.C., Zuravin, S.J. and Orme, J.G. (1994). Factors predicting severity of physical child abuse injury. *Journal of Interpersonal Violence, 9(2).* 170-83.

Johnson, J.M. and Bondurant, D.M. (1995). Revisiting the 1982 church response survey. In C.J. Adams and M.M. Fortune (eds.), *Violence Against Women and Children: A Christian Theological Sourcebook* (pp. 422-427). NY: Continuum.

Lujan, C., DeBruyn, L.M., May, P.A. and Bird, M.E. (1989). Profile of abused and neglected American Indian children in the Southwest. *Child Abuse and Neglect, 13(4).* 449-461.

Malinosky-Rummell, R. and Hansen, D.J. (1993). Long-term consequences of childhood physical abuse. *Psychological Bulletin, 114(1).* 68-79.

Mollica, R.C., Streets, F.J., Boscarino, J. and Redlich, F.C. (1986). A community study of formal pastoral counseling activities of the clergy. *American Journal of Psychiatry, 143(3).* 323-328.

Moncher, F.J. (1995). Social isolation and child abuse risk. Families in Society. *The Journal of Contemporary Human Services, 75.* 421-433.

New Beginnings. (1990). A survey of battered women seeking shelter at New Beginnings, a shelter for battered women in Seattle, Washington.

Office of the Attorney General of California. (1985). *Child Abuse Prevention Handbook.* Sacramento, CA: Crime Prevention Center.

Powers, J.L., Eckenrode, J. and Jaklitsch, B. (1990). Maltreatment among runaways and homeless youth. *Child Abuse and Neglect, 14.* 87-98.

Veroff, J., Kulka, R.A. and Douvan, E. (1981). *Mental Health in America: Patterns of Help-Seeking from 1957 to 1976.* NY: Basic Books.

Wang, C.T. and Daro, D. (1997). *Current Trends in Child Abuse Reporting and Fatalities: The Results of the 1996 Annual Fifty State Survey.* Chicago, IL: National Committee to Prevent Child Abuse.

Weaver, A.J. (1995). Has there been a failure to prepare and support parish-based clergy in their role as front-line community mental health workers? A review. *The Journal of Pastoral Care, 49.* 129-149.

Woodside, M. (1988). Research on children of alcoholics: Past and future. *British Journal of Addiction, 83.* 785-792.

Incest

"Betrayal of Trust"

Katherine was ten years old when her Hebrew school teacher, Mrs. Rosen, approached Rabbi Cohen with her concerns about one of the girls in her class. Mrs. Rosen had begun to notice changes in Katherine. She had become sullen and withdrawn whereas she had previously been a playful child. Katherine laughed infrequently and was less involved in group discussions and activities. She had become shy and irritable with her classmates. When Mrs. Rosen asked Katherine if something was wrong, Katherine had told her that she was afraid of her new daddy and inquired whether she could come to live with Mrs. Rosen. When she asked why Katherine was afraid of her father, she bit her lip and said quietly, "I can't tell you." Mrs. Rosen did not pursue this further with Katherine, but remained worried about her and wondered what she might do.

The rabbi knew that Katherine's mother had recently remarried, and he thought that perhaps the blending of families had something to do with the changes in Katherine's personality. He counseled Mrs. Rosen to discuss her concerns with Katherine's mother, indicating that he would be happy to talk with the child's parents as well.

Katherine's mother, when approached by Mrs. Rosen, agreed with the rabbi's analysis and attributed her daughter's behavior to the changes within the family. She said that Katherine was having a little trouble getting used to things. Mrs. Rosen was left with the impression that Katherine was an overly sensitive girl who was prone to getting herself worked up about imaginary problems. Although she continued to notice Katherine's troubled demeanor, she left the situation alone thereafter.

At home Katherine was scolded for making things up. Her mother was embarrassed and sternly warned her about causing any further trouble with the synagogue. Katherine kept quiet after that. She felt lonely, ashamed, and guilty, believing that the sexual abuse by her stepfather was her own fault. At school Katherine's grades dropped dramatically from high marks to failing grades, and within a year she had started to skip school. By her twelfth birthday, she was drinking frequently, had failed a grade, and had been in trouble with local juvenile authorities. Katherine ran away from home several times, but she was always returned to her mother, where the abuse resumed. Finally, 18-year-old Katherine was hospitalized after a suicide attempt. It was during her hospitalization that she disclosed the abuse she had suffered and was able to begin treatment.

Pastoral Assessment

It has been estimated that 20–40 percent of girls and 2–9 percent of boys are sexually abused by the time they reach the age of 18 (Blume 1998). Incest may occur within the family, by a parent, stepparent, sibling, other relative, or by someone outside of the home, such as a neighbor or teacher. Blood relationship alone does not represent an accurate definition of incest. Unlike stranger or acquaintance abuse, incest is the violation of an ongoing bond of trust between a child and a caretaker. In incest, a person whom the child trusts and depends on for care, nurturance, and support takes advantage of that relationship (Bass and Davis 1994). Force is not a necessary variable; rather, the child's dependency is used against her or him. No child is emotionally prepared to cope with incest. The long-term psychological damage can be devastating (Glod and Teicher 1996).

At the age of 10, Katherine's entire life was affected by a sexual invasion by her stepfather. Her trust, as well as her body, was violated. Mrs. Rosen noticed significant and disturbing changes in Katherine that alerted her that something was wrong. Katherine withdrew from others and evidenced a sullen confusion in her relationships. She became uncomfortable with being touched and voiced her fear to Mrs. Rosen in the hope of being rescued. Despite her innocence, Katherine experienced severe feelings of guilt and shame as she sensed the wrongness of the situation.

The effects of sexual abuse on children are insidious and extreme. Incest represents the ultimate betrayal of a caregiver bond. Katherine's betrayal by a person whom she has trusted to be her protector threatens her entire way of understanding the world. Lacking a way to make sense of the situation, Katherine concludes that she has somehow caused the incest and that there is something wrong with *her*. Incest invalidates children's feelings and sense of reality, teaching them that they cannot trust their own senses or perceptions.

Inadvertently, Mrs. Rosen contributed to Katherine's emotional damage. Although she saw that something was wrong and attempted to intervene on Katherine's behalf, she ultimately let her down, as did Katherine's mother. Neither was able to keep Katherine safe or provide her with the caretaking that all children need and deserve. Katherine's emotional distress was attributed to an overly sensitive nature, which confirmed her belief that she was to blame for her own victimization. Furthermore, failed attempts in seeking help can leave a child feeling hopeless and responsible for the sexual abuse.

Mrs. Rosen and the rabbi might have been able to intervene more successfully if they had directly encouraged Katherine to tell them if anyone was hurting her. By creating a safe opportunity for Katherine to explain what she was experiencing, she might have been able to reveal more about the situation. If during a pastoral assessment one suspects abuse, there are specific ways to intervene that will increase a child's sense of empowerment and safety. Although this does not guarantee that the abuse will be identified or can be stopped, it does let a child know that there are safe places and safe people who care about her or him.

Relevant History

Katherine tells Mrs. Rosen that she is afraid to go home, but she is reluctant to talk about the specific fears she is confronting. A child who has been sexually abused faces complex and conflicting messages. Although Katherine desperately wants the abuse to stop and pleads to be safe, she also feels a need to protect her family. Because Katherine believes that she is to blame for the situation, she does not want others to find out that she has been "bad." Another reason why children may be unable to seek help is that abusers often threaten them or imply that the abuse is the child's fault in order to silence them.

The course of Katherine's emotional decline can be charted from the beginning of the abuse by her stepfather. She does not want to be touched and has trouble in relationships with others because her ability to trust has been severely damaged. She is lonely and depressed and feels alienated. Katherine is unable to concentrate in school—she turns to alcohol to escape from the despair and the hopelessness of her situation. She runs away to try to escape the abuse, but is returned and labeled a bad child by juvenile authorities.

Incest survivors are at an increased risk for suicide (Beitchman et al. 1991). In attempting suicide, incest victims may feel able to reclaim at least some power over their own bodies (see Case 16).

Katherine starts her healing process at age 18, but in a large number of cases, victims of sexual abuse are unable to start this process for many years. People survive by repressing, denying, and minimizing their abuse—taking care of themselves by finding some way to become detached from the memories. This defensive strategy helps them survive the abusive nature of their childhood, but when they become adults, these forgotten events will threaten healthy living. Symptoms can include poor self-image, eating disorders, self-injury, obsessiveness, flashbacks, nightmares, sexual dysfunction, memory loss, disassociation, anxiety, impulsivity, delinquency, depression, and suicide.

Diagnostic Criteria

Once Katherine's sexual abuse is uncovered and she escapes the abusive situation, there are aftereffects of the incest that will require attention. Sexual abuse in adolescence causes severe psychological and emotional consequences. Incest is an extreme trauma, and its effects are virtually inescapable. Post-traumatic stress disorder (PTSD) is the likely diagnosis for Katherine (see Case 7).

There are other diagnoses that are frequently associated with sexual abuse including anxiety disorders, depression, behavioral disorders, and substance abuse. Individual differences affect both the severity and the type of symptoms experienced.

Response to Vignette

It is important that persons who are in a caregiver role with adolescents recognize that their relationship represents a critical and vulnerable bond. Caregivers need to take the time to listen and observe the teens who are depending on them. When a complaint or concern is voiced, it should be taken seriously. Above all things, the young person should be believed and supported. When an adolescent's sense of reality has been invalidated, it is crucial that the teen finds someone who believes her or him and tries to help.

Mrs. Rosen might have been able to provide more support for Katherine had she spent longer talking directly to her. The Hebrew school teacher could have calmly urged Katherine to tell her if she continued to be afraid or if an adult hurt her. Mrs. Rosen might have tried to alleviate any self-blame that Katherine was experiencing, because embarrassment and shame can get in the way of bringing abuse into the open.

Any suspicion of abuse must be reported to the local child protection agency, which will conduct an evaluation and take actions to protect the youngster. The victim of sexual abuse will be physically examined by a physician who specializes in evaluating and treating sexual abuse. This is important because children who have been sexually abused are particularly vulnerable to further traumatization during sensitive medical procedures.

If a teen reports to you that he or she has been sexually abused, listen carefully and believe what you are being told. The response to disclosure of sexual abuse is critical to a young person's ability to resolve the trauma. Do not ask for details, but assure the teen that he or she has done the right thing by telling. Provide reassurance, for there may be guilt or fear of harm for disclosing the secret. Explain that she or he is not to blame for the sexual abuse and that no one deserves it. Finally, offer protection and take immediate steps to follow through.

Treatment Within the Faith Community

People look to their faith community for relationships of trust and support, which casts the leaders into caregiving roles. They must understand that passivity in the face of abuse is itself a violation of caregiver trust. The statistics of sexual abuse are powerful—about 1 of every 3 women will be victims of sexual abuse before reaching adulthood. Faith communities need to understand that some of the children in their care may be vulnerable and that abusers may also be a part of that community. By developing a realistic overview of this problem, a deliberate decision can be made about what kind of involvement the faith community will assume. This may include parental education about incest, sexual abuse, how to evaluate relationships, and spotting warning signs; education for the children about how to say no to people in authority and empowering them regarding the ownership of their bodies; and education for religious leaders about how to handle this sensitive issue when it arises. Unfortunately, there is research evidence that few incest or sexual abuse cases that come to the attention of clergy are reported to child protective services (Johnson and Bondurant 1995).

A referral to a mental health specialist is essential for adequate treatment of the trauma inflicted by sexual abuse or incest. The referral should be to someone who has training and experience in working with incest survivors. Keep in mind that women who have been sexually assaulted will often only accept treatment from a female. Professional evaluation and treatment for the whole family is appropriate to help them understand how to respond to the situation and to facilitate the treatment of the teen who suffered the abuse. If the abuser is a member of the family, professional intervention is imperative.

Indications for Referral

A therapist with special training in the treatment of PTSD (Case 7) and experience working with survivors of incest will be able to help a teen who has been sexually abused. Treatment helps to put the memories into a context that acknowledges the trauma and normalizes the symptoms associated with sexual abuse; it also helps a victim develop alternative coping strategies and provides a safe environment where the teen can heal from the pain. Effective therapeutic interventions are available in individual, family, and group formats.

Treatment by Mental Health Specialist

In past research when health care professionals have been found to have negative attitudes toward incest survivors, those beliefs interfered with providing supportive care. It is hopeful that a recent study of psychiatric nurses reported a high level of acceptance, tolerance, and little blame toward incest and rape survivors among the nurses (Boutcher and Gallop 1996). Education is a key factor in reducing judgmental attitudes. Clergy and congregations need education in the family dynamics of incestual families to reduce negative attitudes and blaming the victim.

Cross-Cultural Issues

National Resources

Resources

National Coalition Against Sexual Assault (NCASA), 125 N. Enola Drive, Enola, PA 17025; ncasa@redrose.net; www.ncasa.org; (717) 728-9764; is a membership organization committed to the prevention of sexual violence through intervention, education, and public policy.

National Organization for Victim Assistance (NOVA), 1757 Park Road, NW, Washington, DC 20010; (800) TRY-NOVA; www.try-nova.org; nova@try-nova.org. This group, founded in 1975, provides support, referrals, and advocacy for victims of violent crime and disasters.

Rape, Abuse, and Incest National Network (RAINN), 635-B Pennsylvania Avenue, SE, Washington, DC 20003; (800) 656-4673; www.rainn.org; rainnmail@aol.com.

Survivors of Incest Anonymous, P.O. Box 21817, Baltimore, MD 21222; (410) 282-3400; www.siawso.org.

VOICES IN ACTION, Inc., P.O. Box 148309, Chicago, IL 60614; (800) 7-VOICE-8; www.voices-action.org; voices@voices-action.org; is an international organization providing assistance to victims of incest and child sexual abuse in becoming survivors.

Parents United International World Headquarters, 615 15th Street, Modesto, CA 95354; (209) 572-3446.

National Organization on Male Sexual Victimization, P.O. Box 207823, West Palm Beach, FL 33416; (800) 738-4181; www.nomsv.org; nomsv@isd.net.

Center for the Prevention of Sexual and Domestic Violence, 936 N. 34th Street, Suite 200, Seattle, WA 98103; (206) 634-1903; www.cpsdv.org; cpsdv@cpsdv.org. The center offers training, consultation, videos, and publications to clergy, laity, seminary faculty, and students.

Interfaith Sexual Trauma Institute, St. John's Abbey and University, Collegeville, MN 56321; www.csbsju.edu/isti; isti@csbsju.edu; (320) 363-3931.

Adults Molested as Children United, P.O. Box 952, San Jose, CA 95108; (408) 453-7616.

Self-Help Resources

Incest Survivors Anonymous, P.O. Box 17245, Long Beach, CA 90807; (310) 428-5599; is an international association based on the twelve-step approach. Women, men, and teens meet to share experiences, strength, and hope so they recover peace of mind. Send a self-addressed stamped envelope for information, if you are a survivor.

Survivors Connections, Inc., 52 Lyndon Rd., Cranston, RI 02905; (401) 941-2548; www.angelfire.com/ri/survivorconnections; scsitereturn@hotmail.com, is a grassroots activist organization for survivors of sexual assault.

Anonymous Sexual Abuse Recovery (Canada) is an electronic support service for victims and survivors of sexual abuse and sexual assault, (905) 389-8969, www.worldchat.com/public/asarc; asarc@asar.org.

Survivors Network of those Abused by Priests, P.O. Box 438679, Chicago, IL 60643; (312) 409-2720; www.teleport.com/~snapmail. This is an international group founded in 1990 to support men and women who were sexually abused by Roman Catholic leaders. It provides extensive phone networking, information, and support groups.

Incest Survivors Resource Network International, P.O. Box 7375, Las Cruces, NM 88006; (505) 521-4260; ISRNI@zianet.com; www.zianet.com/ISRNI.

Sexual Abuse Prevention: A Course of Study for Teenagers, by Rebecca Voelkel-Haugen and Marie M. Fortune. (Cleveland, OH: The United Church Press, 1996).

The Courage to Heal, by Ellen Bass and Laura Davis (NY: Harper Perennial Library, 1994).

Incest and Sexuality: A Guide to Understanding and Healing, by Wendy Maltz and Beverly Holman (NY: Lexington Books, 1991).

Self Help Sourcebook: Finding and Forming Mutual and Self-Help Groups. American Self-Help Clearinghouse, Saint Clare's Health Services, Denville, NJ 07834 (1998). Also online at www.cmhc.com/selfhelp.

References

Bass, E. and Davis, L. (1994). *The Courage to Heal: A Guide for Women Survivors of Child Sexual Abuse.* NY: Harper & Row.

Beitchman, J.H., Zucker K.J., Hood, J.E., daCosta, G.A. and Akman, D. (1991). A review of the short-term effects of child sexual abuse. *Child Abuse and Neglect, 15.* 537-556.

Blume, E.S. (1998). *Secret Survivors: Uncovering Incest and the Aftereffects in Women.* NY: Ballantine Books.

Boutcher, F. and Gallop, R. (1996). Psychiatric nurses' attitudes toward sexual assault/rape and incest. *Archives of Psychiatric Nursing, 10(3).* 184-191.

Glod, C.A. and Teicher, M.H. (1996). Relationship between early abuse, post-traumatic stress disorder, and activity levels in prepubertal children. *American Academy of Child and Adolescent Psychiatry, 34(10).* 1384-1393.

Johnson, J.M. and Bondurant, D.M. (1995). Revisiting the 1982 church response survey. In C.J. Adams and M.M. Fortune (eds.) *Violence Against Women and Children: A Christian Theological Sourcebook* (pp.422-427). NY: Continuum.

Date Rape

"No Means No"

Anne had always been a good student. She generally maintained a B average and was involved in extracurricular activities, including the church youth group. She enjoyed spending time with her friends and liked to hang out with several close friends. Anne has a reasonably close relationship with her parents, although she considered them a little too protective.

She started dating this year, right after her fifteenth birthday. Anne went out several times with Eric, a senior who is popular at their high school. Anne liked him a lot, and on their third date they went to a party where they talked and danced. Most of the kids there were older and were drinking alcohol. Anxious and eager to fit in, Anne had a few beers, too. After a while, they drove to a quiet place because Eric said he wanted to spend some time alone with Anne. They parked and talked about what their future together might be like. Eric told Anne that she was special and that he loved her. They started to kiss; but when he pulled at her clothes, she stopped him. Anne tried to pull away, but he continued to press himself on her. When she continued to resist, Eric questioned whether she was sincere in her feelings for him. The verbal and physical pressure continued until Anne eventually gave in.

After that night, things changed. Anne became withdrawn from her friends and quit most of her activities. She was moody and disagreeable with her parents. She began missing a lot of school, complaining of fatigue and migraine headaches. Her grades dropped substantially.

Her parents brought Anne in to talk with Reverend Nakata to try to "do something about her attitude." In talking with Anne, the pastor asked her about many things, including her dating relationships. In the course of conversation, she relayed the story about Eric as if it were a minor event. Her tone was detached, and she said that it had been her fault. Anne described the situation as "no big deal," but she also said that she now wished to avoid situations where she might have to see him. She said the whole thing had made her feel angry, embarrassed, and ashamed—especially since Eric had broken up with her soon thereafter. Anne admitted that she had been feeling depressed and irritable lately, but she did not believe that this had anything to do with Eric.

Pastoral Assessment

Adolescents are especially vulnerable to sexual abuse in dating situations. Many teens do not understand or identify as rape forced sexual intercourse with someone they are dating (Vicary et al. 1995). This is especially true in a situation like Anne's, which did not involve physical force. When discussing the issue, assume that Anne may not realize that her victimization was a rape. For example, in talking with Anne about the events with Eric, you might refer to "unwanted sexual experience."

Assessment of the trauma must not exacerbate the situation, but proceed with great care taken not to trivialize it. Acquaintance or "date rape" is forced, unwanted sexual intercourse between individuals who know each other or are romantically involved. It is a physical violation of trust, an act of violence.

When talking with someone who has been raped, it is important to be supportive and nonjudgmental, not giving advice or asking for details. In this way, control of the conversation remains with the victim. Even small choices restore a sense of power to someone who has experienced powerlessness in an assault (Hughes and Sandler 1987).

Survivors of sexual assaults need to be believed and should not be made to prove their story. Anne feels, as do most rape victims, that what happened was somehow her fault. It is critical to let her know that she is not to blame. Asking questions such as, "Did you do anything that might have led him on?" will only make these feelings worse.

It is also important not to touch Anne without asking her permission first. When persons have been traumatized, it is natural to want to hug them or hold their hand. Any physical intimacy at this point, however, may be unwanted and unhelpful.

Assessing the effects of the trauma requires listening carefully to what Anne is currently experiencing. It is important to evaluate what resources are available to her, including her coping skills and the strength of her family and social networks. Rape is reacted to in different ways depending on the teen's available emotional and situational resources. Post-traumatic stress disorder (PTSD) symptoms are commonly observed in women after experiences of sexual aggression (see Case 7). Factors influencing Anne's response would include her age and developmental level, her relationship to Eric, her ability to identify and use available support, and the meaning given to the traumatic event by Anne, her family, her friends, and others. The degree of safety and control that Anne is currently experiencing would also affect how she responds (Koss and Harvey 1991).

Avoidant coping reactions, such as dropping away from friends and activities and staying at home, are associated with negative psychological outcomes (Santello and Leitenberg 1993). Since Anne has responded to the situation by withdrawing from social situations, she is at a risk for ongoing and complicated emotional distress.

Anne may not be seeking the support of her family and friends because she is concerned with the way that they will react. Respect her decisions, since Anne needs to feel in control of her life. Do not tell anyone that she was assaulted unless given explicit permission.

Since Anne is denying the impact of the date rape and has not sought counseling herself, assume that this will be the only opportunity for intervention. The focus of the session should be to provide a supportive and reassuring environment; identify immediate needs, such as social support, legal resources, and medical evaluations; allow an opportunity for ventilation of the trauma and associated feelings; address practical problems and develop realistic solutions; provide information about the psychological impact of rape to normalize the process of recovery; and set up a telephone follow-up (Koss and Harvey 1991).

Treatment Within the Faith Community

Available data indicate that date rape accounts for between one-third and one-half of all rapes in this country. The most effective ministry may be the development and implementation of date rape workshops that can provide for the discussion of important topics, which may decrease the likelihood of its occurrence. Structured, open discussions between men and women regarding the risk factors associated with date rape can be aimed at raising awareness, correcting myths and misconceptions, and offering practical recommendations.

When people think of rape, they often envision a woman being forced into a deserted alley by a stranger and violated at gun- or knifepoint. One national survey involving 11- to 17-year-olds found that 92 percent of adolescent sexual assault victims were raped by someone they knew and more than half were assaulted while on a date (Ageton 1988). Males are less likely than females to believe that forced sex between intimates is rape.

The socialization of men and women in America fosters attitudes that women should be passive and dependent and not experiment with their sexuality. Men are socialized to be aggressive and competitive, to have strong sexual feelings, and to experiment with them. These social conventions encourage men to dominate and abuse women and predispose men to accept rape myths (Berkowitz 1992). For example, there is widespread acceptance that force and coercion are legitimate ways to achieve compliance in sexual encounters. Men often do not view verbal intimidation, false promises, ignoring protests, or the use of alcohol and drugs as coercive, but as methods of seduction. In confusing coercion with seduction, the resulting forced intimacy may not be regarded as rape (Ellis 1994).

There are other myths that facilitate tolerance of rape by blaming the victim. These include beliefs such as, "She is asking for it by the way she is dressed" and "When a woman is a tease, rape is at least somewhat justifiable." In a study by Check and Malamuth (1983), 60 percent of the responding males admitted that they would force themselves on a woman if they could be certain of not getting caught. In other research, 12 percent of the girls and 39 percent of the boys believed it was okay to force sex on a girl if the boy had spent a lot of money on her (Giaresso et al. 1979).

Another common myth is "When a woman says no what she really means is yes." Miscommunication and misinterpretation are significant risk factors in date rape. Men may perceive sexual intent when that is not being communicated from the female's perspective. Sometimes, what women consider friendly behavior is regarded as a sexual invitation by a man. Research indicates that there are huge gaps between men's and women's interpretations and expectations of sexual intentions. Studies have also found that men view women as the gatekeepers of sexuality (McLendon et al. 1994). The ability to communicate clearly in social settings and to act definitively is critical.

Alcohol use is one of the most common risk factors in rape. The myth associated with this is that women who are drunk or stoned are fair game. In addition, alcohol may slow an individual's reaction time, impair judgment, and make a response less effective. It should be noted that behaviors that are associated with increased risk do not imply responsibility for being attacked. Whenever a woman is forced against her will to submit to unwanted sexual intimacy, it is rape. If a woman is unable to give consent because she is drunk, it is still rape.

Other risk factors associated with rape include isolation during a date, mixed messages, trying to avoid a scene, age, family alienation, poor peer relationships, and previous sexual assault (Vicary, Klingaman and Harkness 1995).

The identification of these risk factors through group discussions about communication skills, gender differences, alcohol's effects, assertiveness, and rape myths is extremely valuable for young persons who enter the dating world with confusing and complex data. Focused outreach intervention workshops can lessen the likelihood of either men or women becoming involved in date rape situations (Sawyer, Desmond and Lucke 1993).

Indications for Referral

It is essential to refer Anne to a mental health specialist who has training to work with sexual abuse survivors. Women who have been sexually assaulted will often accept only female referrals.

Treatment by Mental

The aftereffects of rape are issues of safety, self-esteem, trust, intimacy, and control. Components in the treatment of rape include: the assessment of related symptoms; the development of a secure relationship;

**Health
Specialist**

processing of the traumatic memories; reformulation of the survivor's thoughts and beliefs; reestablishing a sense of mastery; and treating specific symptoms, such as phobias, depression, and sexual or relationship dysfunction (Koss and Harvey 1991). Individual and/or group therapy is often used.

**Cross-
Cultural
Issues**

Cultural attitudes can be a significant factor when counseling rape victims. A study of African American, Hispanic, and Caucasian females found that Hispanic women may be particularly traumatized by rape because of the greater tendency to believe themselves culpable and tainted by sexual assault. Rape victims who experience shame and self-blame are more likely to avoid treatment than those who do not (Lefley et al. 1993).

Resources

National Resources

Rape, Abuse, and Incest National Network (RAINN), 635-B Pennsylvania Avenue, SE, Washington, DC 20003; (800) 656-HOPE; www.rainn.org; rainnmail@aol.com.

National Coalition Against Sexual Assault (NCASA), 125 N. Enola Drive, Enola, PA 17025; (717) 232-7460; www.ncasa.org; ncasa@redrose.net.

National Clearinghouse on Marital and Date Rape, 2325 Oak Street, Berkeley, CA 94708; www.ncmdr.org.

Women Against a Violent Environment (WAVE), P.O. Box 15650, Rochester, NY 14615; (716) 234-9709; www.mooreresults.com/wave; wave@mooreresults.com.

Center for the Prevention of Sexual and Domestic Violence, 936 N. 34th Street, Suite 200, Seattle, WA 98103; (206) 634-1903; www.cpsdv.org; cpsdv@cpsdv.org. The center offers training, consultation, videos, and publications for clergy, laity, seminary faculty, and students.

Men's Rape Prevention Project, P.O. Box 57144, Washington, DC 20037; (202) 265-6530; www.mrpp.org; info@mrpp.org

People Against Sexual Abuse, Inc. (PASA), 57 Front St., 4th floor, Brooklyn, NY 11201; (718) 834-9467; www.pasa.org; info@pasa.org, is dedicated to ending violence by teaching young people to accept responsibility for and take charge of their lives.

Self-Help Resources

Rape Victim: Clinical and Community Interventions, by Mary P. Koss and Mary R. Harvey (NY: Sage Publications, Inc., 1991).

Stopping Rape: Successful Survival Strategies, by Pauline B. Bart and Patricia H. O'Brian (NY: Pergamon Press, Inc., 1993).

Recovery: How to Survive Sexual Assault for Women, Men, Teenagers, and Their Friends and Families, by Helen Benedict and Susan Brison (NY: Columbia University Press, 1994).

Real Rape, by Susan R. Estrich (Cambridge, MA: Harvard University Press, 1997).

The Gift of Fear: Survival Signals that Protect Us from Violence, by Gavin De Becker (NY: Dell Publishing, 1998) teaches preventive skills to defuse and avoid dangerous situations, decreasing the risk of violent crimes.

Sexual Violence: The Unmentionable Sin, by Marie M. Fortune (Cleveland, OH: Pilgrim Press, 1994).

Trauma and Recovery: the Aftermath of Violence—from Domestic Abuse to Political Terror, by Judith Lewis Herman (NY: Basic Books, 1997).

References

Ageton, S.S. (1988). Vulnerability to sexual assault. In A.W. Burgess (ed.), *Rape and Sexual Assault II*. Garland Reference Library of Social Science 361 (pp. 221-244). NY: Garland.

Berkowitz, A. (1992). College men as perpetrators of acquaintance rape and sexual assault: A review of recent research. *Journal of American College Health, 40*. 175-180.

Check, J.V.P. and Malamuth, N.M. (1983). Sex role stereotyping and reactions to depictions of stranger versus acquaintance rape. *Journal of Personality and Social Psychology, 45*. 344-356.

Davis T.C., Peck, G.Q. and Storment, J.M. (1993). Acquaintance rape and the high school student. *Journal of Adolescent Health, 14*. 220-224.

Ellis, G.M. (1994). Acquaintance Rape. *Perspectives in Psychiatric Care, 30(1)*. 11-16.

Giaresso, R., Johnson, P., Goodchild, G. and Zellman, G. (1979). Acquaintance rape and adolescent sexuality. Paper presented at the Western Psychological Association Meeting, Chicago.

Hughes, J.O. and Sandler, B.R. (1987). "Friends" raping friends: Could it happen to you? *Project on the Status and Education of Women, Association of American Colleges*.

Koss, M.P. and Harvey, M.R. (1991). *The Rape Victim: Clinical and Community Interventions*. NY: Sage Publications, Inc.

Lefley, H.P., Scott, C.S., Llabre, M. and Hicks, D. (1993). Cultural beliefs about rape and victims' response in three ethnic groups. *American Journal of Orthopsychiatry, 63(4)*. 623-632.

McLendon, K., Foley, L.A., Hall, J., Sloan, L., Wesley, A. and Perry, L. (1994). Male and female perceptions of date rape. *Journal of Social Behavior and Personality, 9(3)*. 421-428.

Santello, M.D. and Leitenberg, H. (1993). Sexual aggression by an acquaintance: Methods of coping and later psychological adjustment. *Violence and Victims, 8(2)*. 91-104.

Sawyer, R.G., Desmond, S.M. and Lucke, G.M. (1993). Sexual communication and the college student: Implications for date rape. *Health Values, 17(4).* 11-20.

Vicary, J.R., Klingaman, L.R. and Harkness, W.L. (1995). Risk factors associated with date rape and sexual assault of adolescent girls. *Journal of Adolescence, 18.* 289-306.

Violence and Post-Traumatic Stress

"He Had Repeated Nightmares About the Shooting"

Rodney is a 14-year-old African American youth who recently moved to the community to live with his grandparents for safety. He had nearly been killed in a terrifying drive-by shooting while walking to his inner-city school with his best friend. His friend was shot to death in front of him in a gruesome killing. Rodney, who had been an excellent student with high aptitude in mathematics and art, became scared of school and had difficulty concentrating on his studies. He had repeated nightmares about the shooting and had trouble sleeping. Rodney could be heard screaming at night in his sleep. He is still wary, very edgy, and has outbursts of rage. He recently dived to the ground when a passing car backfired. Rodney, who had been a gregarious teen, now seems emotionally disconnected, preoccupied, and withdrawn. He stays in his room much of the time drawing. His grandparents are concerned that Rodney is "going crazy." They go to their longtime pastor Reverend Cecil Thurman for help.

The effects of psychological trauma of this magnitude—viewing the killing of his best friend—are severe and difficult for any individual to cope with. The word *trauma* comes from a Greek root meaning "wound." In much the same way that a physical trauma may wound the body, bringing disability and suffering, a psychological trauma can overwhelm the thoughts and feelings of a person and bring sustained suffering.

It is important that Reverend Thurman obtain a clear picture of what happened to Rodney. His assessment should include a detailed account of

Pastoral Care Assessment

the traumatic event and a careful summary of current signs of distress. Rodney has clear indications of post-traumatic stress disorder (PTSD) that are similar to those seen in combat veterans. The key sign is his repeated, intrusive thoughts of the event in the form of nightmares. Rodney is probably reliving the horrific experience over and over again in his mind. Reverend Thurman also needs to evaluate Rodney's coping skills and the strength of his social support network.

It is also important to realize that a person who is exposed to this level of stress is at risk of several additional problems for which there needs to be an assessment, including depression (see Case 15), anxiety (see Case 20), and alcohol and drug abuse (see Case 1).

Relevant History

Psychological trauma is more pronounced when it is intentionally inflicted by another person than when the trauma is accidental. The perception of one's life being threatened during a crime, exposure to a grotesque sight, and the violent death of a loved one increase both the likelihood of PTSD and its severity (Resnick et al. 1992). Adolescents are generally more likely than adults to be exposed to many forms of violence including rape, automobile accidents, peer suicide, and street and school violence.

Diagnostic Criteria

The following criteria are involved when a person is diagnosed with PTSD: a traumatic event occurs that involves actual or threatened death or serious injury or a threat to the physical well-being of self or others; and the response is one of intense fear, helplessness, or horror. The traumatic event is reexperienced in specific ways, such as recurrent and intrusive distressing recollections or dreams of the event. Additionally, the individual often persistently avoids situations associated with the trauma and has emotional numbness in general. Often there is hypervigilance and irritability. Post-traumatic stress disorder becomes the diagnosis when these symptoms persist for more than one month and create significant impairment in a person's functioning.

Unfortunately, high numbers of young Americans suffer from PTSD as a result of criminal violence. Exposure to violence among teens in the U.S. is at epidemic levels. African American male adolescents, like Rodney, are at particular risk. Although injury from guns is the second leading cause of death among both African American and Caucasian teens (Koop and Lunderberg 1992), African American adolescents are six times more likely than Caucasian peers to die from homicide. The rate of violent victimization for all those 12 to 19 years of age is twice that of adults over the age of 25 (Bureau of Justice Statistics 1993).

Adolescent males from large urban areas are at the highest risk of victimization and of witnessing severe violence, such as stabbing and shootings. In a study of adolescents and young adults (ages 14–23) in Detroit,

Michigan, 42 percent had seen someone shot or knifed and 22 percent had seen someone killed. Nine percent had seen more than one person killed (Shubiner, Scott and Tzelepis 1993). A national study of more than 11,000 eighth and tenth graders found a high exposure to violence. A full one-third of the students had been threatened with bodily harm, while 15 percent had been robbed and 16 percent had been attacked in their neighborhoods. School offered little safety according to this study—34 percent of the students had been threatened and 13 percent had been physically attacked at school during the preceding year (American School Health Association 1989).

Response to Vignette

It is important to help Rodney and his family understand that post-traumatic stress disorder is a normal reaction to an abnormally stressful event. Psychological trauma is not a sign of being "emotionally weak" or "crazy." Nearly everyone exposed to this type of extreme stress will find their ordinary coping processes overwhelmed. The "shock effect" of the psychologically distressing event (such as witnessing a killing) is outside the range of normal human experience, frequently eliciting intense fear, helplessness, loss of control, and fear of annihilation. People exposed to this type of catastrophic stress are often left suspicious, easily startled, and nervously watchful because they are permanently on alert for a threat that no longer exists. Rodney's diving to the ground when he heard a car backfire is the sort of fear reaction of many people who have been involved in a catastrophic experience. The sound probably reminded him of the gunfire at the time of the shooting, and he reexperienced the terror of the grizzly killing.

At the same time, a person suffering from psychological trauma can cut off feelings in order to suppress anger and tender emotions that are too frightening to acknowledge. This may account for Rodney's withdrawal and emotional detachment from others. Furthermore, unable to use his feelings as a guide to recognizing his emotions, Rodney may have problems moderating his responses to his experiences. His outbursts of rage may be a sign of his internal distress. Rodney could be feeling several complex emotions at once. He may experience anger at those responsible for the traumatic experience and shame for his helplessness in the face of terror. He may also feel guilty for surviving while his close friend died, as well as profound grief over the loss.

Rodney's grandparents were interested in information about post-traumatic stress disorder. It was helpful for them to understand the symptoms of PTSD. They worked with Reverend Thurman to find ways to support their grandson's recovery. Since Rodney had a solid background in the church, the youth director was able to work with Rodney though his interest in art. Rodney began to express his painful emotions through his drawings. The youth director also helped Rodney use his faith as a resource for renewal. Over several months Rodney began to trust others enough to begin working with a psychologist with expertise in treating teenage victims of violence. With the support of his church and family, Rodney regained a sense of hope in his future and a trust in his emotions. He began to process the fear, rage, guilt, and grief that haunted him. Rodney became more emotionally connected to others and less preoccupied with the trauma. He was changed by the experience, but he learned that he could continue his life, guided by the love of others and faith in God. After a year of healing, Rodney began a youth recovery group for victims of violence in his city as a ministry of the church.

Treatment Within the Faith Community

With psychological trauma, an individual's sense of order and continuity of life is shattered. Questions of meaning and purpose recur as a person experiences a loss of control over his or her destiny. Religious faith is a primary coping strategy for many people suffering from psychological trauma with one-half to three-quarters of PTSD sufferers indicating that their faith helped them cope (Weaver et al. 1996). In addition to offering the social support of community, nurturing, nonpunitive religion provides a healing means of addressing the traumatic experience. Faith can enhance well-being, lower distress, and may facilitate faster and more effective emotional recovery (Pargament 1997).

Research indicates that the church is an integral component of African American support networks. African American pastors are more likely to go into the community seeking people in crisis than their colleagues of other ethnic groups (Mollica et al. 1986). In a recent study of 635 African American churches in the northern United States, almost 4 out of 10 of the congregations had a working relationship with the local mental health department, while about one-half of the churches had family support programs (Thomas et al. 1994).

Providing hope and rebuilding trust should not be undervalued. Faith-based, church-sponsored self-help groups can assist survivors in normalizing their experience by working through the healing process with those who empathize with and understand the painful impact of the traumatic encounter. Feedback from others can promote the development of more accurate self-perception and positive change. Individuals become aware of their interpersonal strengths and weaknesses. The group also functions as a caring environment in which members feel safe and secure. Self-help groups can be a natural bridge in the process of reconnecting with the community when survivors are tempted to withdraw and isolate. They can help members move from being helpless victims to coping survivors.

Preventing violence and youngsters' exposure to violence are urgent issues to be addressed by the community of faith. Research suggests that violence prevention programs in schools may be useful in the prevention of aggressive and violent behavior by children. Such programs encouraging nonviolent conflict resolution can reduce aggressive behavior (Cotten et al. 1994), and they may work in church settings. Faith communities should also advocate for less exposure to violence in television and movies and a reduction in the number of handguns in our society.

Most victims of violence never seek professional help to deal with the emotional impact of psychological trauma. Such individuals often feel fearful, suspicious, and threatened. Confrontation with deliberate human cruelty can shatter assumptions of civility and evoke deep feelings of alienation and dehumanization. Victims of violence may be particularly resistant to entering and continuing therapy. A knowledgeable pastor can be helpful in guiding a trauma survivor to treatment and supporting the ongoing therapy.

Indications for Referral

Most psychotherapists who treat PTSD try to provide an opportunity for the teen to feel safe in confronting the traumatic event and understanding its connection with their symptoms. Clients are helped to think about the trauma without reliving it and to exercise self-control without avoidance and emotional numbing. The overall treatment strategy is to help Rodney to understand and integrate the traumatic experience into the ongoing context of his life, so that he no longer continues to reexperience the trauma. Most therapists will concentrate on the present in the aftermath of the trauma by exploring the immediate effects. Victims of violence will need to rebuild self-esteem and self-control as well as develop a renewed sense of personal dignity. A knowledgeable practitioner will assess and support positive coping skills, including appropriate religious expression. The therapist will facilitate the natural grieving process and will assist the teen in formulating concrete, realistic plans to restart his or her life.

Treatment by Mental Health Specialist

Family therapy may be useful for many sufferers of PTSD. This approach uses the primary support group of the family to assist in coping with, integrating, and healing from the traumatic experience. It also recognizes that a psychological trauma affects family members as well as the survivor. Family therapy works best if families are solution-oriented rather than blame-oriented, have open communication, value commitment, and express affection. This therapy model does not work well where family violence is present and family roles are rigid.

Medications are often employed in conjunction with psychotherapy. Antidepressant and anti-anxiety medications may be used to diminish anxiety and agitation, decrease depression, promote sleep, reduce nightmares, and enhance control of aggressive and violent impulses.

Those who work with the traumatized (Backus, Backus and Page 1995) and PTSD survivors who have been surveyed, especially ethnic minorities,

Cross-Cultural Issues

have indicated that religion is used as a primary coping strategy (Weaver, Koenig and Ochberg 1996).

Resources

National Resources

Anxiety Disorders Association of America (ADAA) provides educational materials on PTSD, 11900 Park Lawn Drive, Suite 100, Rockville, MD 20852; (301) 231-9350; www.adaa.org; anxdis@aol.com.

Gift From Within is a nonprofit organization dedicated to helping those who suffer from PTSD. It maintains a roster of trauma survivors who participate in a national network for peer support, (800) 888-5236; R.R. 1, Box 5158, Camden, ME 04843; www.sourcemaine.com/gift; JoyceB3955@aol.com.

National Center for Post-Traumatic Stress Disorder, VA Medical Center, White River Junction, VT 05009; (802) 296-5132; www.dartmouth.edu; dms/ptsd@dartmouth.edu.

International Society for Traumatic Stress Studies, 60 Revere Dr., Suite 500, Northbrook, IL 60062; (847) 480-9028; www.istss.com; www@istss.org.

National Victim Center, 2111 Wilson Blvd., Suite 300, Arlington, VA 22201; (800) 394-2255; www.nvc.org; webmaster@mail.nvc.org. This group, founded in 1985, provides self-help groups and makes referrals to existing groups. It has a quarterly newsletter and conducts conferences.

National Organization for Victim Assistance (NOVA), 1757 Park Road, NW, Washington, DC 20010; (800) 879-6682; www.try-nova.org; nova@try-nova.org. This group, founded in 1975, provides support, referrals, and advocacy for victims of violent crime and disasters. It has a newsletter and conducts conferences.

S.O.S.A.D. (Save Our Sons And Daughters), 2441 W. Grand Blvd., Detroit, MI 48208; (313) 361-5200, was founded in 1987 as a support and advocacy group for survivors of homicide, suicide victims, or victims of other traumatic loss. Weekly bereavement groups, professional grief counseling, training, violence prevention, advocacy, and public education are its focus. Contact this group only if you are interested in starting a similar group in your area. When writing, include a stamped, self-addressed envelope.

Parents of Murdered Children, 100 East 8th St., B-41, Cincinnati, OH 45202; NatlPomc@aol.com; www.pomc.com; (888)818-7662, has 300 chapters in the United States and Australia. The organization was founded to provide self-help groups to support persons who survive the violent death of someone close.

Self-Help Resources

"Post-traumatic Stress Disorder" in the *Clinical Handbook of Pastoral Counseling, Volume 2,* by David W. Foy et al. Edited by R.J. Wicks and

R.D. Parsons (NY: Paulist Press, 1993) offers a helpful chapter on PTSD from a pastoral care perspective.

Coping with Trauma: A Guide to Self-Understanding, by Jon G. Allen, (Washington, DC: American Psychiatric Press, 1995) explains the effects of traumatic experience on the survivor's personality and social relationships. He describes treatment approaches and self-help strategies.

The Gift of Fear: Survival Signals that Protect Us from Violence, by Gavin De Becker (NY: Dell, 1998) teaches preventive skills to defuse and avoid dangerous situations so to decrease the risk of violent crimes.

Assessing and Treating Victims of Violence, edited by John Briere (San Francisco: Jossey-Bass, 1994); *Helping Traumatized Families,* by Charles R. Figley (San Francisco: Jossey-Bass, 1989); *Trauma and Recovery: The Aftermath of Violence from Domestic Abuse to Political Terror* by Judith Lewis Herman (NY: Basic Books, 1997); *Post-traumatic Therapy and the Victims of Violence,* edited by Frank Ochberg (NY: Brunner/Mazel, 1988); *Post-Traumatic Stress Disorder: A Clinician's Guide* by K.C. Peterson, M.F. Prout and R.A. Schwarz (NY: Plenum Press, 1991) are well researched and highly readable texts.

References

American School Health Association. (1989). *The National Adolescent Student Health Survey: A Report on the Health of America's Youth.* Oakland, CA: Third Party Publishing Co.

Backus, C.J., Backus, W. and Page, D.I. (1995). Spirituality of EMTs: A study of the spiritual nature of EMS workers and its effects on perceived happiness and prayers for patients. *Prehospital and Disaster Medicine, 10(3).* 168-173.

Bureau of Justice Statistics. (1993). *Criminal Victimization in the United States. 1992.* Washington, DC: U.S. Department of Justice. Publication NCJ-144776.

Cotten, N.U., Resnick, J., Brown, D.C., Martin, S.L., McCarraher, D.R. and Woods, J. (1994). Aggression and fighting behavior among African American adolescents: Individual and family factors. *American Journal of Public Health, 84(4).* 618-622.

Kilpatrick, D.G., Saunders, B.E., Amick-McMullan, A., Best, C.L., Veronen, L.J. and Resnick, H.S. (1989). Victim and crime factors associated with the development of crime-related post-traumatic stress disorder. *Behavior Therapy, 20.* 199-214.

Koop, C.E. and Lunderberg, G.D. (1992). Violence in America: A public health emergency. *Journal of the American Medical Association, 267.* 3075-3076.

Mollica, R.C., Streets, F.J., Boscarino, J. and Redlich, F.C. (1986). A community study of formal pastoral counseling activities of the clergy. *American Journal of Psychiatry, 143(3).* 323-328.

Pargament, K.I. (1997). *The Psychology of Religion and Coping: Theory, Research, Practice*. NY: Guilford Press.

Peterson, K.C., Prout, M.F. and Schwarz, R.A. *(1991)*. *Post-Traumatic Stress Disorder: A Clinican's Guide*. NY: Plenum Press.

Resnick, H.S., Kilpatrick, D.G., Best, C.L. and Kramer, T.L. (1992). Vulnerability-stress factors in development of post-traumatic stress disorder. *The Journal of Nervous and Mental Diseases, 180(7)*. 424-430.

Rubin, R.H., Billingsley, A. and Caldwell, C.H. (1994). The role of the black church in working with black adolescents. *Adolescence, 29(114)*. 251-266.

Shubiner, H., Scott, R. and Tzelepis, A. (1993). Exposure to violence among inner-city youth. *Journal of Adolescent Health, 14(3)*. 214-219.

Thomas, S.B., Quinn, S.C., Billingsley, A. and Caldwell, C. (1994). The characteristics of northern black churches with community health outreach programs. *American Journal of Public Health, 84*. 575-579.

Weaver, A.J., Koenig, H.G. and Ochberg, F.M. (1996). Post-traumatic stress, mental health professionals and the clergy: A need for collaboration, training and research. *Journal of Traumatic Stress, 9(4)*. 861-870.

Case 8

Divorce

"Forgotten by Her Father"

Anne and her 14-year-old daughter, Emily, had been active members of their church since moving to the community four years ago. Emily's father, James, has a long history of alcohol abuse that became the source of ongoing family conflicts. He had been psychologically abusive and, on several occasions near the end of the marriage, physically abusive toward Anne and Emily during his alcoholic binges. Anne and James were involved in an acrimonious divorce for several years. After the divorce, James had irregular contact with his daughter. Most of the contact with James is now initiated by Emily. Recently, James made no attempt to acknowledge her fourteenth birthday. He lives with his new girlfriend in a nearby town and resents paying child support.

Anne came to the church office with concerns about her teenage daughter and very unhappy with James's conduct toward Emily. Anne fears that the divorce and rejection by James have had negative effects on their daughter. Emily has "temper tantrums," screaming at her mother and saying things like, "You don't understand anything" and "You are my worst problem." Recently, she became more verbally abusive toward her mother. Anne is concerned that some of Emily's friends are "wilder" than those in the past.

In listening to Anne, it became clear that she felt guilty and hurt as a result of the family life prior to and after the divorce. As her pastor, Faye Chang knew that Anne was a devoted and caring parent who had been somewhat indulgent toward her daughter. At times Anne seemed to feel overly responsible for the marital conflict and she had tried to compensate for the divorce by buying expensive gifts for Emily, which she could not afford. Anne had entered counseling for a short period after James became abusive near the end of their eleven-year marriage. She had gained some insight into her personal dynamics and those of the marital relationship.

Pastoral Assessment

In assessing Emily's "temper tantrums," it is essential to understand exactly what behaviors are involved. Is Emily going into extended periods of ranting and uncontrollable rage or are these shorter outbursts of anger often seen in teenagers awkwardly testing limits with parents? Some rebellious, defiant behavior is to be expected in adolescents as a part of their normal development pattern of separation and independence from their family of origin. How much has Emily discovered her tantrums toward her mom to be a successful means of getting her way, especially given Anne's tendency to give in to demands and become indulgent? How much are the tantrums mimicking the hostile, verbally abusive conduct seen by Emily while she was growing up? Is Emily taking much the same bullying role with her mother that she had seen her father take?

It would be important to help Anne evaluate Emily's new "wilder" friends. Are they age-appropriate, do they have responsible adult supervision, and how are they influencing Emily's changing behavior for good or ill? It is normal for each generation of youth to challenge the culture of their parents with new ideas and styles. Simply dyeing one's hair bright green can be normal self-expression in a youth culture, while coming home drunk at midnight is a change in behavior that should be of concern.

At another level there is the need for a mental health specialist to assess Emily for the impact of the rejection by her father. An alcoholic father who has been abusive and now is rejecting causes emotionally wounding experiences. Rejection by a parent is stressful, calling for recognition and care. Are Emily's recent angry outbursts a reaction to the pain she felt from her father ignoring her fourteenth birthday? Perhaps Emily feels safer expressing anger toward her mother than to begin accepting the rejection of her father. Absent fathers are tragically common. One study found that 40 percent of noncustodial fathers have little or no contact with their children in the year following a prolonged separation or divorce (Furstenberg, Morgan, and Allison 1987).

Relevant History

The maternal and paternal grandparents are lifetime active members of the church and very supportive of Anne and Emily. Emily has a solid B average in her studies and is involved in both her school and church choirs. Her teachers report that she is a good student who sometimes appears shy and may lack confidence in her abilities. The church music director recognizes that Emily has singing talent and has encouraged and mentored her.

Diagnostic Criteria

In the past several decades, the number of children affected by divorce has increased dramatically. Parental divorce is one of the most common stressors experienced by children in our society. Every year more than 1 million children in the U.S. experience the divorce of their parents (U.S.

Bureau of the Census 1989). Close to 1 in 3 of the children born in the United States in the 1990s will experience the disruption of a divorce as compared to 1 in 10 in 1970 (Norton and Miller 1992). Approximately 90 percent of the children of divorce are in the custody of their mother.

In legal terms, *divorce* is a discrete event defined as the "dissolution of a socially and legally recognized marital relationship that alters the obligations and privileges of the two persons involved" (Price and McKenry 1988, p. 7). However, in psychological terms divorce is a complex process that can go on for years prior to legal proceedings and is generally a highly stressful series of events for all family members, especially the children. It is common for a family to go through a period of disorganization after the divorce while new relationships are negotiated.

Parents frequently worry about the effects that their divorce has on their children. While the adults may be shattered or relieved by the divorce, children and adolescents are often fearful about their security. Young people can misunderstand the reason for the separation and divorce. It is important to tell teens as much as they need to understand about the reasons for the divorce. Many children and teens assume they are somehow at fault for a divorce and experience emotional distress from the misconception that they are at fault.

Response to Vignette

Pastor Faye Chang recognized that the pastoral care needs of this family called for a mental health specialist experienced in working with teens and their families. Fortunately, the church sponsored a pastoral counseling center with trained marriage and family therapists. One pastoral counselor was Dr. Margo Sanford who sings with Emily in the church choir and has a good rapport with her.

Dr. Sanford met with Pastor Chang and Anne to gather information and make a fuller assessment. She talked with Emily alone to give her a chance to tell her story of recent events. Margo Sanford also spoke to Emily's father on the phone, but he rejected the idea of a meeting with her or his family. Dr. Sanford met with the grandparents and consulted with Anne's teachers at school. This was done after gaining written permission from both the mother and father, who share joint legal custody, to treat Emily.

The family assessment revealed that Emily had experienced multiple stressful life events, including moving, changing schools, being rejected by a parent, and returning home from school each afternoon without an adult in the house. Emily was also suffering from the impact of psychological and physical abuse by her father, which had not been previously addressed. Anne has been under stress from a difficult divorce and the financial strain that has resulted from the loss of family income.

It was equally apparent that Anne and Emily had many personal strengths. Both the mother and daughter are emotionally resilient and, despite their recent volatile relationship, there are good trust and a strong bond of love between them. During the marital turmoil and divorce, Anne and Emily had an excellent support system in their extended family and church. Both of Emily's grandfathers recognized the need to give her extra attention, since her father was unable to give Emily the love and attention she deserved.

Dr. Sanford found that Emily's "temper tantrums" increased after her father forgot her recent birthday. These outbursts appeared more related to her current feelings of rejection and hurt than to a long-standing problem. Dr. Sanford also found that Emily's new "wilder" friends were well-supervised and responsible teenagers displaying age-appropriate rebellious behaviors toward the adult culture of their parents.

Treatment Within the Faith Community

Science tells us that those who pray together are, in fact, more likely to stay together. Commitment to a nurturing faith community can enhance marital stability and deter divorce. Studies show that religious involvement is an important predictor of marital satisfaction, happiness, and adjustment (Hansen 1992). Researchers have found that religious involvement plays a stronger role in marital adjustment than several social or economic factors (Glenn and Weaver 1978). In addition, active religious involvement increases martial commitment (Larson and Goltz 1989) and is a strong deterrent to marital instability and divorce (Heaton 1984; Shrum 1980).

Marriage Encounter programs, designed to improve communication and revitalize marriages, can be helpful for couples. These weekend faith-oriented programs are sponsored by churches to deepen and enrich marriage (see address below).

The church can be helpful in educating the community to understand that sometimes separation or divorce is in the best interest of the children and the adults. For example, it is not in the best interest of Emily or Anne to continue to be exposed to James's abuse. Sometimes marriage does not develop into "holy wedlock" after the wedding, and the religious community needs to show wisdom in understanding that reality—not stigmatizing people who must divorce in the interest of their children's and their own well-being. Research has shown that one stable custodial parent is better for the well-being of a child than two parents in a combative, hostile relationship (Barber and Eccles 1990).

The pastor and the community of faith can be useful in encouraging a couple to consider divorce mediation as an alternative to an adversarial legal battle. Divorce mediation is a voluntary process where couples are guided by a neutral mediation team to negotiate a mutually beneficial settlement. The process is designed to settle such issues as spousal and child support, custody, and visitation with as little emotional turmoil and blaming as possible. The goal of mediation is an amicable and mutually acceptable end to a marriage. Besides reducing financial costs and lowering emotional stress, mediation can foster a better post-divorce relationship between the ex-spouses and children, while modeling a constructive approach to future problem solving.

The stress and negative impact of divorce on parents and teens can be reduced if a strong support system, such as a nurturing church, is available. Not only do the adolescents benefit from nurture (having the care of compassionate congregants), but the custodial parent benefits from the support (emotional encouragement, caregiving, inspiration). Thus, the presence of a faith community can enhance the adjustment of the custodial parent, allowing her or him to offer better care for the teen.

Indications for Referral

Positive adjustment in adolescents is related to the psychological well-being of the custodial parent. It is important that divorcing parents have access to psychological services during the stressful period of the divorce process. Positive psychological adjustment for minors is less likely if the parents are involved in angry, abusive fighting and if the family is under financial strain. Research has consistently shown that it is important to minimize the resentment and bitterness surrounding a divorce (Silitsky 1996).

Treatment by Mental Health Specialist

Typically, a mental health specialist would first see the mother and daughter together to evaluate their communication skills, as well as to educate them in the normal reactions to family conflict and divorce. They would be encouraged to talk about how they see their roles as family members and how they might be more understanding and helpful to one another.

After a few sessions, the therapist would probably meet with the daughter separately to give Emily a chance to share what she might be reluctant to say when her mother is present. Emily would be encouraged to talk about the feelings she may have toward her mother and father. She might wish to talk about her losses and grief resulting from the family conflict and divorce. Emily could be given some alternative ways to express her anger that would be more productive and less threatening to her mother. Beyond problem solving, the therapist would also assess the need for longer-term supportive, insight-oriented psychotherapy. The depth of Emily's wounding by her father's abusive behavior and emotional rejection would be a key issue to be explored. Problems with trust and intimacy may continue into adulthood for children who come from a divorced family. Young adults who experienced a divorce in their family of origin report less trust of a future spouse and lower optimism about marriage (Franklin, Janoff-Bulman and Roberts 1990).

Anne may also see a therapist alone to help her work through some of her hurt and anger. The therapist could help her improve her parenting skills, especially regarding limit-setting with her daughter. Anne might benefit from assertiveness training, and she could use more information about normal adolescent development. Additionally, a skilled therapist would assess the possible need for longer-term supportive, insight-oriented psychotherapy for the mother. The central aspect of the clinical evaluation would be self-esteem issues and dependency needs that might make it difficult for Anne to set appropriate emotional limits with her daughter and former husband.

Cross-Cultural Issues

It is estimated that nearly 4 out of 10 Caucasian children and three-quarters of all African American children born to married couples will experience the impact of parental divorce before they reach the age of 16 (Amato and Keith 1991). About 55 percent of African American children live with one parent, while 20 percent of Caucasian children do so, and 30 percent of Hispanic children reside with one parent (Norton and Miller 1992).

Resources

National Resources

Rainbows, 2100 Golf Road # 370, Rolling Meadows, IL 60008; (800) 266-3206; www.rainbows.org; info@rainbows.org. This is an international organization with 6300 affiliated groups. Founded in 1983, Rainbows establishes peer support groups in churches, schools, and social agencies for children and adults who are grieving a divorce, death, or other painful change in their family. The support groups are led by trained adults. Referrals are also provided.

North American Conference of Separated and Divorced Catholics, P.O. Box 360, Richland, OR 97870; (503) 963-8089; www.conicom/~nacsdc; nacsdc@pdx.oneworld.com. This is an international group founded in 1972 to address religious, educational, and emotional aspects of separation, divorce, widowhood, and remarriage through self-help groups, conferences, and training programs. People from all faiths are welcome.

Association for Children for Enforcement of Support, Inc., 2260 Upton Ave., Toledo, OH 43606; (800) 537-7072; www.childsupport-aces.org; ACES@Childsupport-ACES.org. This national organization with 350 affiliate groups provides information and support for parents who have custody of their children and have problems obtaining child support payments.

The Beginning Experience, 305 Michigan Ave., Detroit, MI 48226; (313) 965-5110. This international Christian organization founded in 1975 provides support programs for divorced, widowed, and separated adults and their children as they work through the grief of a marriage ending.

Divorce Care, P.O. Box 1739, Wake Forest, NC 27588; (919) 562-2112; www.divorcecare.com; 72603.1341@compuserve.com. This is an evangelical Christian organization with 2,900 affiliated groups, funded to help build networks of support groups for those recovering from separation or divorce. It provides information, referrals, support group meetings, and assistance in starting groups.

Grandparent Rights In New Strength, 0689 CR5, Corunna, IN 46730; (219) 281-2384. This group works with religious, local, state, and federal officials to promote uniform laws allowing grandparent visitation rights after a divorce. It offers assistance in court and mediation cases and guidance in starting local support groups.

Grandparents'-Children's Rights, Inc., was founded in 1981 to provide information and advocacy for grandparents being denied visitation rights with grandchildren. It urges grandparents to develop groups to discuss issues and exchange information. Contact Lucile and Lee Sumpter, (517) 339-8663.

Children's Rights Council, 300 I St., NE, Suite 401, Washington, DC 20002; (202) 547-6227; www.vix.com/crc. This national group is concerned with reforming the legal system regarding child custody. It offers a newsletter, information, referrals, directory of parenting organizations, conferences, and group development guidelines.

Parents Anonymous, 675 W. Foothill Blvd., Suite 220, Claremont, CA 91711; (909) 621-6184; www.parentsanonymous-natl.org; parentsanon@msn.com. This national organization founded in 1970 is a professionally-facilitated, peer-led group for parents who are having difficulty and would like to learn more effective ways to parent. It provides group leaders, develops chapters, and has children's groups.

Association of Couples for Marriage Enrichment, P.O. Box 10596, Winston-Salem, NC 271087; (800) 634-8325; home.swbell.net/tgall/acme.htm; wsacme@aol.com, is a national clearinghouse that provides information on marriage enrichment programs.

Self-Help Resources

International Youth Council, 401 N. Michigan Ave., Chicago, IL 60611; (800) 637-7974. This is an international self-help organization sponsored by local chapters of Parents Without Partners, which brings together teens from single-parent homes to share ideas and solve mutual problems, develop leadership skills, and plan teen group activities. Help with starting groups is provided.

World Wide Marriage Encounter, 2210 East Highland Ave., Ste. 106, San Bernardino, CA 92404; (800) 795-5683; www.wwme.org; wwme.office@juno.com; is a religion-based self-help group.

Divorce Online is an electronic resource for those involved in or facing the prospect of divorce. It provides free information on the financial, legal, and psychological aspects of divorce, www.divorce-online.com, information@divorce-online.com.

The Costly Consequences of Divorce, by David Larson, James Sawyers, and Susan Larson (Rockville, MD: National Institute for Healthcare Research, 1995), is a comprehensive assessment of the mental health and social implications of divorce in the United States based on the current research. The text provides useful material to guide a church workshop on the effects of divorce.

Reviving Ophelia: Saving the Selves of Adolescent Girls, by Mary Pipher (NY: Ballantine, 1993), has a good chapter on the effects of divorce on adolescent girls. This is an important book to read.

The Kid's Guide to Divorce, by John Brogann (NY: Fawcett Crest, 1986), is a useful resource focused on the needs and concerns of teens.

The Kid's Book Of Divorce, By, For and About Kids, edited by Eric Rofes (NY: Vintage Press, 1982), addresses divorce from a child's point of view.

Helping Your Grandchildren Through Their Parents' Divorce, by Joan Schrager Cohen (NY: Walker and Company, 1994), provides grandparents with important information on how to strengthen their grandchildren's lives during and after a divorce.

Pastoral Counseling with Adolescents and Young Adults, by Charles M. Sheldon (NY: Crossroad, 1995), has a helpful chapter on teens and divorce from a faith perspective.

Children, Divorce and the Church, by Douglas E. Adams (Nashville: Abingdon Press, 1992), is a useful book written by a pastor on how best to minister to the children and teens of a family affected by divorce.

References

Amato, P.R. and Keith, B. (1991). Parental divorce and the well-being of children: A meta-analysis. *Psychological Bulletin, 110(1).* 26-46.

Barber, B.L. and Eccles, J.S. (1990). Long-term influences of divorce and single parenting on adolescent family and work related values, behaviors and aspirations. *Psychological Bulletin, 111(1).* 108-126.

Franklin, K.M., Janoff-Bulman, R. and Roberts, J.E. (1990). Long-term impact of parental divorce on optimism and trust: Changes in general assumptions or narrow beliefs? *Journal of Personality and Social Psychology, 59(4).* 743-755.

Furstenberg, F.F., Morgan, S.P. and Allison, P.D. (1987). Parental participation and children's well-being after marital dissolution. *American Sociological Review, 52.* 695-701.

Glenn, N.D. and Weaver, C.N. (1978). A multivariate, multisurvey study of marital happiness. *Journal of Marriage and the Family, 40.* 269-282.

Hansen, G.L. (1992). Religion and marital adjustment. In J.F. Schumaker (ed.) *Religion and Mental Health.* NY: Oxford University Press.

Heaton, T.B. (1984). Religious homogamy and marital satisfaction reconsidered. *Journal of Marriage and Family, 46.* 729-733.

Larson, L.E. and Goltz, J.W. (1989). Religious participation and marital commitment. *Review of Religious Research, 30.* 387-400.

Norton, A.J. and Miller, L.F. (1992). *Marriage, Divorce and Remarriage in the 1990s. U. S. Bureau of the Census, Current Population Reports. Series P-23, No. 180.* Washington, DC: U.S. Government Printing Office.

Price, S.J. and McKenry, P.C. (1988). *Divorce.* New Berry, CA: Sage Publications.

Shrum, W. (1980). Religion and marital instability: Change in the 1970s? *Review of Religious Research, 21.* 135-147.

Silitsky, D. (1996). Correlates of psychosocial adjustment in adolescents from divorced families. *Journal of Divorce and Remarriage, 26(1/2).* 151-169.

U.S. Bureau of the Census. (1989). *Statistical Abstract of the United States: 1989.* (109th ed.) Washington, DC: U.S. Bureau of the Census.

Weaver, A.J., Koenig, H.G. and Larson, D.B. (1997). Marital and family therapists and the clergy: a need for collaboration, training and research. *Journal of Marital and Family Therapy, 23.* 13-25.

Stepparenting

"No Instant Love"

Joan and Alex asked to see Pastor Donald Gonzalez for premarital counseling. They were very excited about their upcoming wedding. It was the second marriage for both of them. Joan was divorced with a 13-year-old son, Carlos, while Alex was a widower with a 16-year-old daughter, Lynn. They met at a church-sponsored group, "Parents Without Partners." They had known one another for fourteen months and had a strong bond between them. Their primary concern was their stepparent role with the two teenage children. Carlos is emotionally close to his father and resists getting close to Alex. Carlos has been moody and difficult since he was told of the impending wedding, especially after visits with his father. Lynn sees herself as very grown up and wants to be more independent from her father and stepmother-to-be. Joan and Alex expressed a desire to have an intimate, close relationship with their new stepteens as soon as possible. The couple were particularly pleased to do the premarital sessions with Pastor Gonzalez, who is remarried himself, and the stepfather of two teenagers.

Pastoral Assessment

Forming a new stepfamily unit presents many unique challenges. The management of more relationships takes time and skill. In forming step-families (also called "blended families"), it is important to be flexible and willing to negotiate. Communication that is clear, open, and encourages persons to take responsibility for their thoughts, feelings, and actions is vital. During the first premarital session it was clear that Joan and Alex were good listeners and effective communicators with one another and highly motivated to learn more about being able stepparents.

While a new marriage is a time of joy and excitement for the couple, their teenage children may feel unhappy, vulnerable, and alone. Many newly married parents hope their children will instantly love and bond with the new stepparent. There is no instant love; adjusting to new relationships takes time. Although Joan and Alex have fallen in love and have decided to marry, Carlos and Lynn may not want to be in a stepfamily. How realistic are Alex and Joan concerning the teens' adjustment? Time will be required to adapt to the loss of the former family structure and to accept the new situation.

How clear is the couple about their expectations and roles within the new family structure they will be building together with the teens? How comfortable are Joan and Alex with disciplining and enforcing limits with the teens? What role expectations do the teens carry into the new family? How will Lynn feel about having a "little" brother for the first time? How does Carlos feel about having a new "big" sister? Many children worry that additional youngsters in the family will subtract attention from them. What plan does the couple have to maintain their close relationship despite the new demands of stepparenting? Has the couple accepted the loss of their previous marriages, and will they forgo the hope of trying to re-create an idealized first marriage in the stepfamily? How much have Alex and Joan listened and talked with their teen about the real and unique issues that will arise in the new stepparent? Have they taken the feelings of their teenagers seriously in the midst of their bliss and optimism about the forthcoming wedding?

Relevant History

Lynn has been very close to her maternal grandmother since the death of her mother when she was fourteen.

Alex and Joan make time for themselves apart from the teenagers. Maintaining their privacy in the marital relationship is an important priority for them. Alex and Joan are hoping to have a biological child. More than half (54 percent) of women have a child after remarriage (Wineberg 1990).

Diagnostic Criteria

A stepfamily is generally defined as a family created by remarriage with at least one partner's child from a previous marriage. Stepfamilies are fast becoming the most common family form in the United States. At the beginning of the twenty-first century about 40 percent of all married-couple households will be remarried before the youngest child turns 18 (Glick 1989). The great majority of these stepchildren will live with their biological mother and a stepfather. In the United States remarriages outnumber first-time marriages by 3 to 2 (Norton and Miller 1992).

Response to Vignette

Creating realistic expectations for adults and children is a central task that can enhance positive relationships in stepfamilies. Educating Joan and Alex on "normal" teen reactions to new relationships in a stepfamily is a good starting place. For example, Carlos is probably struggling with both grief and loyalty. He may be grieving the loss of an exclusive relationship with his mother. In addition, the impending marriage may well mean for Carlos the final realization that his parents will not reconcile and that the family he once was a part of is lost and will never reform.

At the same time Carlos may be having feelings of loyalty toward his nonresident father. He may feel that showing affection toward Alex is betraying his biological father. Grief and feelings of loyalty may be the reason for his moodiness and anger toward Alex. Encouraging Joan and Alex to give Carlos "space" and time after a visit with his nonresident father may decrease the conflict potential. It is healthy for Carlos to maintain a good bond with his father. It would also be helpful for Carlos to find an adult that he trusts, such as a grandparent or pastor, to help him express his grief. Healthy grieving requires the recognition and expression of grief-related feelings (Brammer 1988).

A stepparent and an adolescent can experience competing needs. For example, the teenage years are a time when autonomy and independence are to be encouraged. The teen need to be autonomous may be counter to the new stepfamily desire to be more cohesive. Sixteen-year-old Lynn is entering her late teens and may well be at a place in her life where she may naturally be seeking more personal autonomy. Her natural need for autonomy is not a personal rejection or insult. Lynn's relationship with her maternal grandmother may be particularly important as she struggles with her role and status within the new stepfamily.

Courtesy may be expected in a stepfamily, while respect is earned, and love is a bonus. Stepparents are better understood as "friends" to the teens in the early stages. Most teens call their stepparents by their first name or by a special name. Conflicts between a stepparent and the custodial parent are best minimized to foster a parenting coalition. If the custodial parent remains primarily responsible for the control and discipline of the teen, it will allow time for a bond to develop between the stepparent and the youngster. Active parenting by the stepparent can follow after a relationship has been established.

Surveys indicate that many adults enter remarried life with either overly optimistic expectations that their stepfamily would develop a rapid, close bond and/or with little to no planning regarding the unique problems inherent in stepfamily living. Most remarried couples needed to revise their preconceptions and construct a realistic model of remarried life (Pill 1990). Stepfamily life requires a continual and intentional commitment to compromise and change.

Joan and Alex need to take the good communication skills they already have with one another and focus on listening to the teenagers in their family. Pastor Gonzalez should encourage them to spend some time listening and talking privately with the teens about the remarriage. This does not mean the teens dictate the stepparents' private relationship. It does mean that a teen's concerns should be discussed beforehand so that when problems do arise, there is a greater chance to create constructive solutions.

Treatment Within the Faith Community

Research indicates that strong, well-functioning, marital relationships are the essential foundation to successful stepfamilies (Skopin, Newman and McKenry 1993). Married couples report that religious commitment increases family tolerance, improves adjustment, provides moral guidance, facilitates decision making, minimizes conflicts, and increases marital commitment (Weaver et al. 1997; Robinson 1994). These are many of the very qualities associated with strong stepfamily bonds. Church involvement may serve as a positive factor in the success of stepfamily formation. Moreover, a vital faith helps family members cope with the high stress commonly involved in stepfamily life adjustment (Pargament 1997).

Research shows that grandparents take on special importance for youngsters in stepfamilies (Kennedy and Kennedy 1993). Children and teens often seek support and comfort from grandparents who may be experienced as offering a trustworthy and stable relationship in a changing and unpredictable family transition. Attachment to a grandparent can offer continuing and sustaining support that enhances self-identity and family bonds. According to estimates, half of church and synagogue members are seniors (Koenig and Weaver 1997). The faith community can be of great value in educating and supporting grandparents in their roles as effective caregivers in stepfamilies.

In the United States 80 percent of those who divorce remarry, which means that our churches and synagogues have many forms of families with diverse organizational patterns. Educational programs in the faith community that teach effective communication and negotiation skills within different family forms could enhance sensitivity about blended families and their unique needs. Such educational programs could help stepfamilies acknowledge the special difficulties inherent in integrating two families with different histories and expectations and could begin to destigmatize the stepfamily as somehow less than "normal."

Indications for Referral

A parent should consider a mental health evaluation for a teen who feels isolated and has excessive guilt and anger, who is torn between two parents or two households, or who vents excessive anger upon a family member. A referral to a mental health professional is called for when a stepparent or parent favors one teen or if a teen excessively resents a stepparent or parent. Mental health support may help when one of the parents suffers from great stress and is unable to respond to a teenager's needs. Working with stepfamilies is challenging even for experts. Do not hesitate to refer to a mental health specialist if you feel the needs of the stepfamily are beyond your training and experience. A timely referral is an act of responsible pastoral care.

Working with stepfamilies or blended families is best done by someone with specialized training and experience. Knowledge of and sensitivity to the uniqueness of stepfamily dynamics helps a therapist to work supportively and realistically with a blended family. Because stepfamily issues are often multifaceted and emotionally charged, a mental health specialist will need to be therapeutically active, flexible, and resourceful to be effective.

Most therapists who work with blended families use a family systems approach which works with the family as a whole. From that perspective, when families see their members as interdependent parts of a larger whole and understand that the needs, emotions, and actions of each individual affect everyone else, they are more likely to gain empathy for the perspective of the other family members. The American Association for Marriage and Family Therapy has a national listing of family therapists that may be consulted to find experts who specialize in working with blended or stepfamilies (see Resources).

Counseling blended families across cultural and racial lines presents a special need for sensitivities to human diversity.

National Resources

Stepfamily Association of America, 650 J Street, Suite 205, Lincoln, NE 68508; (800) 735-0329; www.stepfam.org; stepfamfs@aol.com. This is a national organization with 60 chapters founded in 1979 that promotes personal and family support through information, education, and advocacy for stepfamilies. The association publishes a quarterly newsletter and other educational materials for adults and children in stepfamilies.

The Stepfamily Foundation, Inc., 333 West End Ave., NY, NY 10023; (212) 877-3244; www.stepfamily.org; staff@stepfamily.org. This foundation provides educational materials on stepparenting issues for parents and professionals.

The American Association for Marriage and Family Therapy, 1133 15th Street, NW, Suite 300, Washington, DC 20005; (202) 452-0109; www.aamft.org; central@aamft.org; offers continuing education programs for those who work with families.

Self-Help Resources

How to Win as a Stepfamily, by Emily B. Visher and John S. Visher (NY: Brunner/Mazel 1991); *Stepparenting*, by Jeanette Lofas and Dawn Sova (NY: Kensington Publishers, 1996); *Strengthening Your Stepfamily*, by Elizabeth Einstein and Linda Albert (NY: Random House, 1987); *Step-By-Step Parenting: A Guide to Successful Living with a Blended Family*, by James D. Eckler (NY: Better Way Publishers, 1993); and *Stepfamily*

Treatment by Mental Health Specialist

Cross-Cultural Issues

Resources

Problems: How to Solve Them, by Tom Frydenger and Adrienne Frydenger (Grand Rapids, MI: Baker Book House, 1997) are helpful books for people in stepparenting situations. They are written to assist in understanding the complexities, difficulties, and opportunities involved in stepparenting.

References

Brammer, L.M. (1988). *The Helping Relationship: Process and Skills.* Englewood Cliffs, NJ: Prentice-Hall.

Glick, P.C. (1989). Remarried families, stepfamilies, and stepchildren: A brief demographic profile. *Family Relations, 38.* 24-27.

Kennedy, G.E. and Kennedy, C.E. (1993). Grandparents: A special resource for children in stepfamilies. *Journal of Divorce and Remarriage, 19(3/4).* 45-68.

Koenig, H.G. and Weaver, A.J. (1997). *Counseling Troubled Older Adults: A Handbook for Pastors and Religious Caregivers.* Nashville: Abingdon Press.

Norton, A.J. and Miller, L.F. (1992). *Marriage and Divorce and Remarriage in the 1990s* (U.S. Bureau of the Census, Current Population Reports. Series P-23, No. 180). Washington, DC: U.S. Government Printing Office.

Pargament, K.I. (1997). *The Psychology of Religion and Coping: Theory, Research, Practice.* NY: Guilford Press.

Pill, C.J. (1990). Stepfamilies: Redefining the family. *Family Relations, 39.* 186-193.

Robinson, L.C. (1994). Religious orientation in enduring marriage: An exploratory study. *Review of Religious Research, 35.* 207-18.

Skopin, A.R., Newman, B.M. and McKenry, P.C. (1993). Influences on the quality of stepfather-adolescent relationships. *Journal of Divorce and Remarriage, 19 (3/4).* 181-189.

Weaver, A.J., Koenig, H. G. and Larson, D. B. (1997). Marital and family therapists and the clergy: A need for collaboration, training and research. *Journal of Marital and Family Therapy, 23.* 13-25.

Wineberg, H. (1990). Childbearing after remarriage. *Journal of Marriage and the Family, 52.* 31-38.

Pregnancy

"She Was Scared to Tell Her Family"

Christine came to see Reverend Ellen Davis because she thought she was pregnant. She wanted to talk to someone, but she was scared to tell her family and worried that her friends would not keep her secret. Christine had just turned 14 years old. She had been going out with Stan, her first real boyfriend, for a few months. She had become very attached, but she was insecure about the relationship. The thought of losing Stan filled her with anxiety and panic. Christine's fears had made her afraid to say no when he had initiated sexual activity, and now she was afraid to tell him that she was pregnant.

Reverend Davis could see that the young woman was overwhelmed by her circumstances. Christine described feeling trapped and hopeless. She paced around the room as she talked and spoke with a desperate tone to her voice. Several times she broke off from her conversation and, dropping her face into her hands, sobbed loudly.

Christine had considered the choices that were available to her and felt that none were acceptable. She did not want there to be an adoption and she refused to consider abortion, and she did not wish to raise the child herself. Moreover, the only scenario she could imagine as acceptable was one that could simply make the situation go away.

A few days after their meeting, Reverend Davis received a call from Christine. She reported, with relief and elation, that she had taken a home pregnancy test and that she was not pregnant after all.

Slightly more than half of American females and nearly two-thirds of males have had intercourse by their eighteenth birthday (Moore et al. 1996). As a result, more than one million U.S. teenagers become pregnant each year, 8 in 10 of which are unintended pregnancies (PPFA 1993). The

Pastoral Assessment

problems associated with teen pregnancy are multiple. Teenage girls who become pregnant are more likely to drop out of school and will probably suffer related long-term educational and economic disadvantages, limited future prospects, and substantially diminished likelihood for their children to achieve their full potential (Koyle et al. 1989). Sexually transmitted diseases (STDs), including AIDS, are a serious risk for sexually active teens. In the past twenty years, the prevalence and severity of STDs have increased steadily among American adolescents (Weinbender and Rossignol 1996). In 1992 the Centers for Disease Control reported that the 15–29 year age-group ranks third highest in incidence of new cases of HIV infection. These statistics suggest that clergy are likely to have teenagers and their families call upon them for help with issues related to sexuality.

In Christine's case, several relevant factors deserve comment. To begin, her behavior in the meeting with Reverend Davis reveals that she is in the midst of a crisis. She cries easily and reports that she cannot see an acceptable resolution to the problem. The first assessment that Reverend Davis must make is to determine the issues that require immediate attention. Once the pastor is clear about the nature of the crisis, she can respond appropriately.

While Christine believes that she is pregnant, she has not yet sought medical verification of her condition. The first step, then, is to help Christine find out whether or not she is pregnant. Taking a look at the information she has given to her pastor, it is clear that Christine has been sexually active and that she has not been using contraception. Thirty-five percent of first intercourse experiences take place without the use of any birth control measures. Sexually active adolescents who do not consistently use contraceptives usually will become pregnant and then face potentially life-altering decisions about whether to resolve the pregnancy through adoption, termination, or parenthood. Seven in ten teen pregnancies occur in girls who were not using any birth control method when they became pregnant (Moore et al. 1996).

If Christine is pregnant, the next step involves addressing the overwhelming distress related to deciding how to resolve the situation. One of the most important factors affecting a decision related to pregnancy outcome is whether or not it was intended. About 85 percent of pregnant teens report that their pregnancy was unintended. For some teenagers, abortion and adoption are not seen as viable options. Only about 2 percent of pregnant adolescents choose adoption to resolve an unwanted pregnancy. Adolescents are more likely than older women to delay seeking an abortion until after the early weeks of gestation, due to denial of the pregnancy, legal barriers, financial barriers, or failing to recognize the early signs of pregnancy (Alan Guttmacher Institute 1994). Teen mothers are likely to have poor prenatal care with consequent medical complications. The children of such pregnancies often become part of the foster care and welfare systems.

They are at risk for abuse, neglect, failure to thrive, and serious illness (American Academy of Child and Adolescent Psychiatry 1997).

Christine tells Reverend Davis that she doesn't feel she can go to her parents with this problem, which points to the need to evaluate her family circumstances. Parents are the earliest and most important influence on an adolescent's developing sexuality (Berkovitz 1985). Family dynamics, communication, and parenting style are important to consider for a full understanding of Christine's situation. Why is she afraid to talk with her parents? Perhaps Christine's family situation is unpleasant, abusive, or chaotic. A pregnancy could provide Christine with a reason to leave home or the hope of creating her own loving family with her boyfriend and baby. Then again, perhaps sex is not an acceptable topic in the home and Christine is afraid of rejection or a punitive response from her folks. In one study, nearly all respondents indicated that they would prefer that sex education come from their parents, yet only 15 percent noted that they were a major source of this information (Sanders and Mullis 1988).

In any event, Christine has chosen to come to Reverend Davis for help, which might put her in an uncomfortable position. Most people are uneasy discussing sexuality; but in order to help teens, it is important to be able to handle this discomfort. If sexuality is not a topic that can be adequately navigated, an immediate referral is warranted. The least helpful response to this situation would be for Reverend Davis to avoid the topic (Knowles 1995).

It is important to take note of Christine's age. She is only 14 years old. Adolescents who initiate sex at young ages are at high risk for an unintended pregnancy. This is because those who begin having sex at young ages are at risk for a long time, are less likely to use contraception, generally have more sexual partners, and tend to engage in high-risk sexual behaviors, such as alcohol or drug use prior to sexual intercourse. The earlier that sexual activity is begun, the greater the risk (Faulkenberry et al. 1987). Because Christine's immediate crisis is averted, it does not mean that she no longer needs counseling from Reverend Davis. The focus just shifts from a crisis orientation to a recognition that Christine is at risk for an unintended pregnancy in the future.

A further subject for exploration is substance use. Alcohol and drug consumption is common with sexual involvement and points to a high-risk factor for unintended pregnancy (Bentler and Newcomb 1986). An assessment of Christine's current substance use will help Reverend Davis identify whether or not this is a relevant area for focus.

Finally, in determining necessary history, it is helpful to figure in the nature of adolescent decision making, which is often reactive and impulsive rather than deliberative. Teen sexual activity is generally infrequent and unpredictable, not reflecting rational and planned behavior. Even if Christine agrees to pursue a particular course of behavior such as abstinence, this does not mean that she will respond to sexual situations based on that decision. In addition to their decision-making style, teenagers tend to see themselves as invulnerable and are apt to believe that pregnancy cannot happen to them. Young adolescents may not have a sufficient level of logical thinking to allow them to recognize issues of choice and consequence relative to their sexuality (Hofferth 1987). For teenagers, sexual activity and later, pregnancy, seem to "just happen."

Diagnostic Criteria

Once the pastor has talked with Christine for a while, she will be able to ascertain Christine's needs: pregnancy screening, crisis counseling, family intervention, information about sexual issues, further information regarding the options related to pregnancy, and/or prenatal care. Clearly, a good evaluation provides many different paths for Reverend Davis to follow.

Response to Vignette

The first response to this situation is to recognize that Christine is in crisis, which presents a heightened risk for suicide. Empathetic listening and supportive reassurance will foster hope during crises. When persons are in crisis, they feel overwhelmed and need help in breaking down their problem into smaller parts that can be successfully managed. It is important to determine the basic causes to which the distress can be attributed.

Christine may be pregnant, but perhaps something else is going on that she is unable to articulate. For example, research indicates that before the age of 15, a majority of first intercourse experiences among females are nonvoluntary. The younger the age of first sexual intercourse, the more likely that the experience was coercive and traumatic (Boyer and Fine 1992). Once Reverend Davis determines whether the distress Christine is experiencing is related to a coercive sexual experience, she can respond in a helpful way (see Case 6). If that is not a problem, Christine's response may be because she is in a frightening situation without having enough information to allow for clarity of thought. Christine may not know about organizations that could help her, or she may be too uncomfortable to call them herself. The pastor can identify local community resources that are able to provide confidential pregnancy screening and counseling. Supportive listening may be enough to establish a trusting relationship so that Christine would allow Reverend Davis to set up an appointment for her.

If Christine is not pregnant, she still faces some critical issues about her sexuality and how she will respond to sexual situations when they arise in the future. Avoiding pregnancy after the first sexual intercourse experience requires consistent abstinence or use of an effective birth control method. Many studies have found that knowledge of basic conception and contraception facts among adolescents to be deficient enough to prevent regular effective use of birth control measures (APA 1995). Reverend Davis and Christine may prefer that the discussion be with her family or an organization experienced in dealing with such issues. Teenagers, left to their own devices, tend to delay seeking contraceptive services because of procrastination, concerns about confidentiality, and ambivalence about sex, contraception, and pregnancy (Moore et al. 1996).

If Christine is pregnant, she is faced with two major choices—termination or continuing the pregnancy to term. If she decides to continue the pregnancy, she must decide whether she will opt for adoption or keep the child. If she decides to keep the baby, she must decide whether she will continue to live with her parents or if she will establish her own home. All of these decisions are important, potentially traumatic, and life-changing. About 37 percent of pregnant adolescents have unintended births and about 35 percent have induced abortions. The rest of teen pregnancies (about 14 percent each) end in miscarriages or result in intended births (Moore et al. 1996). Christine's decisions will be greatly influenced by what her parents, friends, and sexual partners think about the choices (Miller, Christopherson and King 1993). In the process, she will benefit from a nonjudgmental, open relationship with Reverend Davis to provide her with support and information about her options. Christine will need guidance on the transitions facing her and help in setting realistic future goals.

Finally, should Christine be pregnant and decide to continue the pregnancy to term, it is critical that she seek prenatal care. Seventy percent of all pregnant adolescents do not receive adequate prenatal care, although this is the group that needs it the most. Teenage mothers have high rates of anemia and pregnancy-induced hypertension, and their babies are at increased risk of being born prematurely with low birth weight.

Treatment Within the Faith Community

Teenage pregnancy is a serious national problem. There is a significant need for the development of programs for teens and their families that address sexuality and pregnancy. Religious institutions play an important role in the choices of many young people regarding their sexual activity (Studer and Thorton 1987). It is therefore important to understand the interaction between religious involvement and teenage sexual activity. Teenagers who attend worship services frequently and value the role of religion in their lives are less likely to engage in sexual activity (White and DeBlassie 1992). At the same time, religiously involved teens have decreased likelihood that they will use an effective medical method of contraception.

In reviews of programs that seek to address the problem of teenage pregnancy, those that advocate abstinence, or at least the postponement of first intercourse, also tend to lower the probability of using birth control measures and vice versa (Cooksey, Rindfuss and Guilkey 1996). Efforts to discourage sexual activity can backfire to the extent that teaching only abstinence to avoid pregnancy may leave a teenager unprepared to use contraception if his or her resolve not to have sex breaks down. This puts religious leaders and parents in a difficult position when attempting to develop effective programs for teens concerning sexuality and pregnancy. Recent evidence suggests the practicality of emphasizing two fundamental and specific messages in the prevention of pregnancy: that adolescents should delay sexual intercourse and that, if teens do become sexually active, they should consistently use an effective method of contraception (Moore et al. 1996).

Another approach that might be considered is the development of a program to help parents learn how to talk about sex with their children. Teenagers who understand their sexuality are better able to make informed decisions in relationships, cope with peer pressure, and protect themselves from sexual abuse. Many teens will benefit from programs that help them become comfortable discussing sexuality and provide factual information that they need to know. Teens and preteens want information about sex, reproduction, and social and sexual relationships. They need to understand the risks of STDs and pregnancy. Teenagers need to learn how to say no and to be reassured that their concerns, fears, and sexual feelings are normal (Knowles 1995).

Indications for Referral

Christine must be referred to a mental health specialist if she has suicidal thoughts or plans. Referral would also be important should it become apparent that sexual abuse has taken place.

It would be helpful to establish a good relationship with community agencies whose primary goals are to provide education, counseling, and other services related to sexuality and pregnancy. They provide information and materials that will make working with Christine easier.

Cross-Cultural Issues

Data from the 1990 U.S. Census for eight Southeastern states revealed that the teenage birthrate is higher in rural than urban areas. The exception is that African American women aged 15–17 in cities had a higher pregnancy rate (106 per 1,000) than those in rural areas (87 per 1,000). Abortion rates were found to be much lower among rural teens than those in urban settings (Bennett et al. 1997).

National Resources

Resources

America's Crisis Pregnancy Helpline, 2121 Valley View Lane, Dallas, TX 75234; (888) 4-OPTIONS; www.thehelpline.org; acph@dallas.net.

The National Campaign to Prevent Teen Pregnancy, 2100 M St., NW, Suite 300, Washington, DC 20037; (202) 261-5655; www.teenpregnancy.org.

American Medical Women's Association, 801 N. Fairfax St., Suite

400, Alexandria, VA 22314; (703) 838-0500; info@comwa-doc.org; www.amwa-doc. org.

Planned Parenthood Federation of America, 810 Seventh Ave., New York, NY 10019; (800) 230-7526; www.plannedparenthood.org.

American College of Obstetricians and Gynecologists, P.O. Box 96920, Washington, DC 20090; (800) 772-9100; www.acog.com.

National Organization on Adolescent Pregnancy, Parenting and Prevention, 1319 F Street, NW, Suite 400, Washington, DC 20004; (202) 783-5770; www.noapp.org; NOAPP@noapp.org.

National Adoption Center, 1500 Walnut St., Suite 701, Philadelphia, PA 19102; (800) TO-ADOPT; nac.adopt.org; nac@adopt.org.

Self-Help Resources

Parents Anonymous, 675 W. Foothill Blvd., Suite 220, Claremont, CA 91711; (909) 621-6184; www.parentsanonymous-natl.org; parentsanon@msn.com. This national organization, founded in 1970, is a professionally facilitated but peer-led group for parents who are having difficulty and would like to learn more effective ways to parent children. It provides group leaders, develops chapters, and has children's groups.

Trends in the Well-Being of America's Children and Youth. (Child Trends, Inc. 1996). Copies available from Child Trends, (202) 362-5533, aspe.os.dhhs.gov.

How to Talk with Your Teen About the Facts of Life, by J. Knowles (Director of Sexual Health Information, Planned Parenthood Federation of America, 1995). Planned Parenthood Federation of America, Inc., 810 Seventh Avenue, NY, NY 10019; (800) 669-0156; www.ciserv.com/planned parenthood2.

Beginning Too Soon: Adolescent Sexual Behavior, Pregnancy and Parenthood, by K.A. Moore, B.C. Miler, B.W. Sugland, D.R. Morrison, D.A. Glei and C. Blumenthal (Report prepared for the Office of the Assistant Secretary for Planning and Evaluation, 1996) U.S. Department of Health and Human Services; (202) 690-6461; www.aspe.os.dhhs.gov/hsp/cyphome.htm.

When Children Want Children: An Inside Look at the Crisis of Teenage Parenthood, by Leon Dash (NY: Penguin, 1996).

Everything You Need to Know About Teen Pregnancy, by Tracy Hughes (NY: Rosen Publishers, 1989).

Surviving Teen Pregnancy: Your Choices, Dreams and Decisions, by Shirley Arthur and Perry Bergman (NY: Morning Glory Press, 1996).

References

Alan Guttmacher Institute. (1994). *Sex and America's Teenagers.* NY: Alan Guttmacher Institute.

American Academy of Child and Adolescent Psychiatry. (1997). *Council Policy Statement.* Washington, DC: AACAP.

"American Psychological Association written testimony on reducing teen pregnancy" (1995). Submitted to the House of Representatives Ways and Means Subcommittee on Human Resources, Washington, DC: APA.

Bentler, P.M. and Newcomb, M.D. (1986). Personality, sexual behavior, and drug use revealed through latent variable methods. *Clinical Psychology Review,* 6. 363-385.

Bennett, T., Skatrud, J., Guild, P., Loda, F. and Klerman, L.V. (1997). Rural adolescent pregnancy: A view from the South. *Family Planning Perspectives, 29(6).* 256-260.

Berkovitz, I.H. (1985). Healthy development of sexuality in adolescents: The school's contribution. *Medical Aspects of Human Sexuality, 19(10).* 34-49.

Boyer, D. and Fine, D. (1992). Sexual abuse as a factor in adolescent pregnancy and child maltreatment. *Family Planning Perspectives, 24(1).*

Centers for Disease Control. (1992). HIV/AIDS Surveillance Reports. *Morbidity and Mortality Weekly Reports.*

Cooksey, E.C., Rindfuss, R.R. and Guilkey, D.K. (1996). The initiation of adolescent sexual and contraceptive behavior during changing times. *Journal of Health and Social Behavior, 37.* 59-74.

Faulkenberry, J.R., Vincent, M., James, A. and Johnson, W. (1987). Coital behaviors, attitudes and knowledge of students who experience early coitus. *Adolescence, 22(86).* 321-331.

Hofferth, S.L. (1987). Contraceptive decision-making among adolescents. In S.L. Hofferth and Hayes, C.D. (eds.) *Risking the Future* (p. 101). Washington, DC: National Academy Press.

Knowles, J. (1995). *How to Talk with Your Teen About the Facts of Life.* Planned Parenthood Federation of America.

Koyle, P., Jensen, L., Olsen, J. and Cundick, B. (1989). Comparison of sexual behaviors among adolescents having an early, middle and late first intercourse experience. *Youth and Society, 20(4).* 461-475.

Miller, E.C., Christopherson, C.R. and King, P.K. (1993). Sexual behavior in adolescence. In T.P. Gullotta, G.R. Adams and R. Montemayor (eds.) *Adolescent Sexuality.* Newbury Park, CA: Sage.

Moore, K.A., Miler, B.C., Sugland, B.W., Morrison, R.R., Glei, D.A. and Blumenthal, C. (1996). *Beginning Too Soon: Adolescent Sexual Behavior, Pregnancy and Parenthood.* Report prepared for the Office of the Assistant Secretary for Planning and Evaluation, U.S. Department of Health and Human Services.

Planned Parenthood Federation of America. (1993). *Pregnancy and Childbearing Among U.S. Teens.* Planned Parenthood Federation of America.

Sanders, G. and Mullis, R. (1988). Family influences on sexual attitudes and knowledge as reported by college students. *Adolescence*, *23(92)*. 837-845.

Studer, M. and Thornton, A. (1987). Adolescent religiosity and contraceptive usage. *Journal of Marriage and the Family, 49*. 117-128.

Weinbender, M.L.M. and Rossignol, A.M. (1996). Lifestyle and risk of premature sexual activity in a high school population of Seventh-day Adventists: Valuegenesis. *Adolescence, (31)122*. 265-281.

White, S.D. and DeBlassie, R. (1992). Adolescent sexual behavior. *Adolescence, 27(105)*. 183-191.

Runaways

"What Was She Running From?"

The first time that Pastor Brenner met Donna was when she and James showed up together at a potluck dinner held at the church's coffeehouse. Twenty-year-old James attended fairly regularly, often appearing when free food was offered. He had lived on the streets for several years and had struggled with a substance abuse problem. James had been in and out of jail and treatment facilities.

Pastor Brenner introduced himself to Donna. She looked very young and more than a little anxious. She claimed to be 18 and said that she was living with a friend, but she was skittish and uncommunicative. The pastor gave Donna his card with a phone number where he could be reached if she found herself in need. About a week later, Donna called Pastor Brenner asking for help. She admitted to being a runaway and only 16 years old. She had been staying wherever James was, but he had left a few days earlier without a word. Now she was scared and hungry and didn't know where to turn. She was staying at a local shelter, but the staff was suspicious that she was underage, and she was afraid they were going to make her go back home.

When the pastor met with Donna, she explained that home was worse than the streets. She had first run away when she was 14 years old and again several times thereafter. She had returned home each time, but it was always the same. Donna was tearful as she spoke, and Pastor Brenner could see that she was angry as she described her neglectful and chaotic family situation. She was adamant that going home was not an option.

Every year about 700,000 youths run away from home (Gordon 1981). Sometimes, running away is related to a teenager's search for identity, while in other cases it represents personal and family difficulties, neglect, or abuse. Many experts believe that running away is not usually an

Pastoral Assessment

impulsive response to a new problem. Rather, it is a way to escape a long-standing problem that has finally become intolerable (Kurtz, Kurtz and Jarvis 1991). Whatever the reason for running, life on the streets puts young people at risk for substance abuse (see Case 1), impoverished living, and exploitation (Hartmann, Burgess and McCormack 1987).

There are not likely to be easy explanations or solutions in Donna's case. She has run away many times during a period of several years. A youth who runs away from home once may be reacting to a specific problem, but repeatedly leaving home is likely to indicate serious problems with multiple reasons (Spek, Ginther and Helton 1988). It is important to intervene with a runaway as early in the process as possible and try to determine the root of the problem. A good solution will offer resolution of the core problem in a way that eliminates the need for running away in the future.

Relevant History

Since Donna is a teenager, community and social services are less likely to be of help. Adolescents are twice as likely as younger children to be maltreated, yet they are apt to be hidden victims who will never be referred to child protective services. Instead, they will likely find themselves involved with the juvenile justice system (National Center for Child Abuse and Neglect 1988). Abused and neglected teens are more likely to come to the public's attention because of their disruptive behavior than as a result of the maltreatment they have received. Even if she is being sexually or physically abused at home (see Cases 4, 5), 16-year-old Donna is unlikely to ever obtain help for the emotional fallout of this victimization. However, she is at great risk for substance abuse, truancy, and criminal activity, which could bring her into the juvenile justice system.

When a runaway seeks help, it is important to determine how often the teen has run. The severity of the problem increases the more alienated a teenager is from his or her family, making reintegration with the family increasingly difficult (Orten and Soll 1980). To assess the severity of a runaway's behavior, consider the degree to which he or she has turned to running as a response to a stressful situation. The "first-degree" runner is one who is minimally alienated from family members, having run away once or twice, but not as a regular response to family stress. "Second-degree" runaways have more street experience. Their problems are more complex, and they are ambivalent about returning home. The "third-degree" runner tends to be an older teenager who fully identifies with the street culture and has no motivation to return home or enter into treatment. Donna is at least ambivalent about returning home and may already be a third-degree runner.

Diagnostic Criteria

Teenagers who run away are divided in their motives. Some adolescents are "running from" something that they feel unable to solve, such as sexual abuse, family conflict, changes in the family structure, or excessive parental expectations and control. In these cases, running away indicates the limit of their ability to tolerate some situation in the home. Others are "running to" something, such as a romantic relationship or the freedom of living away from home. These runaways tend to be seeking pleasure in places, people, and things that would not be allowed while living at home. However, while the motives for running-from stand alone, the motives for running-to almost always include elements of running-from, usually in relation to things that the home does not permit. The teen who runs-to does so out of a desire to determine her or his own fate, while running-from reflects despair and helplessness (Sharlin and Mor-Barak 1992).

It is important to determine the motive for running away in order to understand the teenager who needs your help. If an adolescent has run away in distress and is seeking rescue from an abusive situation, it is unconscionable to put the teen back where she or he was victimized without a plan that addresses the problems. Otherwise a teen will run again, but will feel unable to trust that there are people who will be able to understand the situation and offer assistance. Residential services may be a reasonable goal for second- or third-degree runners, but in those cases a treatment plan must be developed for the intervention to be successful. The stresses of homelessness and the lack of an adequate support system threaten the psychological and physical well-being of runaways who are trying to survive on the streets. These youth experience exploitation, depression, drug use, and suicidal thoughts (Smart and Walsh 1993).

Response to Vignette

The congregation has set up a coffeehouse program as a ministry within the community. By being available to help, Pastor Brenner has established himself as a firstline resource for Donna. His initial response to Donna was appropriate—unobtrusively giving her a way to contact him if the need arose. When Donna went to see the pastor, she was motivated to work with him to get herself safely off the streets. Donna was in crisis, since her circumstances reflect both danger and an opportunity for positive change.

Referrals for family therapy should be the primary focus for "first-degree" runners, especially when the conflicts do not include physical or sexual abuse. "Second-degree" runners will need a wider system of assistance, including individual, family, and group counseling where various options are explored. For "third-degree" runners, the focus will most productively address issues that will prepare the youth for successful independent living (Miller, Eggertson-Tacon and Quigg 1990).

Treatment Within the Faith Community

Teenage runaways are at risk for mental illness, exploitation, and the establishment of lifelong negative patterns of living. Adolescence is a turbulent age focused on the search for self-identity. As the teen struggles to achieve adulthood, the family often struggles to accommodate this maturation process. The community's ability to recognize teenagers who are at risk for running away will facilitate a positive prognosis for family reintegration. Potential runaways can be counseled on specific problems, and referrals can be made for protection as well as for treatment that focuses on the resolution of the conflicts.

It should be noted that related situations may be encountered. Parents will doubtless seek help when an adolescent is missing. While it may be that the teenager has run away, it may also be that the child has been abducted or has been the victim of some other crime. Care should be taken to consider these possibilities and alert the appropriate legal authorities regarding the status of a missing teen. Families may be reluctant to call the police either because they are denying the severity of the situation or are unaware of their legal responsibilities. Persons younger than 18 years old are considered children, and they are the legal responsibility of their parents, subject to all the laws that have been established for their protection. It is an act of support to help a family understand that contacting the police is the appropriate first response to this situation.

Indications for Referral

Once located, a teenager who has run away from home requires a clinical referral and follow-up. The assessments for severity and motives that have been described in this chapter will provide information and clinical assistance in creating an appropriate living and treatment plan. This diagnostic material can be used to work with the teen to explore the problems that have motivated the runaway situation.

Treatment by Mental Health Specialist

Because running away is both a solution and a problem for adolescents, the reason for the behavior can differ. Treatment by a mental health specialist will differ according to the specific issues that have been identified, the severity of the running behavior, and the teenager's developmental needs. Treatment may focus on family dynamics and the immediate familial crises, especially if the goal is family reintegration. If sexual or physical abuse or neglect has occurred, the trauma may be the initial focus (see Case 7).

Cross-Cultural Issues

Runaways and homeless youth have often been physically or sexually abused by their parents. In a study of 190 adolescent runaways, those who had been sexually abused were more likely than nonabused teens to engage in unprotected sex, have more sexual partners, and use alcohol and drugs. The study found that runaways of African American and Hispanic heritage reported less sexual abuse than the Caucasian runaways (Rotheram-Borus et al. 1996).

Resources

National Resources

National Center for Missing and Exploited Children, 2101 Wilson Blvd., Suite 550, Arlington, VA 22201; (800) THE-LOST; www.missingkids.org.

National Children's Coalition, Streetcats Foundation, 267 Lester Ave., Suite 104, Oakland, CA 94606; (800) 675-KIDS; www.child.net/missing.htm; Ycn@aol.com.

National Runaway Switchboard, 3080 N. Lincoln Avenue, Chicago, IL 60657; (800) 621-4000; www.nrscrisisline.org; info@nrscrisisline.org.

Self-Help Resources

Youth and Children's Resources Net, 267 Lester Avenue, Suite 104, Oakland, CA 94606; (510) 444-6074; www.child.net; YouthKids@aol.com.

Teen Runaways, by Gail Bo Stewart (NY: Lucent Books, 1996), presents the stories of teens who have run away from home, the reasons why, and possible solutions to the problem.

Runaways: In Their Own Words: Kids Talk About Living on the Street, by Jeffrey Artenstein (NY: Tor Books, 1995).

Runaway Me: Survivor's Story, by Evan Cutler (Bloomington, IN: Blooming Press, 1994).

Helping Vulnerable Youth: Runaways and Homeless Adolescents in the U.S., by Deborah Bass (NY: National Association of Social Workers, 1992).

Street Kids: The Tragedy of Canada's Runaways, by Marlene Webber (Toronto, Canada: University of Toronto Press, 1991).

Runaway Adolescents: A Family Systems Perspective, by Brenda Melsen (NY: Garland Publishing, 1995), is a text for pastoral counseling specialists.

References

Gordon, J.S. (1981). Running away: Reaction or revolution. In J.S. Gordon and M. Beyer (eds.) *Reaching Troubled Youth: Runaways and Community Mental Health*. (DHHS Publication No. ADM 81-955, pp. 1-16). Rockville, MD: National Institute of Mental Health.

Hartmann, C.R., Burgess, A.W. and McCormack, A. (1987). Pathways and cycles of runaways: A model for understanding repetitive runaway behavior. *Hospital and Community Psychiatry, 38.* 292-299.

Kurtz, P.D., Kurtz, G.L. and Jarvis, S.V. (1991). Problems of maltreated runaway youth. *Adolescence, 26(103).* 543-555.

Miller, A.T., Eggertson-Tacon, C. and Quigg, B. (1990). Patterns of runaway behavior within a larger systems context: The road to empowerment. *Adolescence, 25(98).* 271-289.

National Center for Child Abuse and Neglect. (1988). *Study of National Incidence and Prevalence of Child Abuse: 1988*. Washington, DC: US Government Printing Office.

Orten, J.D. and Soll, S.K. (1980). Runaways and their families: A treatment typology. *Journal of Family Issues, 1(2).* 249-261.

Rotheram-Buros, M.J., Mahler, K.A., Koopman, C. and Langabeer, K. (1996). Sexual abuse history and associated multiple risk behavior in adolescent runaways. *American Journal of Orthopsychiatry, 66(3).* 390-400.

Sharlin, S.A. and Mor-Barak, M. (1992). Runaway girls in distress: Motivation, background and personality, *Adolescence, 27(106).* 387-405.

Smart, R.G. and Walsh, G.W. (1993). Predictors of depression in street youth. *Adolescence, 28(109).* 41-53.

Spek, N.B., Ginther, D.W. and Helton, J.R. (1988). Runaways: Who will run again? *Adolescence, 23(92).* 881-888.

AIDS/Sexually Transmitted Diseases

"She Didn't Feel Sick"

Trish accompanied her best friend, Shyla, to the health clinic, agreeing to be tested only so that Shyla would be less nervous about her test. When the counselor told Trish that she had tested positive for HIV, Trish fell into a shocked silence. She gave the counselor Gary's name as the only one who could have infected her. It had to be Gary. She had been going out with him for more than a year. They had spoken about getting married after graduating from high school in June. In the beginning he had agreed to use protection, but then he had stopped, complaining the condoms were too uncomfortable.

Several weeks after the results were given to Trish, Shyla went to see her pastor, Gwen Wilson, seeking advice about what she could do for her friend. Shyla explained that Trish was not doing well. Even though Shyla had encouraged her, Trish would not tell her parents about her diagnosis. In fact she had stopped talking to Shyla about it, too. When the Department of Health had contacted Gary about being tested, he became enraged. He had accused Trish of sleeping around and infecting him. He had broken up with her, which had devastated Trish. She had become increasingly depressed and self-destructive. She had started drinking and taking drugs and had, on one recent occasion, told Shyla that she didn't care what happened anymore. Shyla felt helpless and afraid for Trish. She didn't know what to do because she had promised her friend that she would not tell anyone about the diagnosis, but she could see that Trish was in real trouble.

Every hour of every day someone under the age of 20 is inflicted with HIV (Griffin 1996). AIDS is now the fifth leading cause of death among Americans ages 15 to 24 years. In order to protect themselves, teenagers need to know the facts about the human immunodeficiency virus (HIV),

Pastoral Assessment

acquired immunodeficiency syndrome (AIDS), and other sexually transmitted diseases (STDs).

Shyla's concerns for Trish are well founded. Her confusion about what she might do for her friend is understandable. Several areas can be identified to which a response is needed.

Initially, Pastor Wilson can offer valuable assistance by recognizing that there are two people to whom she needs to respond, Shyla and Trish. Shyla is readily seeking support. Helping her to adjust and develop a plan for coping with this difficult situation may be the best initial help for Trish, too. Shyla is confused and anxious and probably feels responsible and helpless as well. The first step is to help Shyla express her feelings and then to assist her in normalizing her distressing experience. People often feel angry and guilty during periods of grief, without knowing that this is normal. When Shyla expresses her fears and concerns, Pastor Wilson will be able to help her understand the difference between helping her friend and feeling that she needs to rescue her. While Shyla may be able to help Trish with factual information and emotional support, this is different from taking responsibility for saving her friend or making complex decisions for her. Trish is not helpless, and it is not constructive to view her as a victim. Shyla needs assistance in identifying a response that addresses her own needs while also being likely to benefit Trish. Trish may never come to see Pastor Wilson, so helping Shyla become informed about the medical and emotional aspects of HIV may be the best chance for Trish to get the information she needs. In addition, helping relieve Shyla's fears about HIV transmission will better enable her to be a supportive friend to Trish.

Should Shyla be able to persuade Trish to talk to the pastor, there are a number of issues that would be useful to examine, recognizing that it may be the single opportunity the pastor has to help her. Trish is bound to be overwhelmed by the severity of her situation. HIV infection can have devastating effects on interpersonal relationships including isolation, rejection, and overall loss of social support (Aguilera 1994). An HIV diagnosis often brings with it multiple psychological effects including depression, anxiety, loss of hope about the future, and issues of death and dying (Perry and Markowitz 1986). The adjustment to the severity of her circumstances is extremely challenging. Trish does not appear to have the coping mechanisms or support system she needs to help her adapt to this new situation.

Relevant History

Most people who are infected with HIV did not believe that they were at risk. Many did not know how to keep from getting infected with HIV. Treatment for HIV is improving significantly; nonetheless, at present, the course of HIV will inevitably lead to AIDS. It is fatal.

In addition to HIV, there are other sexually transmitted diseases (STDs) that sexually active adolescents are at risk of contracting, including chlamydia, trichomoniasis, human papilloma virus (HPV), genital herpes, hepatitis B, gonorrhea, and syphilis. Every year three million teenagers contract an STD (Goldfarb 1997). It is estimated that 25 percent of adolescents will develop an STD by the time they graduate from high school (Scott 1996). STDs can be prevented only through abstinence from sexual contact; however, "safe sex" can greatly reduce the risk of infection. The consistent and correct use of a latex condom can help protect both partners from sexually transmitted diseases, including HIV. Substantial numbers of high school students have had sexual intercourse by age 16, and many do not use protection. Research shows that target HIV/STD programs that emphasize reducing unprotected sex are effective in improving the rates of protected sex (Wellings 1995).

Trish did not believe that she was at risk for contracting HIV because she was sexually active with a single partner, Gary. She also may have believed, as do many teenagers, that asking her partner to use a condom is insulting and indicates a lack of trust. The availability of accurate information might have helped her to make a more knowledgeable decision regarding her sexual activity.

Diagnostic Criteria

People infected with HIV and other STDs may look and feel healthy for years. While they do not feel sick and may not even know they are infected, they can infect others.

HIV is the virus that causes AIDS. A person develops AIDS when his or her immune system becomes so damaged that it can no longer fight off infections. Only a blood test can accurately diagnose HIV, yet sexually active teenagers rarely seek such testing.

HIV is not spread through everyday activities or casual contact. A person will not be infected from drinking fountains, handshakes, hugs, sneezes, swimming pools, sweat, tears, or being around an infected person. Studies of thousands of households where AIDS patients have lived and been cared for have found no instance of transmission from the sharing of kitchen, laundry, or bathroom facilities. HIV is spread to others through sex and blood-to-blood contact.

Response to Vignette

Shyla describes Trish as being overwhelmed and out of control. Trish is clearly in the midst of a crisis after being confronted with a traumatic diagnosis. In addition to education, Trish needs support and counseling to get her through this initial stressful period. A careful assessment should be performed to determine her level of psychological distress and suicidal potential. Support systems can be put in place to help Trish cope with the various challenges she will face.

Trish needs concrete information, emotional support, and empowerment so that she can approach her illness in a positive and proactive manner. Straightforward counseling, giving her credit for being capable, responsible, and intelligent, will be the most helpful.

Trish is likely to feel isolated, helpless, and afraid. Pastor Wilson could best use this opportunity by providing an environment and relationship that will reduce Trish's anxiety long enough to develop a plan of action. The plan should include acquiring education, as well as medical and emotional support. Referral information should be offered to Trish so she can easily access people and agencies that specialize in the treatment of HIV. Since people often have misconceptions about HIV that add to their distress, providing her with factual information may be reassuring. Finally, Trish may need help in identifying what is standing in the way of her being able to talk with her parents. She may need help in determining how best to prepare herself and her family for the disclosure of her diagnosis.

It is critical that Pastor Wilson make herself available to Trish's family. Since many people have little knowledge about HIV and AIDS, factual information may help to address many fears and concerns. Referrals to the many resources and support outlets available may be needed. Family members may experience grief, guilt, blame, stigma, and isolation. They may also harbor irrational fears that can interfere with their ability to provide adequate care. By discussing the topic in an open and nonjudgmental manner, Pastor Wilson will serve as a positive role model for dealing with the disease.

Some people, when diagnosed with HIV or when faced with a family member's diagnosis, adopt denial and avoidance coping strategies that can interfere with their utilization of health and psychological services (Chesney and Folkman 1994). It will be important to discuss this tendency with Trish and to try to motivate her to seek needed services promptly. It is necessary to explain that ignoring HIV will leave her feeling isolated and depressed and may keep her from getting the medical attention that will alleviate symptoms and help her to live longer.

The provision of factual information about HIV will enhance Trish's ability to respond wisely to her situation. Referrals to individuals and agencies that specialize in the treatment of HIV and AIDS will help her to recognize that she is not alone and that she is not helpless in the face of her diagnosis. Once the acute anxiety and depression are stabilized, Trish will need assistance with other issues, including topics that many people are uncomfortable discussing, such as sexuality and death. Clergy are in a unique position to help there.

Confidentiality is an important issue for teenagers seeking help and health care. Providing reassurance about confidentiality will greatly increase the likelihood that Trish will continue to seek help. Other important qualities when working with teenagers include genuineness, respect, and the ability to relate well.

As many as 1.5 million Americans are believed to be infected with HIV. The widespread nature of this disease makes it probable that most people, especially those who counsel, will face this issue, either by direct contact with someone who has HIV or through loved ones of someone who carries a diagnosis. Knowing the facts about HIV and AIDS will increase the provision of accurate information and appropriate referrals, and it will strengthen the support that is offered. In addition to direct services for individuals diagnosed with HIV or AIDS, providing support for their families and caretakers is particularly important. There is often profound psychological distress related to dealing with chronic and deteriorating illness. This is especially true as AIDS progresses into the later stages. Issues likely to come up include grief, lack of needed community support, relationship difficulties, loss, and heightened levels of stress.

People living with HIV infection and AIDS are often thrown into existential crises and find that they have been disaffiliated from traditional sources of spiritual care. The faith community can provide powerful support for individuals with HIV/AIDS. Research indicates that a blending of spiritual practices and mental health approaches positively facilitates the coping of people who are living with these diagnoses (Somlai 1996).

Treatment Within the Faith Community

Shyla would benefit from counseling to help her understand Trish's situation and to provide support for her own grief. Pastor Wilson may offer initial support and assistance, and it may also be appropriate to refer Shyla to a health care professional who specializes in HIV/AIDS. The point is that Shyla is also in crisis and needs education about the illness as well as an opportunity to express her own fears, concerns, and grief.

Trish will benefit from several referrals, including those that will provide appropriate medical care and emotional support. In this scenario, referral to a mental health specialist would be appropriate, due to Trish's obvious distress and inability to seek her family's help or otherwise develop needed social supports. Her drinking and self-destructive behavior are strong indicators of her internal distress and should be taken very seriously.

Indications for Referral

When persons are diagnosed with HIV, they may experience multiple psychological reactions, including anxiety (see Case 20), panic, and depression (see Case 15). Mental health specialists can provide educational information about HIV and AIDS and will work with individuals to develop skills for coping effectively toward positive living with their diagnosis.

Short-term therapy that focuses on depression and anxiety will be helpful in alleviating Trish's acute symptoms of distress. Social support groups are then appropriate to establish critical peer support and emotional coping. Other treatment strategies may include holistic and natural treatments, relaxation training, and visualization.

Treatment by Mental Health Specialist

Cross-Cultural-Issues

Among teens and adults the proportion of HIV cases is higher among ethnic minorities than Caucasians (Karon et al. 1996). African American pastors who received HIV/AIDS training reported that they were more comfortable counseling persons with AIDS and much more active in educating their congregation on the topic (Crawford et al. 1992).

Resources

National Resources

National Association of People with AIDS (NAPWA), 1413 K St., NW, 7th floor, Washington, DC 20005; (202) 898-0414; www.napwa.org; napwa@napwa.org. A national network of persons with AIDS founded in 1986 as a voice for health, social, and political concerns.

Centers for Disease Control (CDC), National Prevention Information Network, P.O. Box 6003, Rockville, MD 20849; (800) 458-5231; www.cdcnac.org; info@cdcnpin.org.

Critical Path AIDS Project, 2062 Lombard Street, Philadelphia, PA 19146; (215) 545-2212; kiyoshi@critpath.org; www.critpath.org.

Advocates for Youth, 1025 Vermont Ave., NE, Suite 200, Washington, DC 20005; (202) 347-5700; www.advocatesforyouth.org; info@advocatesforyouth.org; provides information on STDs for youth and parents.

American Social Health Association (ASHA), P.O. Box 13827, Research Triangle Park, NC 27709; (800) 783-9877; hivnet@ashastd.org; www.sunsite.unc.edu/asha; has free and confidential information on the Web site about STDs. The group has hotline information.

Sexuality Information and Education Council of the United States (SIECUS), 130 West 42nd St., Suite 350, New York, NY 10036; (212) 819-9770; www.siecus.org; siecus@siecus.org; has a fact sheet on STDs.

National Catholic AIDS Network, P.O. Box 422984, San Francisco, CA 94142; (707) 874-3031; www.ncan.org; ncan@sonic.net.

HIV/AIDS Ministries Network, Health and Welfare Ministries, United Methodist Church, General Board of Global Ministries, 475 Riverside Dr., Room 350, New York, NY 10115; (212) 870-3909; gbgm-umc.org/programs/hiv/aids.html; aidsmin@gbgm-umc.org.

AIDS National Interfaith Network, 1400 I Street, NW, Suite 1220, Washington, DC 20005; (202) 842-0010; www.thebody.com./anin/aninpage.html; Aninken@aol.com.

AIDS Advocacy in African American Churches Project, 611 Pennsylvania, SE, Suite 359, Washington, DC 20003; (202) 546-8587.

Union of American Hebrew Congregations/Central Conference of American Rabbis, Joint Committee on AIDS, 75 2nd Ave., Suite 550, Needham Heights, MA 02194; (617) 449-0404.

The Ark of Refuge: HIV/AIDS Ministry, 1025 Howard Street, San Francisco, CA 94103; (415) 861-1060; www.sfrefuge.org./Ark.html;

serves people of color, women, low-income and homeless with HIV.

Self-Help Resources

Teens Teaching About AIDS; (800) 234-TEEN; Hotline staffed by teens for teens, 4 P.M.–8 P.M. Eastern Standard Time.

KAIROS Support for Caregivers, 2128 15th Street, San Francisco, CA 94114; (415) 861-0877; eros.the-park.com/kairos; kairos@hooked.net.

AIDS Education and Research Trust, 4 Brighton Rd., Horsham, West Sussex, RH13 5BA, England; www.avert.org; avert@dial.pipex.com.

Centers for Disease Control (CDC) National AIDS Hotline, (800) 342-2437 or CDC National STD Hotline, (800) 227-8922.

Growth House, Inc., HIV and AIDS links, www.growth house.org/hivlinks.html; info@growthhouse.org, (415) 255-9045.

HIV In Site: Gateway to AIDS Knowledge, hivinsite.ucsf.edu; Web site is also available in Spanish.

Herpes Anonymous, P.O. Box 278, Westbury, NY 11590; (516) 334-5718; is dedicated to helping others like themselves overcome the social stigma of herpes. Contact this group if you are interested in starting a similar group in your area.

Herpes Resource Center, P.O. Box 13827, Research Triangle Park, NC 27709; (800) 230-6039; www.ashastd.org; is a national network of 90 groups founded in 1979 to offer emotional support and education for persons with herpes.

AIDS and Your Religious Community: A Hands-On Guide for Local Programs, by Warren J. Blumenfeld (Boston: Unitarian Universalist Association, 1991).

References

Aguilera, D.C. (1994). *Crisis Intervention: Theory and Methodology* (pp. 257-301) St. Louis, MO: Mosby-Year Book, Inc.

Chesney, M.A. and Folkman, S. (1994). Psychological impact of HIV disease and implications for intervention. *Psychiatric Clinics of North America, 17.* 163-182.

Crawford, I., Allison, K.W., Robinson, W.L., Hughes, D. and Samaryk, M. (1992). Attitudes of African-American Baptist ministers towards AIDS. *Journal of Community Psychology, 20(4).* 304-308.

Goldfarb, A.F. (1997). Adolescent sexuality. *Annals New York Academy of Sciences, 816.* 404-410.

Griffin, C.B. (1996). "Living Healthy," *Blue Cross and Blue Shield of Massachusetts, 3.* 3.

Karon, J.M., Rosenberg, P.S., McQuillan, G., Khare, M., Gwinn, M. and Petersen, L.R. (1996). Prevalence of HIV infection in The United States, 1984–1992. *Journal of the American Medical Association, 276(2).* 126-131.

Perry, S.W. and Markowitz, J. (1986). Psychiatric interventions for AIDS-spectrum disorders. *Hospital and Community Psychiatry, 37.* 1001.

Scott, M.A.K. (1996). Reducing the risks: Adolescents and sexually transmitted diseases, *Nurse Practictioner Forum, 7(1).* 23-29.

Somlai, A.M., Kelly, J.A., Kalichman, S.C., Mulry, G., Sikkema, K.J., McAuliffe, T., Multhauf, K. and Davantes, B. (1996). An empirical investigation of the relationship between spirituality, coping and emotional distress in people living with HIV infection and AIDS. *Journal of Pastoral Care, 50(2).* 181-191.

Wellings, K., Wadsworth, J., Johnson, A.M., Field, J., Whitaker, L. and Field, B. (1995). Provision of sex education and early sexual experience: the relation examined. *British Medical Journal, 311.* 417-420.

Sexually Transmitted Diseases (STDs)

Once called venereal diseases, STDs are among the most common infectious diseases in the United States. In spite of all the publicity surrounding AIDS, STDs are on the increase. According to the National Institutes of Health, more than twenty STDs have been identified affecting more than 13 million Americans.

Acquired Immunodeficiency Syndrome (AIDS)

AIDS is caused by the human immunodeficiency virus (HIV), which destroys the body's capacity to fight infections. There are an estimated 1 million cases in the United States and 30 million worldwide. People who have AIDS are very susceptible to other diseases. Transmission of the virus primarily occurs during sexual activity and by sharing needles used to infect intravenous drugs. Pregnant women with AIDS can transmit the virus to their child.

Chlamydial Infections

These infections are the most common of all STDs, with an estimated 4 million new cases each year. Many people with chlamydial infection have few or no symptoms. Pelvic inflammatory disease (PID), a serious complication of the infection, has emerged as a major cause of infertility among women. Once diagnosed, chlamydial infections are treatable with antibiotics.

Genital Herpes

An estimated 23 percent of adult Americans suffer from this infection with one-half million new cases each year. The major signs of herpes are painful blisters or open sores in the genital area. The sores disappear in two or three weeks, but the virus remains in the body and the lesions may recur occasionally. Genital herpes symptoms can be helped with antiviral medication, but the virus remains in the body. Women who acquire genital herpes during pregnancy can transmit the virus to the baby, which can result in serious health risks to the child if left untreated.

Genital Warts

Genital warts are caused by the human papilloma virus (HPV). The warts first appear as hard, painless bumps in the genital area. Genital warts are spread by sexual contact with an infected partner and are very contagious. An estimated 1 million new cases are diagnosed in the United States each year. Scientists believe that HPV may also cause several types of genital cancer. The warts are treated with a topical substance or by freezing.

Gonorrhea

There are about 1.5 million cases in the U.S. each year. The early symptoms of gonorrhea often are mild, and most women have no symptoms of the disease. If symptoms develop, they usually appear within two to ten days after sexual contact with an infected partner. The common signs of gonorrhea are a discharge from the vagina or penis or painful/burning urination. It can be treated with antibiotics. The most common complication for women is infertility.

Hepatitis B

This is an inflammation of the liver caused by a virus (HBV). In the severe form, it is a serious threat to health and can sometimes lead to liver failure and death. HBV is most commonly passed on to a sexual partner during intercourse, especially during anal sex. It is estimated that 300,000 persons in the United States become infected annually. At present, there are no specific treatments for the acute symptoms of this virus.

Syphilis

This infection has been on the increase in many cities in the United States in recent years. An estimated 100,000 cases occur annually. Syphilis is a sexually transmitted disease caused by a bacterium. The initial sign is a painless open sore in the genital area that generally appears within two to six weeks after sexual contact. If untreated, the disease can damage the central nervous system and cause death. Penicillin is commonly used to treat the disease.

Trichomoniasis

Trichomoniasis, sometimes referred to as "trich," is a common STD that affects 2 to 3 million Americans each year. It is caused by a parasite and often occurs without symptoms. If symptoms occur, they are in the form of genital discharge. This STD is treatable with medication.

Chronic Medical Problems

"She Had Been a Trouper"

Jill Daniel was becoming progressively withdrawn and isolated. Her parents were concerned. They spoke after church with Father Norwood and arranged to meet with him later that day. Thirteen-year-old Jill accompanied her parents.

"We think Jill is depressed. Over the past year she's spent less and less time with her friends, and she doesn't want to go anywhere with the family. We are worried." As the story unfolded, Jill recounted how she had suffered from severe asthma since early childhood. At least twice a year, bad attacks resulted in frightening trips to the emergency room. She had always handled it "like a trouper," but this year it was different.

Jill was required to restrict her physical activities. This year she entered junior high school; and like lots of teenage girls, she dreamed of becoming a cheerleader. But it was clear that the exertion required precluded her from cheerleading. For the first time, her chronic illness began to matter a lot.

Her parents commented, "We've told her there are many other things she can do." Jill chimed in, "They just don't understand!"

Pastoral Assessment

During his thirty years as a priest, Greg Norwood had seen many children who were starting life with some form of medical condition or physical disability. There were those with epilepsy, cerebral palsy, diabetes, and heart conditions. One girl had a colostomy, youngsters had been in bad accidents, and a few children had cancer. He knew that Jill's reaction was typical for teenagers. Simply trying other activities, as her parents suggested, does not work most of the time. Adolescents are dominated by the need to make connections with friends and to do "normal" teenage activities. Jill was expressing entirely appropriate feelings of disappointment.

And, she did not feel accurately understood by her parents. Since she was, reportedly, becoming more withdrawn, Father Norwood took these concerns seriously. He knew that he needed to do an assessment to determine if Jill was depressed (see Case 15). Jill had a problem, and her parents were also in the midst of a crucial family issue; they needed to be helped to know how to respond.

Diagnostic Criteria

Significant medical illnesses and chronic physical limitations have a number of different impacts on children and teenagers. Many variables will influence how such circumstances affect a child. Let's consider the following factors that may contribute to how one copes with illness:

The family attitude about physical pain and suffering. This will vary tremendously from family to family. On one end of the continuum are those who insist on stoicism; in the extreme there may be messages such as "If you complain, you are weak and should feel ashamed." At the other end are parents who feel overwhelmed by their child's suffering and may respond by *excessive* caretaking to the point of overprotecting the child. (Such parents inadvertently transmit the message to children that they are completely helpless, which can interfere with appropriate maturation and can serve to frighten children.) Of course, in the middle are those sensitive and compassionate parents who find a balance between caretaking and treating their teenagers in age-appropriate ways.

The course of the disorder. Is it a static condition—not likely to get worse but also not likely to improve? Is it a transient disorder? Is it a condition subject to improvement, but with a protracted course of recovery? Is it a disorder that results in deterioration and progressive disability? Is it a terminal illness? To what degree does the illness or condition interfere with important life activities, such as normal socialization, school, and so forth?

Is it likely to carry some form of negative social stigma and thus result in peer rejection? Examples of this might be cerebral palsy or disfiguring burns. What toll has the illness or condition taken on the family? For example, some illnesses begin with ample amounts of parental care and involvement; but after months or years of heartache and strain, family members begin to get "worn out."

Has the illness or condition radically changed the person *of the child?* This is often the case in neurologic diseases or head injuries. Despite some recovery, many of these children are changed. They may have lost cognitive abilities, they may have become persistently aggressive and violent or lost all capacity for empathy. Parents of these children, in many respects, feel that they have lost *their child* and are left with the burden of caring for someone they hardly know.

The availability or lack of important resources: financial, social, health care, respite, spiritual. The types of circumstances can vary tremendously and a complete discussion of the impact of childhood illnesses is beyond the scope of this book. However, it is important for clergy to be alert to the following issues that commonly arise in the context of significant medical problems.

For the Child
- Missing out on important life activities.
- Peer rejection and social isolation.
- Suffering from chronic pain.
- Fears about the illness and implications for the future—issues frequently not openly discussed with adolescents, but often on their minds.
- Sadness, grief, or depression regarding the multitude of losses accompanying such circumstances.
- Some adolescents become defiant—this may be seen in an unwillingness to cooperate with treatment or rehabilitation.

For the Parents
- Worries about the future of their child.
- Grief and loss over "what might have been" were it not for the issues.
- Anger toward other families who have healthy children, toward insensitive children who may say hurtful things to their child.
- Guilt—the sheer exhaustion of caring for a very ill child may lead to some parents secretly wishing the child had died and then feeling terribly guilty for this feeling. This is especially common in parents of children with severe mental retardation or other forms of serious brain injury.
- Significant time is required for caring for the child, thus taking time away from work, recreation, and parental intimacy.
- There may be serious financial burdens associated with the illness.

For the Family
- Accommodation of a sick or injured child often results in marked alterations of a family's lifestyle. The ill teenager often requires a good deal of attention, thus siblings many times feel left out or neglected.

Pastors should be sensitive to these issues. In addition it will be important to evaluate for the presence of the following, which may be a part of a teen's reaction to their illness or condition:
- Depression
- Excessive worry, fear, or anxiety
- Substance abuse
- Uncontrolled pain (note: some people do not like to complain and thus may not report that they suffer from excessive pain unless directly asked)

Relevant History

In Jill's case, although she minimized the impact of her asthma prior to this year, upon questioning she revealed the following, which was a surprise to her parents. She spoke of feeling terrified during severe episodes and of almost constant worries regarding "When will it happen again?" and "Will I die?"

She had become moderately depressed over the past year. With some prompting she acknowledged that she had had some suicidal ideas, but absolutely no intent to actually kill herself. She had withdrawn from many social activities, which probably fueled her depression.

Her mother and father were both clearly loving parents. They initially spoke of her problems in a concerned but rather matter-of-fact way. However, when Jill spoke about being afraid to die, her mother became tearful and shared similar fears.

Indications for Referral

The decision to refer for mental health treatment in such cases depends on the nature and severity of the child's response to the illness.

Response to Vignette

The discussion with Father Norwood was extremely helpful. It opened many doors to issues the family had not fully understood. This particular family was able and willing to acknowledge that Jill was suffering a lot, and they followed Father Norwood's advice to see a mental health professional.

The entire family met with a counselor for three sessions, and then Jill continued to see her for six months. Jill was able to speak openly about her worries and fears. Her sense of desperation lessened. At some point, the counselor intervened with the school; and Jill was ultimately able to join her school's "spirit team," acting in a less strenuous way as she once again became involved in activities.

Treatment Within the Faith Community

All Christians and Jews know the story of Job. And many persons conclude that in the wake of physical illness or injury, they too should be patient and strong. But people, especially children, must be encouraged to express their physical and emotional suffering. Even Jesus shed tears of anguish. This human experience is easier to bear when shared with another.

It is important to remind the congregation to keep in mind those who have chronic illnesses or conditions. It is usual for tremendous concern to be expressed at the time of an accident or the diagnosis of an illness. However, social isolation is very common in the many months and years that follow. It is during these times that ongoing pastoral availability is crucial.

Treatment by Mental Health Specialist

The particular focus of mental health treatment will, of course, depend on the nature of the teenager's emotional response to the illness or condition. In any case, supportive psychotherapy is often quite helpful.

Beyond this, a useful approach is to teach adolescents active communication and assertiveness skills. Not only will these help the teen deal more effectively with teachers, medical care providers, peers, employers, and such; but they can, in an important way, reduce feelings of helplessness and powerlessness, which so often accompany the experience of chronic illness.

If illnesses or injuries are static or lead to deterioration, almost invariably a part of mental health treatment will involve grief work. This may take many forms, but generally involves the gradual facing of painful realities and mourning the loss of normal life opportunities. However, such treatment also requires active problem solving and encouragement to explore new ways to get needs met. These teens ultimately must find ways to enhance their sense of mastery and self-worth, along with ways to make meaningful connections with peers. The latter may be accomplished by involvement in a support group—in some communities there are specialized groups for teenagers with particular disorders, such as diabetes.

Cross-Cultural Issues

Religion may be particularly helpful for ethnic minority families who experience high levels of stress (Pargament 1997). Religion appears to enhance well-being, lower distress, and facilitate faster recovery from high stress. In a study of Orthodox Jewish families with a disabled child, religion was found to be a source of strength important to adjustment and positive adaptation (Leyser 1994).

National Resources

Resources

Association of Birth Defect Children, 930 Woodcock Road, Suite 225, Orlando, FL 32803; (800) 313-2232; abdc@birthdefects.org; is a national network that gives support for families of children with birth defects and developmental disabilities caused by environmental agents.

National Fathers' Network, Kindering Center, 16120 NE Eighth St., Bellevue, WA 98008; (206) 747-4004; www.fathersnetwork.org; jmay@fathersnetwork.org; is a national organization offering networking and support for men who are committed to giving quality care to their children with special needs.

National Parent Network on Disabilities, 1130 17th Street, NW, Suite 400, Washington, DC 20036; (202) 463-2299; www.npnd.org; NPND@cs.com; is a national group with 175 affiliates founded to advocate for parents of persons with disabilities.

People Living Through Cancer, 323 Eighth St., SW, Albuquerque, NM 87102; (888) 441-4439; cancerhope@aol.com; was founded in 1983 to help cancer survivors and their loved ones make informed choices and improve the quality of life by sharing in a community of people who have faced the disease. Conducts national training for American Indians who are interested in developing programs. Contact this group only if you are interested in starting a similar group.

The Center for Attitudinal Healing, 33 Buchanan Drive, Sausalito, CA 94965; (415) 331-6161; healingcenter.org; is a national organization founded in 1975 with 100+ affiliate groups. It supports programs for children, adolescents, and adults facing their own, or a family member's, life-threatening illness, loss, and grief. All services are free of charge.

Candlelighters Childhood Cancer Foundation, 7910 Woodmont Ave., Suite 460, Bethesda, MD 20814; (800) 366-2223; www.candlelighters.org; info@candlighters.org; is an international foundation with 400 groups, founded in 1970. It provides support for parents of children and teens with cancer by linking families. It has a long-term survivors network, youth newspaper, and Internet linkage.

National Information Center for Children and Youth with Disabilities, P.O. Box 1492, Washington, DC 20013; (800) 695-0285; www.nichcy.org; nichcy@aed.org.

Self-Help Resources

National Parent to Parent Support and Information Systems, Inc. (NPPIS), P.O. Box 907, Blue Ridge, GA 30513; (800) 651-1151; judd103w@wonder.em.cdc.gov; nppsis.org, is a national network linking together parents who have children with special health care needs or rare disorders. The network provides information, referrals, and assistance in starting support groups.

Rainbows, 2100 Golf Road #370, Rolling Meadows, IL 60008; (800) 266-3206; www.rainbows.org; info@rainbows.org. Rainbows is an international organization with 6,300 affiliated groups. Founded in 1983, Rainbows establishes peer support groups in churches, schools, and social agencies for children and adults who are grieving a divorce, death, or other painful change in their family. The support groups are led by trained adults. It also provides referrals.

MUMS: National Parents Network, 150 Custer Ct., Green Bay, WI 54301; (920) 336-5333; www.waisman.wisc.edu/~rowley/mums; mums@netnet.net, was founded in 1979 as a national parent-to-parent organization to provide networking for families with children with rare birth defects, chromosomal abnormalities, or medical conditions. It can match families with rare disorders using an extensive database.

References

Leyser, Y. (1994). Stress and adaptation in Orthodox Jewish families with a disabled child. *American Journal of Orthopsychiatry, 64(3)*. 376-385.

Pargament, K.I. (1997). *The Psychology of Religion and Coping: Theory, Research, Practice*. NY: Guilford Press.

General References Regarding Chronic Medical Problems

Melamed, R.G. and Siegel, L.J. (1980). *Behavioral Medicine*. NY: Springer.

Melamed, R.G. and Siegel, L.J. (1985). Children's reactions to medical stressors: An ecological approach to the study of anxiety. In A.H. Tuma and J. Maser (eds.) *Anxiety and the Anxiety Disorders* (pp. 369-388). Hillsdale, NJ: Erlbaum.

Bereavement

"He Took the Death Hard"

It had been six weeks since the funeral. Eighteen-year-old Ron Taylor had been killed in an automobile accident, and his death had stunned and saddened the whole congregation. The Taylors had been members of the church for more than fifteen years, and they were well known in their small community. Pastor Martinez received a call from Ron's mother, Betty. "I'm concerned about Billy. Can we come and talk to you?" Billy was Ron's 15-year-old younger brother.

Stan Martinez knew Billy fairly well and could see that he was reluctant to come in to talk to the minister when his mother motioned him into the pastor's study. Betty did most of the talking at first as she described how Billy "seems to be taking it hard." Billy remarked, "Well, I'm sad, but I'm doing OK." Betty chimed in, "He's just so quiet and withdrawn. He's spending a lot of time in his room and he's lost his appetite. I'm worried." Billy rejoined, "Mom . . . I'm OK, it's not that big of a deal." However, his mother and Pastor Martinez suspected that this was not entirely true. Billy was a good, solid, caring kid; and he'd been very close to his brother. Of course he was taking it hard, and it is very common for teenagers (especially boys) to minimize or downplay their emotional pain.

Pastoral Assessment

Stan Martinez is now confronted with a rather common situation. There has been a tragic loss, and such events have a significant impact on all people. However, not all people respond to the death of a loved one in the same way. The questions pastors must consider are: Is this a normal response to loss? and, How can I help?

The process of mourning (what mental health professionals refer to as normal or uncomplicated bereavement) needs to be differentiated from more severe or pathological reactions. The most common pathological response to loss is severe clinical depression, but the distinction between healthy grief and depression sometimes is not completely clear.

Grief, or what some call the work of mourning, is often a prolonged, terribly painful process. Major losses dramatically change people's lives, but normal grief must be appreciated as a healthy process, essential to ultimate emotional healing. In contrast, depression and other maladaptive responses to loss do not promote emotional recovery. They intensify suffering and prolong the course of healing.

In studies of normal bereavement, it is clear that emotionally healthy people do not all respond in the same way. While many people experience sudden and intense sadness, a number of folks emotionally shut down in a state of emotional shock manifested by a lack of strong feelings, social withdrawal, and feelings of numbness. Following a loss, if persons experience this type of reaction, they may tell others that they feel like something is wrong with them or that they feel guilty because they (at least intellectually) expect to feel a wave of sadness. This can be a perplexing reaction to both the individual who experiences it and to those around him or her. It is not uncommon for friends or relatives who see such a person to wonder "whether he or she cares," failing to understand that the individual is simply in a state of emotional numbness. Usually this state of shock gives way in a few days, several weeks, or a number of months. At that time, the person may be surprised to encounter a tidal wave of intense sadness.

Mindful of this, Pastor Martinez is careful not to jump to conclusions. Billy may just be in this "shutdown" mode. Stan will need to be accepting of Billy's attitude that "it's no big deal." He also must listen carefully and gently ask some questions to determine if Mrs. Taylor's concerns are warranted. The pastor knows that the process of grieving is unique for each person and that it cannot be rushed.

Relevant History

Certain factors have been determined that may greatly increase the risk of *complicated grief* reactions. These include:

- Sudden and unexpected death
- Loss of a child
- Death occurring after a very lengthy illness
- Death due to suicide or homicide
- Violent death (especially with mutilation)
- A death that was preventable
- Multiple deaths or a history of significant loss
- Personal or family history of clinical depression
- Lack of a stable and available support system (Rando 1984 and 1991; Marmar 1991)

In Billy's case, the loss of his brother was sudden, unexpected, and violent; perhaps it was preventable. However, there had been no prior losses, no family or personal history of depression, and his parents are capable and supportive. Thus, some factors suggest increased risk for complicated bereavement, but the one factor that certainly is positive is the presence of a close, loving family.

In the United States many misperceptions exist regarding the impact of significant losses. Our fast-paced society seems to think that people must "get on with their lives," which often translates into expectations that people will complete mourning within a few months. Unfortunately, hearts do not heal that fast. It is not uncommon for significant grieving to continue for a period of from one to four years (and much longer for parents who have lost a child).

Diagnostic Criteria

As noted previously, no one pattern exists that characterizes grief—the responses vary tremendously. However, they broadly fall into either a state of emotional rawness (aware of intense sadness, loneliness, and missing the loved one) or of relative numbness. Also, for teenagers two other related manifestations are commonly seen. The first is anxiety. Losses for everyone tend to markedly destabilize people. Following the death of a loved one, the world may seem much less safe and secure. For teens who are not yet fully mature, this is especially common. Adolescents may experience tension headaches, sleep disturbances, difficulty concentrating, generalized nervousness, and often, irritability.

Another common reaction seen with teenagers is a version of "numbness" where the child becomes extremely involved (to a fault) in distracting activities. This may take the form of immersion in schoolwork or obsessive pursuit of athletics. More destructive versions include promiscuity or substance abuse, which can be seen as attempts to avoid awareness of inner painful feelings. Usually these adolescents are not consciously aware of the motive to avoid emotions and may resist if parents or others imply that they are in denial.

The following signs may alert a pastor or mental health professional that the process of mourning has taken a pathological turn:

- Preoccupation with thoughts about death and (especially) suicide
- Extreme nervousness or agitation
- Marked weight loss
- Substance abuse
- Low self-esteem
- Feelings of hopelessness
- Significant physical symptoms for which the family doctor fails to find any organic cause (such as headaches, stomachaches)
- Severe sleep disturbances (especially very early morning awakening and being unable to return to sleep)

- No outward signs of joy, aliveness, or vitality
- Marked withdrawal from life activities for more than two weeks

Sadness, uneasiness, loneliness, and a sense of loss may continue for a number of months after the loss of a loved one. This is especially so when children lose parents, since that involves both a terrible loss and often marked changes in the teenager's life and lifestyle (such as much less parental involvement, financial strains). The presence of these "red flags" suggests that you may not be witnessing normal grief. These signs clearly suggest depression and require a referral to a mental health specialist.

Response to Vignette

Billy's reaction to the loss of his brother is understandable. Pastor Martinez carefully asked him about his sleep, his activities, and emotional reactions (including an inquiry about any suicidal ideas). It became apparent that except for social withdrawal and some decrease in appetite, Billy did not exhibit signs of clinical depression. Pastor Martinez then said to Billy and his mother, "Billy, you said it's 'no big deal.' But, I think you and I both know that in your heart of hearts, Ron's death was a big deal and still is. It's entirely normal for people to need a long time to come to terms with very painful losses. Now you have kind of shut down, but it wouldn't surprise me if, at some point in the future, you start to experience some painful feelings. I want you to keep in mind that when this happens, it is very normal and human."

The pastor continued, "I think it would be good for us to meet again in a few weeks to just talk a bit about how things are going. Also, I want you to think about something. It's often said that 'sadness is easier to bear if you share it with someone.' You can call me at any time. Or if you want, I can help you find a group of other teenagers who meet and talk to one another about losses they have experienced. And let me encourage you to open up to your parents."

Pastor Martinez had from time to time included in his sermons the idea that "people do not get over major losses quickly." He has always wanted those in his congregation to know that they can provide much-needed support to one another by maintaining emotional care and availability over the many, many months of grief that follow the loss of a loved one. Three weeks later, Billy's mother called to report that she noticed Billy had been crying. Apparently his numbness had given way to more visible mourning. Ultimately Billy was not interested in talking with Pastor Martinez, but the minister did provide support to the family as they healed together.

Some 75 to 85 percent of people encountering major losses do not experience pathological grief. They suffer a lot, but stay involved in life. This large group of mourners rarely want or need psychological counseling, finding that the support of their family and faith community aids greatly as they begin to heal. The smaller group of "at-risk" folks can potentially suffer for many years and are the ones for whom psychotherapy may be very beneficial.

Each year 8 million people in the United States experience the death of a family member. There are over 800,000 new widows and widowers each year. Other losses lead to bereavement, too (including divorces, separations, miscarriages, and serious illnesses like Alzheimer's disease, which results in the loss of a *person*, long before physical death). Beyond the way a pastor may interact with individuals or a family, the entire congregation often plays a significant role in responding to losses. This can be influenced profoundly by the attitudes of clergy, which are demonstrated both in personal interactions and in messages conveyed in sermons.

After six months or so following a loss, two events commonly occur. The first is the inaccurate assumption by friends that "they are getting over it." Second, for the bereaved, a new wave of more profound loss is often experienced. At this time (give or take a few months) the reality and finality of the loss start to sink in. An important message to share with the congregation is that we should not abandon a mourner after a few months; often a greater need emerges later on and continued support is extremely important.

Treatment Within the Faith Community

A good deal of "grief work" is done within one's family and/or with one's pastor. Also, a tremendously helpful resource is bereavement support groups.

When the situation dictates mental health treatment, two main options are commonly recommended. The first is psychotherapy, where the person first establishes a safe and trusting relationship with a therapist. Then grieving is encouraged. This is often facilitated by asking the mourner to speak in great detail about the lost loved one (not only the painful events of the death, but also positive memories). This approach is based on the understanding that ultimately painful realities must be faced and losses mourned, but with a deep appreciation that each person must do this according to an inner timetable. This encouragement to remember, reflect, and feel is done with gentleness and much support.

Sometimes the mourner is asked to bring in photos of the loved one or encouraged to write a heartfelt letter to the deceased, expressing thoughts or feelings to that person.

For some people, psychotheraphy may involve just a few sessions; for others it may be more lengthy, depending on the circumstances.

A second approach, almost always taken in conjunction with psychotherapy, is medication. In cases of acute, traumatic loss, sometimes it is helpful and appropriate to make use of antianxiety medications (minor tranquilizers) for a few days or a week to help people sleep. However, on-

Treatment by Mental Health Specialist

going use of tranquilizers is rarely appropriate. If, however, there are signs of severe depression (suicidal ideas, severe agitation, marked and persistent sleep disturbances, weight loss) antidepressants *may* be indicated. No pill can fill empty lives or mend broken hearts, but antidepressants often are helpful in reducing symptoms of major depression. Once the depression lifts, the work of continued mourning can continue.

Cross-Cultural Issues

Attitudes regarding death and mourning vary tremendously across cultures. For this reason, the pastor must be attuned to prevailing beliefs among parishioners and to unique values that may be culturally-specific to minority groups.

Resources

National Resources

Hospice Helpline, National Hospice Organization, 1901 N. Moore St., Suite 901, Arlington, VA 22209; (800) 658-8898. The majority of hospice programs provide support groups for family members.

The Compassionate Friends, Inc., P.O. Box 3696, Oak Brook, IL 60522; (630) 990-0010; www.compassionatefriends.org; tcf_national@prodigy.com; a group that gives support to parents who have lost a child and siblings who have lost a brother or sister.

Parents of Murdered Children, 100 East 8th St., B-41, Cincinnati, OH 45202; (888) 818-POMC; www.pomc.com;NatlPOMC@aol.com, has 300 chapters in the United States and Australia. The organization was founded to provide self-help groups to support persons who survive the violent death of someone close.

Rainbows, 2100 Golf Rd. #370, Rolling Meadows, IL 60008; (800) 266-3206; www.rainbows.org; info@rainbows.org, is an international organization with 6,300 affiliated groups. Founded in 1983, Rainbows establishes peer support groups in churches, schools, and social agencies for children and adults who are grieving a divorce, death, or other painful change in their family. The support groups are led by trained adults. Rainbows also provides referrals.

There are several computer accessible Internet Web sites that provide information on grief and bereavement resources. *GriefNet* is a directory of resources of value to those who are experiencing loss and grief, sponsored by the nonprofit Rivendell Resources, P.O. Box 3272, Ann Arbor, MI 48106; griefnet.org; griefnet@griefnet.org; fax (313) 761-1960.

Teen Age Grief, P.O. Box 220034, Newhall, CA 91322; (805) 253-1932; www.smartlink.net/~tag; tag@smartlink.net.

Self-Help Resources

After the Death of a Child: Living with Loss Through the Years, by Ann K. Finkbeiner (NY: Free Press, 1996) and *When the Bough Breaks: Forever*

After the Death of a Son or Daughter, by Judith Bernstein (NY: Andrews and McMeel, 1997) are highly recommended.

The Minister as Crisis Counselor, by David Switzer (Nashville: Abingdon Press, 1985 revised) offers a very informative chapter on pastoral responses to persons with normal and complicated grief reactions.

Clinical Management of Bereavement, by George M. Burnell and Adrienne L. Burnell (NY: Human Sciences Press, 1989) and *Helping the Bereaved*, by Alicia S. Cook and Daniel S. Dworkin, (NY: Basic Books, 1992) are instructive books written from a mental health professional's point of view.

Grief, Transition, and Loss: A Pastor's Practical Guide, by Wayne Oates (Minneapolis, MN: Fortress, 1997).

References

Marmar, C.R. (1991). Grief and bereavement after traumatic loss. *Audio Digest Psychiatry, 20(5)*.

Rando, T.A. (1984). *Grief, Dying and Death: Clinical Interventions for Caregivers*. Champaign, IL: Research Press.

Rando, T.A. (1991). *How to Go on Living When Someone You Love Dies*. New York: Bantam Books.

Depression

"Totally Bored and Gloomy"

Amy is 15 years old, and the past several years have been marked by family instability. Her mother had protracted suffering before dying of cancer. Amy had been sent to live with her grandparents for a year in another town, since her father was unable to cope with the stress. When Amy moved back home to attend high school, she was upset to find out her father was dating a neighbor. Amy's mother had been a devout woman who took her to Mass and church activities all of her life. George, the parish nurse, came to see Father Coyne about Amy.

George reported that Amy's behavior had changed markedly over the last few months since her return. She writes morbid poems about death, wears black clothes, and has become increasingly preoccupied with music that focuses on pessimistic and nihilistic themes. She is uncharacteristically short-fused, grouchy, and restless. She complains of low energy and feeling worthless. Amy's father told the parish nurse that Amy often watches television half the night and then has difficulty getting to school. Her grades have dropped significantly. She has lost a lot of weight, and her father has found numerous empty bags of candy and cookies hidden under her bed. She has grown increasingly distant and wary of adults. She stopped going to church youth activities, saying she "did not believe in anything anymore." She complained to George of feeling "totally bored."

Pastoral Assessment

Depression in teens has essentially the same symptoms as in adults, though adolescent symptoms can require more assessment savvy to recognize and translate. For example, pervasive sadness is expressed by Amy in writing morbid poems about death, by wearing black clothing, and in her preoccupation with nihilistic music. Irritability is a common expression of depression among teens. Watching television into the night and difficulty with school attendance may reflect sleep disturbance, which is common in depressed individuals. Her drop in grades may be a sign of decreased concentration and slowed thinking, also common signs of depression. Boredom is often a synonym for depression among suffering teens.

It is important to obtain a full picture of Amy's current situation and assess her resources. Highly stressful life events such as the death of a parent and bereavement are risk factors for depression in teens, especially when adolescents have poor coping skills. It is always important to consider whether a depressed teen is using alcohol or other substances. Research indicates that about one-fourth of depressed adolescents use drugs or alcohol to cope (Fleming and Offord 1990). Two issues often associated with a major depression in teens need to be explored immediately. First, depression and morbid thoughts about death must always be fully investigated to gain a clear picture of suicide potential (see Case 16). Second, the hidden food wrappers under Amy's bed may be evidence of an eating disorder called bulimia, which is characterized by binge eating followed by throwing up or purging (see Case 17). This can be a serious health risk, especially when significant weight loss is involved.

Diagnostic Criteria

An adolescent is diagnosed with a major depression when there have been two weeks or more of feeling sad, gloomy, depressed, irritable, or experiencing a loss of interest, motivation, or enjoyment in usual activities (APA 1994). Along with a depressed mood or loss of interest, the person must also have had two or more weeks of at least four of the following eight symptoms: fatigue or loss of energy; lethargy or increased restlessness (agitation); loss of appetite and weight or excessive appetite and weight gain; difficulty sleeping or sleeping too much; loss of social or sexual interest; feelings of worthlessness or excessive guilt; difficulty concentrating; feeling that life is not worth living, wanting to die, or feeling suicidal.

Depressed adults recalling their early family experiences indicate that the family interactions of their youth were marked by more conflict, greater rejection, poorer communication, less expression of feelings, and more abuse than persons with nondepressive histories. Depression has also been associated with low self-esteem, high self-criticism, and perfectionistic standards (Birmaher et al. 1996).

Approximately 10 percent of adults who have a major depression also have a "manic" episode. These individuals are usually suffering from "manic-depressive" or "bipolar" disorder. About 20 percent of those who suffer from manic-depressive disorder have their first manic experience during their teen years (McClellan and Werry 1997). The predominant mood during mania is elevated, expansive, elated, or extreme irritability. During a manic episode individuals may sleep very little; talk rapidly, loudly, and continually; experience racing thoughts; and take little time to eat. They often have uncharacteristically poor judgment, extreme distractibility, and may lose touch with reality. They may become impulsive, making serious financial, social, and occupational blunders. Persons with this illness are at high risk for suicide attempts. The medication Lithium has been found to be remarkably effective in the treatment of this disorder.

Both Amy's mother and maternal grandmother have a history of depression. Teenagers and children with parents who have been depressed are about three times more likely to have a major depression in their lifetime than those with nondepressive parents and grandparents.

Amy is not using alcohol or drugs. Research has found that alcohol and drug use usually follow several years of depression in adolescents. This means that early and effective intervention can lower the risk of substance abuse in depressed teens (Birmaher et al. 1996).

Relevant History

Father Coyne, after consultations with Amy's father, grandparents, and church youth workers, decided to talk with Amy. The priest and the parish nurse had visited Amy's home almost daily during the preceding year while her mother struggled with the devastating effects of cancer. Amy had seen Father Coyne administer her mother's last rites, holding her hand in the final moments of her life on earth.

At first Amy was guarded and wary, resisting talking to her priest. However, Father Coyne was an experienced pastor with good listening skills who could communicate compassion and nonjudgmental care. His many years of pastoral work with the family had built an underlying intimacy and trust that broke through Amy's pain and fear. She was able to tell him about her bitter feelings of betrayal and resentment toward her father. She related her devastation at the loss of her mother who had adored her. She talked about feeling alone and living in an increasingly gloomy world of despair. She had begun to dwell on thoughts of death and had recently contemplated suicide. She also hid her increasingly uncontrollable eating binges.

Father Coyne was helpful and supportive of the need to have a mental health specialist fully evaluate Amy's depression and related problems. He continued to work and pray with Amy and her family through her treatment, helping her process her grief and offering spiritual direction. Father Coyne and the parish nurse had working relationships with several mental health professionals who understood the important and positive effects that nurturing, nonpunitive faith and a caring pastor have in mental health recovery. Father Coyne knew that early and effective interventions were important, and he expressed optimism for a positive outcome for Amy. He was also careful about developing clear understandings of confidentiality with Amy, her family, and the mental health professionals.

Response to Vignette

Treatment Within the Faith Community

Depression is one of the most pervasive forms of emotional problems in young people. Experts estimate that about 1 in 20 teens are depressed (Reynolds 1995). Professor Marty Seligman, a leading researcher in the field, has found that depression has increased tenfold in the United States since the Second World War. In large measure, this astronomical increase is a result of a high-stress society with a diminished sense of community and faith (Seligman 1990). Given these epidemic levels of depression, it is not surprising that clergy report in several studies that depression is one of the most common problems among people seeking their help. Unfortunately, these same studies reveal that clergy are inadequately trained to identify depression and suicide risk (Weaver 1995). In a national survey of clergy and pastoral care specialists, only 1 in 4 thought the church was offering effective programs for depressed teenagers. Pastors ranked their effectiveness with teen depression as the second poorest out of ten areas of ministry to troubled youngsters (Rowatt 1989). Adolescent depression is underreported and undertreated. A sound clergy evaluation can be critical since about 15 percent of people with untreated major depressions take their life.

Pastors, church leaders, and other adults can educate and enlighten a congregation by providing factual information about teen depression and other mental health issues. There is considerable societal bias against those with mental illness, which is one of the reasons that adults and teens are reluctant to admit to being in distress or to seek help. Educating the faith community about teen depression can decrease bias and increase advocacy for mental health services for teens (Brent et al. 1993).

Indications for Referral

Amy will need to work with a specialist in mental health. She has signs of severe depression and needs to be assessed for suicide risk and for an eating disorder. Sometimes severe depression can have psychotic symptoms such as auditory or visual hallucinations (hearing or seeing things that do not exist in reality) or delusions (fixed false beliefs without a rational basis), which need immediate referral and treatment.

Treatment by Mental Health Specialist

A combination of medication, cognitive therapy, and family therapy has become a common standard of treatment for teen depression. The mental health specialist must assess Amy's potential for suicide and take actions that are needed. Grave risk usually requires hospitalization. The specialist will determine if she is suffering from the eating disorder bulimia and intervene as required. Psychological testing can be useful in making an accurate assessment for depression. Because depression in adolescence often recurs, treatment planning should include a long-term component that addresses relapse prevention.

Depressive symptoms in teenagers are often treated with medications. The usefulness of antidepressant medications for young persons does not currently have the scientific research evidence that is available for adults.

Any medication for minors should be carefully questioned, given the ongoing physical and psychological development of young people (Gadow 1991).

Cognitive interventions focus on "automatic thoughts," defined as what people think about themselves in particular situations. Depressed teens often think negatively about themselves, their future, and their environment. The cognitive approach attempts to identify negative thought processes and logical errors. The interventions are designed to modify these assumptions, errors, and views. Usually treatment involves self-monitoring of mood and activities, often in the form of keeping a daily log.

Insight-oriented psychotherapy may be helpful when treating depression. In this model, persons are unaware of negative beliefs that are rooted in early childhood experiences, such as repeated parental rejection or unrealistic family expectations. Therapy aims at guiding the person to understand and change these underlying beliefs. This is done gradually, beginning with supportive interventions. Over time, the therapist clarifies and points out issues to develop helpful ways to gain self-esteem and autonomy. At this point, family therapy may be indicated to increase adjustment.

Family therapy will be important for Amy and her family. It can enhance communication and provide a setting in which relatives can become more aware of one another's feelings and can see the impact of their behavior on other family members. Sessions can help Amy explore the feelings of rejection and betrayal that have cut off communication and have caused a breach in her relationship with her father. Amy can also be helped by relatives to work through her pain and grief over the loss of her mother. In teens, depression is often related to the struggle for independence, and the wise therapist will foster appropriate autonomy.

Relaxation training may be used in the treatment of depression. It can reduce feelings of anxiety that tend to magnify unpleasant experiences and undermine pleasurable experiences.

Cross-Cultural Issues

In children, major depression occurs at approximately the same rate in girls as it does in boys. In the teenage years, a girl is twice as likely to have a major depression as a boy, paralleling the adult ratio (Lewinsohn et al. 1994).

Resources

National Resources

There are many organizations that offer assistance and information about depression that can be useful to congregations, parents, and clergy:
National Youth Crisis Hotline, (800) 442-4673; Children's Rights of America, 500 Sugar Mill Rd., Bldg. B, Suite 220, Atlanta, GA 30350; www.cra-us.org; cra@cra-us.org, provides counseling and referrals to local

counseling services. Responds to youth dealing with pregnancy, molestation, suicide, depression, and child abuse. Operates twenty-four hours a day.

Boys Town National Hotline, (800) 448-3000; 13940 Gutowski Road, Boys Town, NE 68010; www.ffbh.boystown.org; Helpkids@Boystown.org; provides short-term counseling and referrals to local resources, including U.S. territories and Canada. Counsels on parent-child conflicts, suicide, depression, pregnancy, runaways, and abuse. Spanish-speaking operators are available. Operates twenty-four hours a day.

National Mental Health Association (NMHA), 1021 Prince St., Alexandria, VA 22314; (800) 969-6642; www.nmha.org; nmhainfo@aol.com, provides information on clinical depression.

Depression Awareness, Recognition, Treatment (D/ART), sponsored by the National Institute of Mental Health, 5600 Fishers Lane, Rockville, MD 20857; (800) 421-4211; www.nihm.nih.gov/newdart; provides free information and literature on depressive disorders, symptoms, treatments, and sources of help. Publications available in Spanish, Asian languages, and Russian.

National Foundation for Depressive Illness, Inc., P.O. Box 2257, New York, NY 10116; (800) 239-1265; www.depression.org; a twenty-four-hour recorded message describes symptoms of depression and manic depression and gives an address for more information, physician, and support group referrals by state.

National Depressive and Manic-Depressive Association, 730 N. Franklin St., Suite 501, Chicago, IL 60610; (800) 826-3632; www.ndmda.org; myrtis@aol.com.

Self-Help Resources

Lonely, Sad and Angry: A Parent's Guide to Depression in Children and Adolescents, by Barbara D. Ingersoll and Sam Goldstein (NY: Doubleday, 1996) and *Helping Your Depressed Teenager: A Guide for Parents and Caregivers,* by Gerald D. Oster and Sarah S. Montgomery (NY: John Wiley and Sons, 1995) are designed to help parents with depressed teens.

Depression and Related Affective Disorders Association (DRADA) is a nonprofit organization that works in association with the Johns Hopkins University School of Medicine. It offers support groups and peer support programs for youth as well as educational materials and programs for school counselors and teachers on adolescent depression and manic depression. It regularly reviews books and videos helpful on the topic of depression. *Carrie's Story* is a sixteen-minute videotape DRADA has produced that gives an account of a teen and her family coping with depression. DRADA, Meyer 3-181, 600 North Wolfe Street, Baltimore, MD 21287; (202) 955-5800; drada-g@welchlink.welch.jhu.edu; www.med.jhu.edu/drada.

The Link, Internet Mental Health offers useful self-help information related to depression; www.mentalhealth.com/dis/p20-md01.html.

References

American Psychiatric Association. (1994). *Diagnostic and Statistical Manual of Mental Disorders*, Fourth Edition. Washington, DC: APA.

Birmaher, B., Ryan, N.D., Williamson, D.E., Brent, D.A., Kaufman, J., Dahl, R.E., Perel, J. and Nelson, B. (1996). Childhood and adolescent depression: A review of the past ten years. Part I. *Journal of the American Academy of Child and Adolescent Psychiatry, 35(11)*. 1427-1439.

Brent, D.A., Poling, K., McKain, B. and Baugher. M. (1993). A psycho-educational program for families of affectively ill children and adolescents. *Journal of the American Academy of Child and Adolescent Psychiatry, 32*. 770-774.

Fleming, J.E. and Offord, D.R. (1990). Epidemiology of childhood depressive disorders: A critical review. *Journal of the American Academy of Child and Adolescent Psychiatry, 29*. 571-580.

Fisher, R.L. and Fisher, S. (1996). Antidepressants for children. *Journal of Nervous and Mental Disease, 184(2)*. 99-102.

Gadow, K.D. (1991). Clinical issues in child and adolescent psycho-pharmacology. *Journal of Consulting and Clinical Psychology, 51(6)*. 842-852.

Lewinsohn, P.M., Clarke, G.N., Seeley, J.R. and Rohde, P. (1994). Major depression in community adolescents: Age at onset, episode duration, and time to recurrence. *Journal of the American Academy of Child and Adolescent Psychiatry, 33*. 809-818.

McClellan, J. and Werry, J. (1997). Practice parameters for the assessment and treatment of children and adolescents with bipolar disorder. *Journal of the American Academy of Child and Adolescent Psychiatry, 36(1)*. 138-157.

Reynolds, W.M. (1995). Depression. In V.B. Van Hasselt and M. Hersen (eds.) *Handbook of Adolescent Psychopathology* (pp. 297-348). NY: Lexington Books.

Rowatt, G.W. (1989). *Pastoral Care with Adolescents in Crisis*. Louisville, KY: Westminster/John Knox Press.

Seligman, M.E.P. (1990). Why is there so much depression today? The waxing of the individual and the waning of the commons. In R.E. Ingram (ed.) *Contemporary Psychological Approaches to Depression* (pp. 1-9) NY: Plenum Press.

Weaver, A.J. (1995). Has there been a failure to prepare and support parish-based clergy in their role as frontline community mental health workers? A review. *The Journal of Pastoral Care, 49*. 129-149.

Suicide

"He Felt Like Killing Himself"

The phone rang in my office. The woman's voice was distressed. "Pastor Henderson," she said, "can I come over to talk? I'm worried about Zach, my 16-year-old."

"Sure," I replied, "come over to the church office." She was the single parent of two teenage boys. The family had been in some turmoil since the divorce. Zach's brother, the father's favored son, began to live with his dad. After the divorce, Zach felt rejected by his father. Zach's mother arrived with red, swollen eyes—this was a worried parent.

"Pastor," she began, "I don't know what to do." She explained that Zach had been doing poorly in school and had become increasingly irritable following a breakup with his girlfriend last month. He moped around the house a lot and had isolated himself. "I thought he would get over it in a couple of days," she said. "But last night he became angry at me, said life was not worth living, and that he wants to kill himself." Then she told me that Zach's favorite teacher had killed himself a few months ago.

Pastoral Assessment

One might be tempted to view the 16-year-old teenager's statement that he felt like "killing himself" as a manipulative threat. Don't! Any threat of self-harm by a teen requires a careful assessment. Gather more information. A role-model, such as a favorite teacher, committing suicide, places vulnerable youth at a risk of self-harm (Davidson 1991). What does it mean that Zach is increasingly irritable, mopes around the house a lot, and is isolating himself? Is Zach depressed, and if so, how seriously? How much has the recent divorce, coupled with his father's rejection, affected the teenager? Is the loss of his girlfriend the last straw? It is always useful to rule out possible alcohol and drug abuse, which, when combined with depression, places a teen at risk of suicidal behavior. Does Zach have access to a firearm? Most teen suicides are committed with a gun. You might consider one or two sessions with Zach and his mother to gather information and clarify concerns before referring the teenager and family to a mental health professional who has an expertise in working with families and teenagers in crisis.

Diagnostic Criteria

It is important for pastors to be aware of the warning signs of suicide. You can use the pneumonic device SADPARENTS to assist you in remembering them.

Sex—The ratio of male to female completed suicides is 4 to 1. However, young women attempt suicide four times more frequently. Males tend to use the more lethal means—firearms.

Age—One in seven deaths among those 15–19 years of age is a suicide. Caucasian males 16 and older are at the greatest risk among teens.

Depression—Intense feelings of depression and hopelessness are strongly associated with suicide. Depressed teens often become withdrawn and isolated, which adds to the risk.

Previous attempts—A history of suicide attempts is the most significant indicator of suicide risk. Unfortunately, only about 1 in 5 teens who attempt suicide seek professional help (Garrison et al. 1993).

Alcohol and drug abuse—Substance abuse is a significant factor in one-third to one-half of teen suicides. The combination of depression and active alcohol/drug abuse places an adolescent at significant risk for suicide (Burstein et al. 1993).

Reckless or delinquent behaviors—High-risk behaviors such as reckless driving can be an indicator of suicidal potential. There is also an association between delinquent or antisocial behavior and suicide risk, especially when linked with depression and substance abuse (Burstein et al. 1993).

Easy access to firearms—Two-thirds of teens who take their lives use firearms. The presence of guns in the home, even when stored and locked, increases the risk of suicide in teens (Brent et al. 1991).

Nonstable family—Family disruption or turmoil, separation from or rejection by parents, poor family communication and problem-solving skills, serious mental health problems in a parent, or a family history of suicide have been identified as risk factors for teen suicide (Brent 19881).

Thought-out plan—An organized plan for suicide is a high-risk factor. The more specific the plan, the greater the danger. An organized plan with an available means places a person at very high risk and demands immediate attention.

Stress—Highly stressful situations, such as a breakup with a girlfriend, failure at school, excessive pressure to succeed, or an unwanted pregnancy are risk factors for teens. Sometimes the suicide of an important person can trigger self-harm in a youngster.

Zach had a history of experimentation with alcohol and drugs. His father is a very self-involved individual with little empathy for others. Zach has access to a handgun at the father's home, but he does not have a history of delinquent or high-risk behaviors (such as recklessly driving a motorcycle).

Zach's story presents us with a set of factors that call for a crisis management approach. The most disturbing factor in the story is his statement that he feels life is not worth living, that he would like to kill himself. Given the possible combination of depression and substance abuse along with high family stress and several personal losses, Pastor Henderson needs to approach this situation with high risk for suicide in mind. Zach has suffered the rejection of his father who chose to split the family by favoring his brother. This sort of rejection by a parent can set up a vulnerable youth for self-rejection and potential self-harm. It is vital that he be kept from any firearms that may be at his father's house. Zach needs treatment for being a danger to himself and depression, as well as assessment for substance abuse. Inpatient mental health care may be required during the crisis period.

Pastor Henderson, as a sacramental presence, is in a unique position to offer hope and reassurance to Zach and his family. Faith calls them to hope, transformation, and renewal. Faith that affirms life is a sustaining resource in crisis. Persons with an active religious life have much lower risk of suicide (Weaver and Koenig 1996).

Teen suicide is an urgent issue to be addressed by the faith community. Each year about 5,000 youths take their lives, while an estimated fifty to one hundred times that number attempt suicide. The primary focus of the church must be prevention. Youth ministry can help educate families and teens about the warning signs of suicide and support mental health treatment for those at risk. Surveyed teenagers suggest that increased family counseling services, more qualified adults with counseling skills, and crisis phone hotlines are good preventive ministries (Gallup and Bezilla 1992). Crisis phone hotlines may be a particularly effective ministry to teens who tend to use the phone as a favorite communication device.

Teen groups designed to help adolescents develop more effective problem-solving skills as well as better communication and interpersonal skills is suggested by research. Teens at risk for suicide may magnify their problems and show poor social judgment. Support and understanding from peers are a valuable suicide preventive measures, especially when the adolescent mistrusts and resents adults.

Furthermore, the church must advocate rational handgun control as an important means to reduce suicide. Easy firearms availability is a major contributor to increased suicide among youth and adults.

The church can also be a place of support in the aftermath of suicide. Although many suicides can be prevented by early recognition of warning signs and referral to mental health specialists, the fact remains that they do occur. Suicide is the second leading cause of death among youth in the United States. Sooner or later this tragic situation will occur in most congregations, often with a devastating impact on the family, the clergy, and the congregation as a whole. An important fact that must be faced by all people involved with suicidal individuals is that, as caregivers and fellow human beings, there are limits to what can be done to help others. It is guilt that takes the greatest toll on survivors of a suicide—family, friends, and those who tried to help.

One important message that can be conveyed to the family and, if appropriate, the congregation following a suicide is that most suicides are the result of serious emotional illness—not personal weakness, lack of faith, cowardliness, or failure of loved ones to be supportive.

Finally, it is important not to allow the romanticizing or glamorizing of teen suicide in a funeral or memorial service. Because adolescents can view suicide as a clean, quick fix to all their problems, a realistic view of suicide needs to be articulated. Teens need to clearly see its tragic aftermath.

Indications for Referral

A referral is called for any time a serious threat of suicide is present. An assessment should be based on the risk factors noted, such as an organized plan with access to a means, prior attempts, alcohol or drug abuse, depression and hopelessness, family instability, reckless behaviors, or high stress. A referral is always appropriate when a pastor feels the case is beyond his or her expertise. Most teens who attempt suicide do not seek professional help. A pastor can be critical in supporting the family and teen through the process of seeking mental health treatment. Nine out of ten suicidal youth are suffering from a treatable mental health disorder, which means that most teen suicides are preventable (Brent and Perper 1995).

Treatment by Mental Health Specialist

The primary goal in working with a suicidal teen is safety. Treatment may involve hospitalization or outpatient care. Inpatient treatment is indicated when the teen is psychotic or intoxicated, has a brain disorder, and/or when his or her social support system is inadequate. Voluntary hospitalization is preferable to involuntary placement, although the latter is often necessary to ensure safety. Outpatient care is sufficient when the risk of suicide is determined to be low or the crisis that precipitated suicidal thinking has diminished. Zach will also need treatment for depression (see Case 15 and perhaps substance abuse, Case 1).

Cross-Cultural Issues

About 3 of 4 young adult suicides (ages 15–24) are Caucasian males. Caucasian teens are more than twice as likely to take their lives as are African Americans. However, since 1987, the incidence of suicide among youth has increased most rapidly among African Americans (Shaffer, Gould, and Hick 1994).

National Resources

There are several organizations that offer assistance and information about suicide prevention programs that can be useful to congregations and clergy.

National Committee of Youth Suicide Prevention, 66 5th Ave., 13th Floor, NY, NY 10103; (212) 597-9292.

American Association of Suicidology, 4201 Connecticut Ave. N.W., Suite 310, Washington, DC 20008; (202) 237-2280; www.cyberpsych.org/aas/index.html; amyjomc@ix.netcom.com.

Samariteens, 500 Commonwealth Ave., Boston, MA 02215; (800) 252-TEEN, dedicated to assisting teens in despair.

The Compassionate Friends, Inc., P.O. Box 3696, Oak Ridge, IL 60522; (630) 990-0010, www.compassionatefriends.org; tcf_national@prodigy.com, a group that gives support to parents who have lost a child and siblings who have lost a brother or sister.

Survivors Helping Survivors, St. Lukes Medical Center, 2900 West Oklahoma Ave., Milwaukee, WI 53215; (414) 649-4638; gives support to those who lose loved ones to suicide.

Camp Fire Boys and Girls, 4601 Madison Ave., Kansas City, MO 64112, (816) 756-1950; www.campfire.org; info@campfire.org; has a suicide prevention program for adolescents in many communities in the United States. The program is cosponsored by the National Mental Health Association, 1021 Prince St., Alexandria, VA 22314.

National Youth Crisis Hotline, (800) 442-3673, www.cra-us.org, cra@cra-us.org, provides counseling and referrals to local counseling services. Responds to youth dealing with pregnancy, molestation, suicide, and child abuse. Operates twenty-four hours a day.

Boys Town National Hotline, (800) 448-3000, www.ffbh.boystown.org, Helpkids@/Boystown.org provides short-term counseling and refers to local resources. Counsels on parent-child conflicts, suicide, pregnancy, runaways, and abuse. Spanish-speaking operators are available twenty-four hours a day.

Handgun Control Inc./Center To Prevent Handgun Violence, advocates for rational gun control to protect youth from violence to self or others, 1225 Eye Street, NW, Suite 1100, Washington, DC 20005; (202) 898-0792; www.handguncontrol.org/index.htm.

National Suicide Foundation, 1045 Park Ave., NY, NY 10028; (800) ASF-4042; 76433.1676@compuserve.com, provides state-by-state directories of survivor support groups for families and friends of a suicide.

Self-Help Resources

The Minister as Crisis Counselor, by David Switzer (Nashville: Abingdon Press, 1985 revised) and *Pastoral Care with Adolescents in*

Crisis, by G. Wade Rowatt Jr. (Louisville, KY: Westminster Press, 1989) offer helpful sections on suicide from a faith perspective. *Clergy Response to Suicidal Persons and Their Family Members,* David C. Clark (ed.) (Chicago: Exploration Press, 1993) is a comprehensive interfaith resource book for clergy on suicide across the life-span. *The Hatherleigh Guide to Child and Adolescent Therapy,* chapter on adolescent suicide, by James C. Brown (NY: Hatherleigh Press, 1996) and the *American Psychologist* journal article on adolescent suicide prevention, *48(2),* 169-182 by Ann F. Garland and Edward Zigler, offer excellent summaries of the topic from a mental health specialist perspective. *Coping with Adolescent Depression and Suicide; Caring for Your Adolescents* is the title of a booklet published by the American Academy of Pediatrics, P.O. Box 927, Elk Grove Village, IL 60000.

References

Brent, D.A. and Perper, J.A. (1995). Research in adolescent suicide: Implications for the training, service delivery, and public policy. *Suicide and Life-Threatening Behavior, 25(2).* 222-230.

Brent, D.A., Perper, J.A., Allman, C.J., Moritz, G.M., Wartella, M.E. and Zelenak, J.P. (1991). The presence and accessibility of firearms in the homes of adolescent suicides. *Journal of the American Medical Association, 266.* 2989-2995.

Brent, D.A., Perper, J.A., Goldstein, C.E., Kolko, D.J., Allan, M.J., Allman, C.J. and Zelenak, J.P. (1988). Risk factors for adolescent suicide: A comparison of adolescent suicide victims with suicide inpatients. *Archives of General Psychiatry, 45.* 581-588.

Burstein, O.G., Brent, D.A., Perper, J.A., Moritz, G., Baugher, M., Schweers, J., Roth, C. and Balach, L. (1993). Risk factors for completed suicide among adolescents with a lifetime history of substance abuse. *Acta Psychiatrica Scandinavica, 88.* 403-408.

Davidson, L. (1991). Psychological perspectives. In J.T. Clemons (ed.) *Perspectives on Suicide* (pp. 11-21) Louisville, KY: Westminster/John Knox Press.

Gallup, G.H. and Bezilla, R. (1992). *The Religious Life of Young Americans.* Princeton, NJ: The George Gallup International Institute.

Garrison, C.Z., McKeown, R.E., Valois, R.F. and Vincent, M.L. (1993). Aggression, substance abuse, and suicidal behavior in high school students. *American Journal of Public Health, 83(2).* 179-84.

Schaffer, D., Gould, M. and Hick, R. (1994). Increasing rate of Black suicide in the U.S. *American Journal of Psychiatry, 151.* 1810-1812.

Weaver, A.J. and Koenig, H.G. (1996). Elderly suicide, mental health professionals and the clergy. *Death Studies, 20(5).* 495-508.

Case 17

Eating Disorders

"Carla's Secret Diet"

Nina called Reverend Don Casey because she was concerned about Carla, her daughter. Carla had always been very sensitive about her weight and has been on and off diets since she was 13 years old. Now 18, Carla diets almost continuously. She exercises a lot, some days for hours at a time, and often worries aloud about getting fat. Recently, Nina found empty laxative packages in Carla's trash can and has heard her vomiting in the bathroom after meals. Nina also has noticed that when Carla goes off her diet, she eats everything she can get her hands on. Nina is worried that her daughter has become obsessed with her weight; but when she tries to discuss it, Carla becomes defensive and angry and they soon begin to argue.

When she arrived to see Pastor Casey, Carla appeared sullen and withdrawn. She was defensive, and she seemed somewhat depressed. Despite her frequent dieting, Carla was not really thin. In appearance, Carla was about average weight for her height.

The pastor tried to start a conversation. Carla sat slouched forward in her chair, chewing on a long strand of her hair. She made very little contact and would not respond to the pastor's questions. Finally, Carla sarcastically announced that she was only there because her mother had made her come. She admitted to frequent dieting but quickly added that all of her friends dieted and that it was no big deal. When Reverend Casey brought up her mother's concerns about the laxatives, Carla became angry and stormed out of his office.

Although embarrassed by her eating habits, Carla continued to deny that she had a problem. Privately, she was worried that she was out of control. Her never-ending diet was extremely restrictive. She allowed herself to eat only once a day, and no fats or carbohydrates were acceptable, ever. Inevitably she would fail on this diet and give in to her urges to eat other things. When she did, Carla would go to the other extreme, bingeing excessively, eating huge amounts of sweets. Afterward Carla would purge her body with strong laxatives, vomiting, and exercise. She was preoccupied with food and with her weight. Her lack of control overwhelmed her with disgust and despair.

Pastoral Assessment

Anorexia nervosa and *bulimia nervosa* are serious eating disorders—about 90 percent of those affected are young women (Schlundt and Johnson 1990). Eating disorders are not limited to any race or socioeconomic status. Among young women in America, preoccupation with thinness and body image is the norm rather than the exception.

Both bulimia and anorexia involve a preoccupation with body image and food. Bulimia is the more common of the two eating disorders and is characterized by a repetitive cycle of bingeing and purging. Bulimics tend to feel out of control in relation to the food they consume. Anorexia is a state of starvation that is accomplished by severely limited intake of food and/or purging. Anorexics will continue to regard themselves as overweight regardless of their emaciated appearance. Individuals with anorexia intensively strive to control the kinds and amounts of food they eat. Features that are common to both bulimia and anorexia include depression, secrecy, and obsessions with food and weight.

A good pastoral care assessment will try to sort out the nature of the eating patterns. To make an accurate assessment, it is important to understand the extreme secrecy and shame associated with most eating disorders. It will be necessary to take the time to establish a good rapport with a teenager in crisis. Once a little trust has been established, it may be possible to get a better snapshot of the dysfunctional eating behaviors. For example, it would be valuable to determine whether Carla has been bingeing and purging in addition to restrictively dieting. Further, it is important to learn whether she has been losing weight or whether her weight fluctuates. This information will lead to a better understanding of Carla's eating disorder and the kind of intervention that will be most appropriate.

It is critical to determine how Carla has been feeling emotionally. Depression (see Case 15), anxiety (see Case 20), and unstable moods are commonly associated with eating disorders (Brewerton et al. 1995). Has Carla been depressed, overwhelmed, or less involved with her friends? If so, a suicide risk assessment would be essential.

Finally, individuals with bulimia nervosa frequently have problems with alcoholism and other substance abuse (Holderness, Brooks-Gunn and Warren 1994). A thorough assessment would include collecting information regarding substance use history. By determining whether or not there is now a substance abuse problem, the pastor will be better able to make appropriate referrals.

Relevant History

Carla's mother, Nina, has provided the pastor with important information about Carla's disorder. Nina reports that Carla has been dieting for a long time and that her diets are very restrictive. Bulimia often begins after a period of dieting, inadequate nutrition, hunger, fatigue, and feelings of self-denial. Restrictive dieting also leads to dieting failure. These factors may trigger powerful urges to binge eat.

The laxative containers that Nina found in Carla's room indicate that Carla is probably abusing laxatives to get rid of the food that she consumes. To avoid gaining weight after a binge, bulimics may utilize several methods to purge, including self-induced vomiting, laxative abuse, diuretic abuse, fasting, and/or excessive exercise. Purging acts to reduce anxiety about gaining weight, and it creates the feeling of being thin. Keep in mind that some of the feelings of being thin are a direct by-product of dehydration and the electrolyte imbalance that is created by purging (Whitaker 1992). Extreme purging may cause dangerous imbalances to the body's sodium, potassium, and other chemicals that may have medical implications including irregular heartbeat and seizures.

There are many theories about the causes of bulimia nervosa, but there is no single answer. Rather, there are contributing factors including biological predisposition, psychological precipitants, and social pressures. Maladaptive eating behaviors may develop as a way of handling stress and anxieties. Low self-esteem and poor body image contribute to the likelihood of developing an eating disorder. It also appears that life crises, such as the loss of a significant relationship, may be another trigger.

It is of note that Pastor Casey views Carla as appearing depressed. Between 40 percent and 80 percent of all eating disorder patients experience depression (Herzog et al. 1991).

Diagnostic Criteria

Nina reports that her daughter's habit is to restrictively diet and then to binge and purge. This is the pattern that most clearly points to a diagnosis of bulimia nervosa. Carla's weight is normal, so she does not appear to be starving herself to the point of emaciation as is seen with individuals who are anorexic. Many people with bulimia maintain a nearly normal weight and appear generally healthy. While bulimia may give the feeling of thinness and control over food, bulimia is not the weight loss method it is believed to be.

A diagnosis of bulimia or anorexia has specific symptoms (APA 1994):

Bulimia Nervosa
- recurrent episodes of binge eating (minimum average of two binge-eating episodes per week for at least three months)
- a feeling of lack of control over eating during binges
- regular use of one or more of the following to prevent weight gain: self-induced vomiting, use of laxatives or diuretics, strict dieting or fasting, vigorous exercise
- persistent over-concern with body shape or weight

Anorexia Nervosa
- refusal to maintain weight that's over the lowest weight considered normal for age and height
- intense fear of gaining weight or becoming fat, even though underweight
- distorted body image
- in women, three consecutive missed menstrual periods without pregnancy

Response to Vignette

From the outset of this situation, Reverend Casey is in a difficult position. Carla did not come to see him of her own volition, and she denies that she has a problem. It is often true that one of the biggest obstacles in the effective treatment of eating disorders is admitting that there is a problem. The embarrassment, guilt, and disgust associated with anorexia and bulimia frequently make eating disorders secretive conditions. Many individuals develop bulimia during late adolescence, but ashamed of their dieting habits, they do not seek help until their thirties or forties. By this time, their eating behavior has become a deeply ingrained style and is very difficult to change. Even when family members, physicians, or mental health professionals directly confront people with their behavior, they often continue to deny that there is a problem.

Those with eating disorders who get early treatment have a much better chance of full recovery than persons who wait years before getting help (Fallon 1991). Referral to a mental health professional who specializes in eating disorders is indicated.

Treatment Within the Faith Community

Nina has taken a big step for her family by calling Reverend Casey. It is often as difficult for the family to admit to the problem as it is for the individual with an eating disorder.

When families are struggling with a member who has an eating disorder, it is always useful to help the family learn as much as possible about the condition. Many local mental health organizations, colleges, counseling centers, and self-help groups will provide free literature on the subject.

Bringing the problem out into the open may initially cause the person with an eating disorder to feel threatened and defensive because the secret has been exposed. Anger and family conflict are therefore likely to occur. The family should gently encourage the individual to seek professional help and to stay in treatment, while recognizing that the responsibility for change is not theirs. The family's and clergy's role is to give information, love, and support, but not to monitor eating behaviors or pass judgment.

If an individual with an eating disorder goes directly to a pastor, it would be appropriate to explain in a caring way the dangerous and unhealthy nature of the eating behaviors. It is important to understand that such persons are terrified of gaining weight and becoming fat. This irrational fear is very real, even if the individual is actually underweight. Explain that nonfood factors are at play and that with help from someone who knows what they are going through, the situation can get better. Encourage her to seek professional help.

If an eating disorder is suspected, particularly if it involves weight loss, a referral to a physician should be made immediately to rule out other medical causes and to determine physical status. Left untreated, eating disorders can become chronic conditions with severe medical and emotional complications. In addition to the problems that Carla's mother has noticed, there are other common effects of bulimic behavior. Constant vomiting erodes tooth enamel, causing dental complications, and chronic throat and gastric inflammation can also occur.

Indications for Referral

Once it has been determined that a teen has an eating disorder, referral to a mental health professional who specializes in this problem is always appropriate. It cannot be overemphasized how important professional treatment is, since most people find it difficult to stop their bulimic behavior without professional help. The emotional effects of this secretive behavior may have profound effects on an individual's personality. Professional treatment should be sought as soon as possible.

The complexities of the physical and emotional problems inherent in eating disorders call for a comprehensive treatment plan. Mental health professionals need to work with others to obtain the best result. Physicians treat medical complications, nutritionists advise on diet, and mental health professionals provide therapy. The plan may include individual psychotherapy, family therapy, antidepressant medications, behavior modification, and support groups.

Treatment by Mental Health Specialist

Eating disorders cause great distress for an individual as well as for family and friends who are confused about how best to cope with the situation. The family is often asked to help in the treatment of individuals with eating disorders, since their support can play an important role in successful treatment.

Most eating disorders can be effectively treated on an outpatient basis; however, some conditions may develop that would require hospitalization. The mental health professional will determine whether the individual is experiencing symptoms severe enough to require hospital care. Life-threatening conditions may include serious weight loss, metabolic disturbances, severe depression, or risk of suicide.

In a study of sixth- and seventh-grade girls in northern California, Hispanic and Asians were found to have greater body dissatisfaction than their Caucasian counterparts. This was especially true of the leanest ado-

Cross-Cultural Issues

lescent girls in the study. Body dissatisfaction has been linked to subsequent development of eating disorders (Robinson et al. 1996).

Resources

National Resources

American Anorexia/Bulimia Association, Inc. (AABA), 165 West 46th Street, New York, NY 10036; (212) 575-6200; amanbu@aol.com; members.aol.com/AMANBU.

Center for the Study of Anorexia and Bulimia, 1 West 91st Street, New York, NY 10024; (212) 595-3449.

National Eating Disorder Organization, 6655 S. Yale Ave., Tulsa, OK 74136; (918) 481-4044; www.laureate.com/nedointro.html.

National Association of Anorexia Nervosa and Associated Disorders, P.O. Box 7, Highland Park, IL 60035; (847) 831-3438; members.aol.com/anad20; anad20@aol.com.

Family Resources for Education on Eating Disorders (FREED), 9611 Page Ave., Bethesda, MD 20814; (301) 493-4568; cpcug.org/user/rpike/freed.html; ludewign@ors.od.nih.org.

Anorexia Nervosa and Bulimia Association (ANAB), 767 Bayridge Drive, P.O. Box 20058, Kingston, Ontario K7P 1C0 Canada; (613) 547-3684; www.ams.queensu.ca/anab; anab@www.queensu.ca.

Healing Connections, Inc., 1461A First Ave., Suite 303, New York, NY 10021; (212) 585-3450; HealConn@aol.com; www.something-fishy.com/healingconnections, raises funds to help defray cost of treatment for people with eating disorders who could not otherwise afford care.

Self-Help Resources

Eating Disorders Awareness and Prevention (EDAP), 603 Stewart Street, Suite 803, Seattle, WA 98101; (206) 382-3587; hometown.aol.com/edapinc/home.html.

Anorexia Nervosa and Related Eating Disorders (ANRED), P.O. Box 5102, Eugene, OR 97405; (541) 344-1144; www.anred.com; jarinor@rio.com.

Ask NOAH About: Mental Health—Eating Disorders: Anorexia and Bulimia Nervosa, noah.cuny.edu/wellconn/eatdisorders.html. This Web site can also be viewed in Spanish.

Lucy Serpell's Eating Disorders Resources Web site offers a wide variety of information, www.iop.bpmf.ac.uk/home/depts/psychiat/edu/eat.htm.

Hunger Pains: The Modern Woman's Tragic Quest for Thinness, by Mary Pipher (NY: Ballantine, 1997) is an interesting account of the way society worships thinness and forces many girls and women to extremes in attempts to create an "ideal" image.

Bulimia Nervosa and Binge-Eating: A Guide to Recovery, by Peter J. Cooper (NY: New York University Press, 1995).

Bulimia: A Guide for Family and Friends, by Roberta Trattner Sherman and Ron A. Thompson, (NY: Jossey-Bass, 1997).

American Psychiatric Association. (1994). *Diagnostic and Statistical Manual of Mental Disorders, Fourth Edition*. Washington, DC: American Psychiatric Association.

Brewerton, T.D., Lydiard, R.B., Herzog, D.B., Broatman, A.W., O'Neil, P.M. and Ballenger, J.C. (1995). Comorbidity of Axis I psychiatric disorders in bulimia nervosa. *Journal of Clinical Psychiatry, 56(2)*. 77-80.

Fallon, B.A., Walsh, B.T., Sadik, C., Saoud, J.C. and Lukasik, V. (1991). Outcome and clinical course in outpatient bulimic women: A 2- to 9-year follow-up study. *Journal of Clinical Psychiatry, 52(6)*. 272-278.

Holderness, C.C., Brooks-Gunn, J. and Warren, M.P. (1994). Co-morbidity of eating disorders and substance abuse: Review of the literature. *International Journal of Eating Disorders, 16(1)*.1-34.

Herzog, D.B., Keller, M.B., Lavori, P.W. and Sacks, N.R. (1991). The course and outcome of bulimia nervosa. *Journal of Clinical Psychiatry, 52 Suppl.* 4-8.

Robinson, T.N., Killen, J.D., Litt, I.F., Hammer, L.D., Wilson, D.M., Haydel, F., Hayward, C. and Taylor, C.B. (1996). Ethnicity and body dissatisfaction: Are Hispanic and Asian girls at increased risk for eating disorders? *Journal of Adolescent Medicine, 19*. 384-393.

Schlundt, D.G. and Johnson, W.G. (1990). *Eating Disorders: Assessment and Treatment*. Boston: Allyn & Bacon.

Whitaker, A.H. (1992). An epidemiological study of anorectic and bulimic symptoms in adolescent girls: Implications for pediatricians. *Pediatric Annals, 21(11)*. 752-759.

References

Attention Deficit Disorder

"He Can't Sit Still"

This kid is driving me nuts!" The remark was made by an exasperated mother in her Bible-centered women's support group. The comment was also accompanied by a good deal of guilt and shame. Ella Dunning is a bright, mature, good-hearted woman. She loves her three children and wants with all her heart to be a good mother. But her middle son, John, is driving her to distraction.

She went on to complain that he can't sit still, and he is rude, always interrupting others. John is clumsy, picks fights with his younger brother, and has chronic academic problems.

Ella sighs, "I just don't know what is wrong with me. I feel like a failure as a mother."

Many things may account for the behavior she describes in her son. For 3 to 5 percent of children, it is traced to a neurological condition known these days as ADD (attention deficit disorder, also referred to as hyperactivity). If Ella is like most moms of an ADD child, rather than feeling guilty, she should be given some kind of endurance award. This disorder results in extremely difficult behavioral problems that love and nurturing alone cannot cure.

Pastoral Assessment

Reverend Linda Long, the women's group leader, suggested that she have a private meeting with Ella, which took place later that day. Linda was aware of ADD both from her own reading and recent media coverage of the disorder. And she also was aware that a host of emotional problems and stressful events can lead to restless, hyperactive behavior. So she spoke with Ella and gleaned some background information.

In actual cases of ADD, pastoral counseling alone will not be enough to deal with the problem. However, Reverend Long knew from experience that parents in Ella's circumstances often engaged in inappropriate self-blame. The pastor can be helpful in lending a supportive ear, making a global assessment, and (if appropriate) giving a referral to a mental health professional.

Diagnostic Criteria

Key to the diagnosis of ADD is the history. Many types of acute stress reactions cause hyperactivity, restlessness, impulsivity, poor school performance, and so forth, and superficially may look like ADD. Many of these children are actually suffering from stress reactions (such as in response to marital discord), anxiety disorders, or agitated depressions. Some may be manifesting the earliest signs of an emerging mental illness (such as schizophrenia) or another form of neurological disorder.

What is unique about ADD is that most youngsters (more than 80 percent) will have shown notable behavioral problems since early childhood. The signs and symptoms seen from a developmental perspective include the following:

Infancy and Early Childhood
- Unstable patterns (sleep and feeding)
- Excessive irritability and restlessness
- When upset, the infant is difficult to soothe
- May not like being held
- Extremely active ("into everything")
- Intense crying spells/temper tantrums

Preschool and Kindergarten
- Inability to follow rules or wait their turn
- Can't sit still for group activities
- Pesters other children and teacher in elementary school
- Great difficulties following directions and staying "on task"
- Impaired ability to pay attention, poor concentration, easily distracted
- Impulsive (sometimes aggressive)
- Easily emotionally upset
- Makes disruptive noises, can't stay in seat
- Won't play games "by the rules"

Almost invariably parents can recall (vividly) how these problems emerged early and have been persistent. Early onset and persistence are key to an ADD diagnosis. Also many of these children appear to function normally in some settings (such as when playing video games or actively involved in sports). The environmental conditions that elicit problem behavior are when they must sit still (such as in class or in the car during long trips) and almost any time when interacting with their siblings.

Such children tend to wear on the nerves of the most patient parent or teacher. Ultimately, people become frustrated with them, and the child is then subject to frequent critical remarks, "Can't you sit still?" "For heaven's sake, just settle down!" "Just stop bugging me." When such children get bombarded with these comments, coupled with peer rejections and academic failures (almost always an eventual outcome of untreated ADD), it's no wonder they usually develop low self-esteem.

Many of these children are basically good-hearted kids. However, 50 percent will also develop noticeable aggressiveness and conduct problems (see Case 19). These kinds of behavior do not invite compassionate concern, but rather are often responded to with anger, criticism, and sometimes harsh punishment.

Since the early part of the twentieth century there has been speculation that ADD was caused by some type of brain dysfunction. This initially was suspected because these troubled children often came from healthy, loving, intact families. During the past decade, the causes of ADD have been more clearly understood. First, it is generally agreed that in 80 percent of ADD children, the underlying neurologic problem can be traced to genetics. For the remaining 20 percent, the problem is caused by various factors that have resulted in subtle brain impairment (such as head injuries, adverse prenatal events, encephalitis, metabolic disturbances). The most well-accepted theory suggests that ADD can be traced to neurochemical irregularities in the frontal cortex of the brain and that the most likely neurochemical involved is *dopamine*.

A complete diagnosis is based on taking a careful history and ruling out certain physical illnesses and other psychological disorders. When diagnosed, many of these youngsters can be successfully treated both medically and with behavioral techniques.

One of the most important things to underscore is that without professional treatment, the disorder stubbornly persists despite a host of parental efforts. About 30 percent of ADD children do show noticeable improvement by mid to late adolescence, but 70 percent go on to become ADD adults.

Relevant History

In John's case, he did in fact have most of the early markers of ADD-related behavior. His mother revealed that the problems had persisted throughout his childhood and that there had not been any significant changes or stresses in the family. The one area that has concerned her most is his progressive academic deterioration and most recently his "I'm giving up" attitude.

Although most ADD children are recognized during early elementary school, some go undetected. These youngsters may be seen as having a "bad attitude about school" or in some cases labeled as troublemakers or delinquents.

In John's case, he did not show signs of a concurrent conduct disorder (he was not aggressive), and he did show the capacity to love others and to feel attached.

Indications for Referral

Persistent signs and symptoms noted above always indicate the need for professional treatment. ADD does not in most cases spontaneously resolve. And standard child-rearing approaches are often grossly inadequate to address this problem.

Response to Vignette

Reverend Long clearly recognized the signs of an apparent ADD adolescent and shared her hunches with John's mother. She said, "I think it would be a good idea to have John evaluated for ADD. In the meantime, I want you to know that if he has this problem, you need to give yourself a break. Ella, you are pretty hard on yourself. Sounds to me like you are into a lot of self-blame. If John has ADD, then you need to know that it is a biological disorder; *and* fortunately, it is very treatable."

Linda Long's role is to help spot the problem, do a brief assessment, share conclusions or impressions with Ella, provide support, and point her toward helpful resources (a professional evaluation, an ADD support group, and some reading material).

Mrs. Dunning followed the advice and sought out an evaluation from her pediatrician and a child psychologist. John did, in fact, have ADD, and soon was started in treatment (counseling and medication). Within three months, his behavior had improved radically.

Treatment Within the Faith Community

Many emotional and psychological problems result in "invisible pathology," where the adolescent suffers inwardly and does not reveal outward signs of distress. In contrast, ADD is a "loud" disorder. These children can't help but be noticed since their behavior is so disruptive. Church is one of the environments likely to elicit and even magnify ADD behavior since services include times of silence and personal reflection. The expectation that they "sit still and be quiet" drives these youngsters nuts. It is very difficult for them to restrain their inwardly-driven need to move about and create noise. Three to 5 percent of all children have ADD, and you won't be able to ignore it!

Within the faith community, it can be helpful for everyone to know a bit about ADD (and other neurologic disorders such as mental retardation, head injuries, Tourette's syndrome, and epilepsy) and to help the community understand that behavioral disturbances in these children are not the result of poor parenting. The parents of neurologically impaired children deserve an extra measure of support and compassion.

The most important interventions that occur between a pastor and the family involve helping them to find appropriate resources and working with parents to dispel unrealistic guilt.

In properly diagnosed ADD children and teenagers, psychiatric medication has been found to be very effective (success rates vary from 83 to 95 percent of those treated). The medications used generally fall into two categories: stimulants such as Ritalin (methylphenidate), Dexedrine (dextroamphetamine), Adderall (dextroamphetamine), and Cylert (pemoline); and antidepressants such as Wellbutrin (bupropion) and Tofranil (imipramine) (Preston and Johnson 1997).

These medications target certain, specific ADD symptoms including impulsivity, poor attention, and emotional reactivity. If the medication is taken as prescribed, improvement is generally noted within a few days to a couple of weeks. It is important to know that there is no evidence to suggest that these drugs are abused by ADD children. It should also be emphasized that failure to treat ADD has grave consequences—often untreated adolescents get into problems with the law, experience academic failure, develop chronic feelings of low self-esteem, and turn to alcohol and other drugs. Many parents are apprehensive about the use of psychiatric medications and may reject such a treatment. It is important to honor their feelings, but it is helpful to encourage them to seek more information to become informed, albeit skeptical, consumers. Good books exist (listed below) and a number of well-run support groups provide up-to-date information about treatment options.

Especially if ADD is first recognized in adolescence, you can anticipate that the teen with ADD will have suffered from demoralization and feelings of low self-esteem. Beyond medical treatment, individual and/or family counseling can be necessary and effective.

Finally, it may be important to contact the adolescent's school. Many educational systems offer free evaluation services for children suspected of having learning disabilities (including ADD). Some schools also provide specialized programs for such students.

ADD and hyperactivity are significantly influenced by cultural norms. In some cultures (such as British, German, Japanese) there are strong demands for emotional control and disciplined academic performance. Communities infused with such values may find it harder to tolerate the restless, off-task behavior of ADD children. In certain rural areas of America, there is much more acceptance of nonacademic pursuits—there are courses that deal with agriculture and after-school activities, such as participating in the harvest.

For these reasons it is difficult to determine in a precise way the prevalence of ADD cross-culturally. There will be vastly different responses from parents depending on cultural and personal values.

National Resources

National Attention Deficit Disorder Association, 9930 Johnnycake Ridge Rd., Suite 3E, Mentor, OH 44060; (800) 487-2282;

Treatment by Mental Health Specialist

Cross-Cultural Issues

Resources

www.add.org; NatlADDA@aol.com, is an organization dedicated to advocate for adults and children with attention deficit disorders. It assists in starting support groups and holds national conferences.

Feingold Associations of the U.S., 127 E. Main St., Suite 106, Riverhead, NY 11901; (516) 369-9340; www.feingold.org; help@feingold.org, is a national group founded in 1976 to help families of children with learning or behavioral problems including Attention Deficit Disorder. It provides telephone support and has a newsletter.

Attention Deficit Information Network (ADIN), 475 Hillside Ave., Needham, MA 02194; (781) 455-9895; www.addinfonetwork.com; adin@gis.net. This national network provides information and support to persons whose lives have been affected by ADD. It has referrals to self-help groups.

Children and Adults with ADD (CHADD), 8181 Professional Place, Suite 201, Landover, MD 20785; (800) 233-4050. www.chadd.org

National Center for Learning Disabilities, 381 Park Avenue, South, Suite 1401, NY, NY 10016; (888) 575-7373; www.ncld.org.

Self-Help Resources

ADD Anonymous, P.O. Box 421227, San Diego, CA 92142; (609) 560-6190; addanon@aol.com, gives assistance in starting recovery groups for those with ADD, based on the twelve-step model.

ADDult Support Network, 20620 Ivy Place, Toledo, OH 43613.

Adolescents and ADD: Gaining the Advantage, by Patricia O. Quinn (NY: Magination, 1995).

The ADHD Parenting Handbook: Practical Advice for Parents from Parents, by Betty Osman (NY: John Wiley & Sons, 1997).

ADD News for Christian Families, Penrice Publishing, P.O. Box 530905, Livonia, MI 48153; members.aol.com/addnews; addnews@aol.com.

References

American Psychiatric Association. (1994). *Diagnostic and Statistical Manual of Mental Disorders-IV.* Washington, DC: APA.

Barkley, R.A. (1981). *Hyperactive Children: A Handbook for Diagnosis and Treatment.* NY: Guilford Press.

Barkley, R.A. (1989). Attention deficit hyperactivity disorder. In E.J. Mash and R.A. Barkley (eds.) *Treatment of Childhood Disorders* (pp. 39-72). NY: Guilford Press.

Kendall, P.C. and Braswell, L. (1984). *Cognitive Behavioral Therapy for Impulsive Children.* NY: Guilford Press.

Parker, H.C. (1988). *The ADD: Hyperactivity Workbook.* Manassus, VA: Impact Publications.

Preston, J. and Johnson, J. (1997). *Clinical Psychopharmacology*. Miami, FL: Medmaster.

Rosenberg, D.R., Holttum, J. and Gershon, S. (1994). *Textbook of Psychopharmacology for Child and Adolescent Psychiatric Disorders*. NY: Brunner/Mazel Publishers.

Weiss, G. and Hechtman, L. (1986). *Hyperactive Children Grown Up*. NY: Guilford Press.

Wender, P. (1987). *The Hyperactive Child, Adolescent and Adult: Attention Deficit Disorder Through the Lifespan*. NY: Oxford University Press.

Conduct Disorder/ Delinquency

"He Was Constantly in Trouble"

The voice at the other end of the phone was frantic and obviously filled with shame. It was Nikki Cummings, a longtime church member. She said, "Reverend Grayson, I just can't believe that this is happening. I feel so bad about calling you. This is so embarrassing." After some encouragement from her pastor, Nikki continued, "My son, David, is in trouble with the police." George Grayson asked her to come to his office, and the two met later that day.

Mrs. Cummings was uneasy as she confessed her bad news. Her 14-year-old son, David, and another neighborhood boy, Mitch, had been caught vandalizing a house, not two blocks from her home. She was not only upset but also in a state of confusion, since nothing like this had ever happened before. David was a sweet youngster—he made good grades, went to church on a regular basis, and almost never got into trouble. It is to Mrs. Cummings's, credit that she had the courage to approach her pastor. When such things happen in church families, almost invariably they cause a tremendous sense of embarrassment.

Let's also consider the other boy, Mitch. He had had some sporadic involvement in the church and was known to Reverend Grayson. However, in his case, there was a history of serious family problems (parents engaged in vicious arguments and had recently separated). Mitch lives with his mother, one older sister, and two younger sisters. During the past two years Mitch, also 14 years old, had gotten into fights at school, had been truant, was making failing grades, and was once caught stealing baseball cards from a store.

Both boys vandalized the house. From outward appearances, each had committed a juvenile crime. However, upon closer inspection there were important differences between David and Mitch that have bearing on our understanding of conduct disorder and related behavioral problems.

Pastoral Assessment

Reverend Grayson was sympathetic to Mrs. Cummings's plight. He reassured her, saying, "Obviously this is very upsetting, but let's not jump to conclusions. I'd like to take some time to talk with you about David." His noncritical, nonjudgmental stance helped to put her at ease. Parents of children who have committed a crime often anticipate that they will be blamed. George Grayson was there to understand, not to condemn.

Mrs. Cummings talked about how David was a very nice boy; he always had been. However, he didn't have many friends, was very shy and rather withdrawn. Six months ago, Mitch moved into the neighborhood. "And that's when I started to get worried," she explained. "I just felt that there was something wrong with Mitch. But David seemed to like him and started spending a lot of time with him."

Reverend Grayson was now confronted with a dilemma. He certainly could not condone vandalism; however, he had enough experience to know that outward behaviors often do not reveal inner motives. He was wise to take a supportive, wait-and-see approach with David's mother.

Diagnostic Criteria

Many children exhibit behaviors that may suggest what is commonly referred to as conduct disorder. Some of these behaviors include: defiance, violation of rules, irritability and aggressiveness (behaviors often seen in children with ADD, mood disorders, and some types of acute adjustment reactions), and/or academic problems. However, it is important to emphasize that true conduct disorders must be distinguished from more transient stress reactions or other psychological disorders.

Conduct disorder is characterized by the following behaviors (APA 1994): A *repetitive* and *persistent* pattern of behavior manifested by the presence of three or more of the following during the past twelve months:

- bullies, threatens, or intimidates others
- initiates physical fights
- has used a weapon
- has been physically cruel to people
- has been physically cruel to animals
- has stolen while confronting a victim (such as purse snatching)
- has forced someone into sexual activity
- has deliberately engaged in fire setting
- has deliberately destroyed others' property
- has broken into a home or car
- lies, has shown deceitfulness
- has stolen items (such as shoplifting)
- often stays out late despite parental prohibitions

- has run away from home at least twice
- is often truant from school

And the behaviors cause significant problems in social or academic functioning.

Many clinicians have noted that at the heart of the true conduct-disorder child, there are a profound lack of attachment to others, little empathy, little true guilt, and often evidence that they experience sadistic gratification when harming someone (or an animal) or violating social norms.

Relevant History

David: He has been a good student and a kind child and sibling. Of the criteria above, he has broken into a house and destroyed property. However, this by all accounts was a single episode (neither repetitive nor persistent). The other criteria do not apply to David. He has shown good social skills, a sense of attachment to his family members, and in the aftermath of the recent event, is genuinely remorseful. This boy misbehaved, but does not have a conduct disorder.

Mitch: Mitch is often a bully. He intimidates his younger sisters, has tortured animals, and has started several small fires (mainly to frighten neighborhood children). He has engaged in shoplifting and now vandalism—each time failing to show any sign of guilt or remorse. He lies often, frequently cuts classes, and has run away from home five times. He is a very different kind of boy from David. He likely suffers from a conduct disorder.

Indications for Referral

Two occasions call for referral to a mental health specialist. The first is when an actual conduct disorder (as described above) is strongly indicated. Such adolescents will not respond to the kind of supportive encouragement offered in a pastoral counseling and are *very* high risk for repeated offenses.

A second group of teenagers are those that show *some* signs of misbehavior, but more likely are suffering from other emotional problems. These youth may have one or more of the following:

- A long-standing history of ADD or learning disabilities.
- A sad or depressed look. Many depressed teenagers act out in defiant or aggressive ways in an attempt to avoid experiencing their inner pain. They may initially come across as "Mr. Tough Guy—I don't give a damn about anything." But as you listen and watch carefully, many of these teens have sad eyes or they tell you that they are a loser or a failure. Often the tough veneer gives way as their underlying sadness leaks through. Be prepared for them to deny inner distress, yet place trust in your perceptions. These teens don't have true conduct disorder; they are in pain and need counseling.

- A family that is undergoing incredible stresses, and the defiant or delinquent behavior has only recently surfaced as stress has increased.
- A personal or family history of major mental illness (such as manic-depressive illness or schizophrenia). The defiant behavior may be the early manifestations of an emerging psychiatric problem.
- A living environment where it is the norm to be aggressive (such as in an inner-city setting). In such situations, adopting group normative behavior may be a necessity for survival.

And finally, there are teens like David who have a good heart, a solid history, but who have been pressured by friends to engage in inappropriate behavior. These youth are often passive, dependent, lonely, and easily influenced.

Response to Vignette

After George Grayson listened carefully and obtained background information, it was fairly clear to him that David did not suffer from a hard-core conduct disorder. He spoke with David's mom and reassured her that sometimes these things happen, and it was not a sign that David was inherently bad or the victim of inadequate parenting. At the same time, such behavior must be taken seriously. Reverend Grayson, with Nikki's permission, intervened on David's behalf. He spoke with the assistant district attorney who agreed not to seek a juvenile hall sentence, but to have David ordered to attend twenty weeks of counseling.

David and his mother were relieved that he would not be sent to juvenile hall. A week later David entered counseling, which involved both individual therapy and several sessions of family counseling.

Six months later, David, Nikki, and David's father, Bart, visited with George Grayson. David looked great. His parents reported that David had been able to work on a number of things in counseling, including developing better social skills. As a result he had been able to make new friends and was feeling more self-confident.

David was not the kind of teenager destined for a life of crime. The way things were handled by his parents, the pastor, and juvenile authorities transformed a potential tragedy into a growth experience.

Unfortunately, Mitch took another path. After his release from juvenile hall, he continued to engage in petty crimes, dropped out of high school, and began using drugs. At the age of nineteen, he died of a heroin overdose. Unfortunately, by the age of 14 or 15, those adolescents exhibiting classic signs of a conduct disorder do not fare well. As most mental health specialists will attest, this is one of the few psychological disorders that have a poor response to treatment and a rather grim prognosis.

Treatment Within the Faith Community

Conduct disorder is not rare. Prevalence rates vary from 6 to 19 percent of males and 2 to 9 percent of females (APA 1994). It is one of the most frequently diagnosed psychological disorders among children and adolescents. There may be many cases of this in every church.

In David's case, the pastor was in a pivotal position to guide him toward psychological counseling. This outcome depended heavily on the minister's ability to withhold judgment and to approach the situation with compassion. His assessment was important in reducing some of Nikki's guilt and opening the door to a helpful intervention.

When a congregation learns about such "crimes," it is common for some people to jump to conclusions and to assume that someone is to blame. Despite religious teachings about compassion, there seem to be natural inclinations to assume the worst and blame others. A recurring theme throughout this book is that one should never jump to quick conclusions based on scant information or superficial behavior. In David's case, he was given the benefit of the doubt, and his pastor and parents were able to hear his truth.

Treatment by Mental Health Specialist

As noted above, misbehavior (such as defiance, aggression) can occur in many different contexts. If this is simply one aspect of another psychological disorder (such as depression, ADD), the treatment of choice is to focus on the primary underlying disorder (see Cases 15 and 18).

Should it be determined that a teenager has a conduct disorder (for those over 18, it is called antisocial personality disorder), treatment options are very limited.

Prior to puberty, some minors destined to develop antisocial tendencies can be helped with individual and/or family counseling. However, by age 14 or 15, the traits seen in true conduct disorder often become quite rigidified and very resistant to modification. Sadly, most of these adolescents end up being "treated" by the judicial system rather than by mental health professionals.

Therapists and clergy alike can be of most help in supporting family members. We may be able to offer assistance along three lines: accepting difficult realities of a child gone amiss; grieving lost hopes and dreams of a child becoming a loving, productive citizen; and supporting the family in setting limits. Often delinquent and antisocial adolescents inflict tremendous injuries upon their families by stealing, lying, using, abusing, and so forth. Limit-setting, which in its extreme may involve estrangement, can be very difficult to do, both in terms of the effort it takes and the inevitable heartache it causes. These parents and siblings need our encouragement, guidance, and empathy.

Cross-Cultural Issues

There are marked differences across cultures regarding what constitutes appropriate social behavior. Particular types of aggressive behavior, such as gang violence, may be a dominant aspect of some cultures and thus may not reflect a mental disorder or a diagnosis of conduct disorder.

Immigrants coming to America, especially from war-ravaged countries, may have had to adopt certain behaviors (such as deceptiveness, intimidation, combativeness) to survive in the culture of origin. Finally, there are widely recognized differences between genders. Almost without exception, hostility and aggression are much more likely to be seen in males than in females (true also for aggressive behavior displayed in non-human mammals). As with many disorders, notions of "normality" are strongly culture-bound.

Resources

National Resources

American Academy of Child and Adolescent Psychiatry, 3615 Wisconsin Ave., NW, Washington, DC 20016; www.aacap.org; (202) 966-7300.

Federation of Families for Children's Mental Health, 1021 Prince St., Alexandria, VA 22314; (703) 684-7710; www.ffcmh.org; ffcmh@crosslink.net. This national, parent-run organization has 122 affiliated groups that focus on the needs of children and teens with emotional, behavioral, and mental health problems. They provide information, advocacy, and family support.

Parents Anonymous, 675 W. Foothill Blvd., Suite 220, Claremont, CA 91711; (909) 621-6184; www.parentsanonymous-natl.org; parents anon@msn.com. This national organization, founded in 1970, is a professionally facilitated peer-led group for parents who are having difficulty and would like to learn more effective ways to parent children. They provide group leaders, develop chapters, and have children's groups.

Self-Help Resources

Toughlove International, P.O. Box 1069, Doylestown, PA 18901; (800) 333-1069, www.toughlove.org; service@toughlove.org, was founded in 1979 as a self-help program for parents, youth, and communities dealing with out-of-control behavior of a family member. Parent support groups help parents take a firm stand to help youth take responsibility for their behavior. It offers group development guidelines.

Before It's Too Late: Why Some Kids Get into Trouble and What Parents Can Do About It, by Stanton Samenow (NY: Times Books, 1989).

Winning Cooperation from Your Child!: A Comprehensive Method to Stop Defiant and Aggressive Behavior in Children, by Kenneth Wenning (NY: Jason Aronson, 1996).

Treating the Unmanageable Adolescent: A Guide to Oppositional Defiant and Conduct Disorders, by Neil Bernstein (NY: Jason Aronson, 1997), is a text useful to pastoral care specialists.

American Psychiatric Association. (1994). *Diagnostic and Statistical Manual of Mental Disorders, Fourth Edition*. Washington, DC: APA.

Dadds, M.R., Sanders, M.R., Behrens, B.C. and James, J.E. (1987). Marital discord and child behavior problems: A description of family interactions during treatment. *Journal of Clinical Child Psychology, 16*. 192-203.

Dadds, M.R., Schwartz, S. and Sanders, M.R. (1987). Marital discord and treatment outcome in behavioral treatment of child conduct disorders. *Journal of Consulting and Clinical Psychology, 55*. 396-403.

Hinshaw, S. and P. (1987). On the distinction between attentional deficits/hyperactivity and conduct problems/aggression in child psychopathology. *Psychological Bulletin, 101*. 443-463.

Kendall, P.C. and Braswell, L. (1985). *Cognitive-Behavioral Therapy for Impulsive Children*. NY: Guilford Press.

McMahon, R.J. (1987). Some current issues in the behavioral assessment of conduct-disordered children and their families. *Behavioral Assessment, 9*. 235-252.

Olweus, D. (1980). Familial and temperamental determinants of aggressive behavior in adolescent boys: A causal analysis. *Developmental Psychology, 16*. 644-660.

Patterson, G.R. and Dishion, T.J. (1985). Contributions of families and peers to delinquency. *Criminology, 23*. 63-79.

Porter, B. and O'Leary, K.D. (1980). Marital discord and childhood behavior problems. *Journal of Abnormal Child Psychology, 8*. 287-295.

References

Anxiety Disorders

"He Was Seen as High-Strung and Fearful"

Josh was always a sensitive and high-strung child. As a young boy he had multiple fears. He refused to go on amusement park rides, he was afraid of big dogs and deep water, and his fears of the dark persisted well beyond those normally seen in children. Slightly scary or intense movies often caused nightmares. The first week of school each year was accompanied by stomachaches. Finally, Josh had a hard time with separations. His folks had put off a weekend getaway without the children for years because they knew Josh would become upset.

Josh's problems were probably amplified because his father was a rather fearless, macho guy. He loved his son, but secretly felt ashamed of his timidity.

Reverend Lucas always knew the shy children. He had been shy as a youngster, too, and felt a special kinship with them. He had known Josh since he was in kindergarten, although Josh did not attend Sunday school until he was a sixth grader. According to Josh's mother, the boy would get upset and have stomachaches, so Josh accompanied his parents to church while his brother and sister attended Sunday school.

Thus it was not a complete surprise when Josh's mother contacted Reverend Lucas to talk about the current problem. Josh was a freshman in high school, and most of his friends at church were planning an exciting summer work camp in Mexico. As the time for the trip approached, Josh began to complain. His mother explained to Reverend Lucas, "He's scared to leave home, and I'm concerned. His father and I think Josh needs the experience of a trip away from home, and I'm worried that he'll back out. The work camp is in two months, and I don't know what to do!"

Pastoral Assessment

Some of the common sources of anxiety in children and adolescents are triggered by acute situational stressors or are seen in those who are subject to chronic family dysfunction (such as long-term marital conflicts, parental substance abuse, and so forth). Thus the pastor will want to inquire about such stressors (many of which are discussed in detail in other chapters). A central component of anxiety for most people is the experience of powerlessness, which may be characterized as a sense of insecurity, lack of control, or threat to safety. Children are dependent on their families to provide a sense of stability and security, consequently a variety of significant stressors can leave them feeling vulnerable and insecure.

It is, however, important to understand that certain types of anxiety problems may be traced to biological causes and may not be in response to significant life stresses. For this reason, the pastor must inquire carefully about recent or ongoing life stresses without automatically assuming that difficult life events are inevitably the cause of anxiety symptoms (see side bar).

When talking to teenagers, especially to those with long-term anxiety problems, it is important to know that they often have experienced significant shame and sometimes ridicule regarding their fearfulness. This may be especially true for boys who are socialized in our culture to be tough and fearless. Many avoid social and recreational activities, especially those who have what mental health professionals call "social phobias." Thus they miss out on important life activities and frequently begin to feel odd or different from their peers. In discussing anxiety problems, the pastor may benefit from asking teenagers specifically how their nervousness, worry, or fear has affected them personally. Many of these teens are quite open to talking about their problems when they feel that they won't be criticized or shamed.

Anxiety Disorders: Nature or Nurture

Anxiety problems are common in children and adolescents. Among the severest anxiety disorders, three subtypes have been shown to have their roots in a biological disturbance. These disorders tend to run in families, and the risk for developing them may be genetically transmitted. It is important to note that increased risk of inheriting a genetically transmitted disorder does not mean it will always be passed on to children. It does, however, suggest that there is increased likelihood of developing a particular disorder. There is significant research to support the role of abnormal brain chemistry in these disorders.

The anxiety disorders that appear to be biologically based include the following:

Panic Disorder is characterized by the periodic eruption of extreme intense anxiety symptoms. Generally such panic attacks come on abruptly, reach their full intensity in one to ten minutes and then subside. Most attacks are transient, lasting from one to twenty minutes. They are extremely frightening experiences of overwhelming fear or dread accompanied by sudden physical symptoms such as shortness of breath, smothering feelings, trembling, light-headedness, sweating, and a racing heart. Often panic attacks occur spontaneously. Although they *may* be provoked by acute stressful events, many attacks come "out of the blue" during nonstressful times. Often youngsters will believe that they are either going crazy or about to die.

Generalized Anxiety Disorder (GAD) is characterized by long-standing feelings of tension, insecurity, and nervousness. The hallmark of GAD is constant worry. Teens with GAD experience the stresses of everyday life in an overly intense way. There is speculation that such children are constitutionally sensitive and naturally more prone to risk-avoidance and worry.

Obsessive-Compulsive Disorder (OCD) typically begins in childhood or adolescence, and if untreated, may last a lifetime. It is a type of anxiety disorder accompanied by two groups of symptoms: obsessions (recurring, intrusive, very worrisome thoughts) and compulsions (repetitive ritualistic behaviors). Examples of obsessions include intense worries about dirt, germs, or contamination. Common rituals involve actions like repeated hand washing, counting rituals, or a driven need to have one's surroundings neat and symmetrical. Most people experience *occasional* obsessive thinking or compulsive behaviors, but those with OCD are continuously plagued by these very disturbing symptoms.

In all three disorders there is a pronounced feeling of loss of control. Teenagers with these conditions cannot simply stop the symptoms by willpower alone because a part of the disorder can probably be traced to abnormal neurochemistry. Good medical and psychological treatments have been developed for these oftentimes serious afflictions.

If it is determined that family crises or significant situational stress are *not* evident and if the symptoms are severe and/or long-standing, the pastor can assume that the child *may* have a biologically mediated anxiety disorder, and a referral to a mental health professional is in order.

Many people believe that having faith in God should alleviate worries and fears. However, for those facing significant life stresses or suffering from biologically based psychiatric disorders, the picture is much more complicated. The pastor can play an important role in reducing shame and self-criticism and in encouraging the teen to consider professional intervention.

Diagnostic Criteria

Anxiety symptoms are numerous and can generally be classified into three groups:

Physical Symptoms
- tension
- sleep disturbances, especially difficulty in falling asleep
- generalized aches and pains, including stomachaches and headaches
- trembling, shakiness
- cold hands and feet
- numbness in hands or feet
- dry mouth
- shortness of breath, often accompanied by tightness in the chest and/or a smothering sensation
- sweating
- frequent diarrhea and/or urination
- rapid heart rate
- dizziness or light-headedness

Cognitive and Emotional Symptoms
- feeling nervous, edgy
- fearfulness (fear of situations or objects, fear of death, fear of loss of control)
- excessive worry ("what-ifing")
- phobias (specific fears, such as fear of flying)
- obsessions
- difficulty concentrating

Anxiety-Driven Behaviors
- avoidance of fear-provoking situations, such as social interactions
- compulsions or rituals
- agitation or restlessness
- biting fingernails or pulling out strands of hair
- substance abuse, often used to reduce anxiety

Anxiety symptoms are classified as appearing in two major forms. The first is anxiety or panic attacks—sudden explosions of intense anxiety (see sidebar). The other version is generalized anxiety symptoms that may be almost continuous—lasting for a few days, several weeks, many months, or years. Generalized anxiety symptoms are often quite unpleasant, but not as intense as full-blown panic attacks.

Critical in the diagnostic process is the assessment of three factors that *may* influence the emergence of anxiety symptoms: the role of situational stress factors, such as serious family or marital conflicts; the presence or absence of substance abuse (many illicit drugs, including alcohol, may cause significant anxiety symptoms); and the presence or absence of a primary medical disorder, for example, a disorder such as thyroid disease.

Treatment depends upon the assessment of the cause of anxiety symptoms. Since medical disorders can, on occasion, cause anxiety disorders, a referral to the primary care physician is warranted. Obviously, if substance abuse is a factor, it must be addressed aggressively.

Situational stresses account for a large number of anxiety disorders in young people, and counseling (pastoral or psychotherapy) is always indicated. If it is determined that a teenager suffers from a biologically-based disorder, medication is often indicated and is frequently a very successful option.

Relevant History

Pastor Lucas obtained some background information from Josh's parents. There were no significant stresses in his life, and he had a long-standing history of nervousness and fearfulness. Like many anxious youngsters, Josh had shown an intense response to separations from his parents through childhood.

The pastor also learned that "nervousness" was a widespread problem in Josh's mother's family. She, herself, had numerous phobias, and her two sisters suffered from panic disorder. The history is suggestive of a generalized anxiety disorder.

Response to Vignette

Reverend Lucas met with Josh for a private talk. Although at first he seemed evasive, eventually Josh admitted that he was worried about the summer trip. The pastor had a good talk with him in which Josh discussed his difficulties. He found Reverend Lucas to be understanding and supportive. A comment that was received especially well was when Reverend Lucas said, "It sounds to me like you are just a naturally sensitive kid.... There are probably a lot of us around. I suspect sometimes people just don't understand how you feel." Josh replied, "No kidding!"

This compassionate, nonshaming interaction was the key to getting Josh interested in seeing a psychologist. He and his parents were open to this referral, and Josh met with a psychologist later that week. During the next two months, Josh met weekly with the psychologist and was able to develop some specific techniques for reducing anxiety. This sensitive boy was not "cured," but he experienced a new sense of mastery as he used techniques to help him cope with anxiety. His confidence gradually grew, and Josh was able to successfully go with his friends to the work camp.

Anxiety disorders of this magnitude seldom spontaneously cease. Likewise, "pull yourself up by your bootstraps" lectures rarely do more than induce shame. Short-term pastoral counseling, as we saw with Josh, can be effective in accomplishing two objectives: to reduce shame and self-criticism and to encourage the person to seek professional counseling.

Treatment Within the Faith Community

Don't worry about anything, but in all your prayers ask God for what you need. (Philippians 4:6 TEV)

Anxiety and its cousin fear are common human experiences. There are numerous Bible passages dealing with fear and worry that can be a comfort (Psalms 4:8; 91:1-2; Proverbs 3:24; Isaiah 26:3; Matthew 6:25-34; John 14:27; Philippians 4:6-7; 1 Peter 5:7). Memorizing these verses and repeating them during times of fear and anxiety can bring relief in high-stress situations.

Many people, despite their best efforts, encounter overwhelmingly stressful life events and/or suffer from biologically based anxiety disorders. One of the most important messages a pastor can offer his or her congregation is to accept human limitations without shame. Only about 1 in 4 individuals with an anxiety disorder receive treatment. Much of the resistance to treatment results from the fear of stigmatization.

Indications for Referral

Teens with anxiety symptoms will vary widely with regard to two important issues: how long the symptoms have occurred and the magnitude of severity (such as how much they are suffering and what impact it has on normal living). In Josh's case, in addition to his discomfort from feelings of anxiety, he also experienced considerable amounts of shame and an increasing sense of low self-confidence. Additionally, the fears were beginning to interfere with his ability to engage in important life activities. Anxious children often cope with their difficulties by avoidance and withdrawal. As a consequence, they miss out on important experiences such as social interactions and the opportunity to develop social skills, a sense of belonging, and connection to peers.

Josh's problems were long-standing. The referral to a psychotherapist was clearly in order.

Treatment by Mental Health Specialist

For adolescents experiencing anxiety attributable to situational stresses, counseling or psychotherapy (often family therapy) is the treatment of choice. In such cases, the anxiety symptoms are simply a part of the teen's reaction to a basic sense of insecurity or worry associated with stressful circumstances.

For more severe and chronic anxiety disorders (panic disorder, OCD, and severe GAD), two treatments have a documented record of effectiveness. The first is behavior therapy, a specialized form of psychotherapy. The second is medication. In recent times, the mainstay of drug treatment for these disorders has been the use of antidepressant medications, specifically the serotonin antidepressants (such as Prozac, Paxil, Celexa, Serzone, and Zoloft). These *nonaddictive* medications are effective and safe treatment options. Drug treatment is generally most successful if combined with behavior therapy (Preston and Johnson 1997).

Although the prevalence of some anxiety disorders may be higher among African Americans than the general population, little research has been done to investigate the problem in adults or children (Neal and Turner 1991).

National Resources

Anxiety Disorders Association of America (ADAA), 11900 Parklawn Drive, Suite 100, Rockville, MD 20852; (301) 231-9350; www.adaa.org; anxdis@aol.com; provides a list of professionals in your area that offer specialized treatments for anxiety disorders.

Association for the Advancement of Behavioral Therapy, 305 Seventh Avenue, 16th Floor, NY, NY 10001; (212) 647-1890.

American Psychological Association, 750 First Street, N.E., Washington, DC 20002; (202) 336-5500; www.apa.org; public interest@apa.org

American Academy of Child and Adolescent Psychiatry, 3615 Wisconsin Ave., N.W., Washington, DC 20016; (202) 966-7300; www.aacap.org.

National Institutes of Mental Health has a Panic Disorder Education Program that provides helpful educational materials, (888) 8-ANXIETY; NIMH, Publications List, Room 7C-02, 5600 Fishers Lane, Bethesda, MD 20892.

National Alliance for the Mentally Ill (NAMI), 200 N. Glebe Road, Suite 1015, Arlington, VA 22203; (800) 950-6264; www.nami.org; helpline@aol.com.

National Anxiety Foundation, 3135 Custer Drive, Lexington, KY 40517; (606) 272-7166; lexington-on-line.com/naf.html.

Obsessive Compulsive Foundation, Inc., P.O. Box 70, Milford, CT 06460; (203) 878-5669; www.ocfoundation.org/indright.htm; info@ocfoundation.org, is dedicated to intervention, to finding a cure for obsessive-compulsive disorders, and to improving the welfare of those who suffer from this disorder. It provides education, research, and mutual help. It has videotapes and books available as well as a nationwide listing of 250 support groups.

National Mental Health Association, 1021 Prince St., Alexandria, VA 22314; (800) 969-NMHA; (800) 433-5959 for the hearing impaired; www.nmha.org; nmhainfo@aol.com, has a fact sheet series on anxiety disorders.

Dean Foundation, Obsessive Compulsive Information Center; (608) 827-2390; 2711 Allen Blvd., Middleton, WI 53562; has an information computer database available, along with listings of mental health referrals and support groups working with OCD issues.

Self-Help Resources

Phobics Anonymous, P.O. Box 1180, Palm Springs, CA 92263; (619) 322-2673; is an international organization founded in 1985 for the mutual support of persons with anxiety and panic disorders that uses the 12-step recovery program.

Obsessive Compulsive Disorder: A Guide, by John H. Greist (Dean Foundation, 1997). Obsessive Compulsive Disorder Information Center has a useful discussion of medication and behavioral therapy treatment options for the disorder.

Learning to Live with Obsessive Compulsive Disorder, by Barbara L. Van Noppen (Milford, CT: OCD Foundation, 1989, 1997), provides information for family members of those suffering from OCD.

Minister's Handbook of Mental Disorders, by Joseph W. Ciarrocchi (NY: Paulist Press, 1993), has an informative chapter on anxiety disorders from a faith perspective.

References

Achenbach, T.M. (1985). Assessment of anxiety in children. In A.H. Tuma and J.D. Maser (eds.) *Anxiety and the Anxiety Disorders* (pp. 707-734). Hillsdale, NJ: Erlbaum.

American Psychiatric Association. (1994). *Diagnostic and Statistical Manual of Mental Disorders, Fourth Edition.* Washington, DC: APA.

Bamber, J.H. (1974). The fears of adolescents. *Journal of Genetic Psychology, 125.* 127-140.

Barker, P. (1984). Family dysfunction and anxiety in children. In V.P. Varma (ed.) *Anxiety in Children* (pp. 89-104). London: Croom Helm.

Barrios, B.A. and Hartmann, D.P. (1988). Fears and anxieties. In E.J. Mash and L.G. Terdal (eds.) *Behavioral Assessment of Childhood Disorders,* Second edition (pp. 196-262). NY: Guilford Press.

Campbell, S.B. (1986). Development issues. In R. Gittelman (ed.) *Anxiety Disorders in Childhood* (pp. 24-57). NY: Guilford Press.

Neal, A.M. and Turner, S.M. (1991). Anxiety disorders research with African Americans: Current status. *Psychological Bulletin, 109(3).* 400-410.

Preston, J. and Johnson, J. (1997). *Clinical Psychopharmacology.* Miami, FL: Medmaster.

Learning Disabilities

"She Was Not Stupid"

It had been hard to hear other parents singing the praises of their children's academic successes. "Suzi has gotten a scholarship." "Jeff is on the dean's list." "Mary was just chosen to compete on the statewide debate team." And it was embarrassing and disappointing to glance at Becky's material, which she recently brought home from Sunday school. On the top of the page her daughter had drawn a beautiful sunset and beneath it written, "God is Grate."

"I know Becky is not stupid. She can carry on a very appropriate conversation. She understands TV shows, she seems interested in learning new things, and she's not lazy either. I've seen her work very hard to complete homework assignments, but her grades are terrible—they always have been. And the other day I heard her in her room crying and heard her say, 'I hate myself. I'm just so retarded!'" Becky's mother, Jill, confided to the associate pastor in her church over lunch one day. "I just don't know what to do."

Reverend Robertson felt bad for Jill. His congregation was made up of a number of affluent families, many of whom were professionals. Academic stardom was commonplace in his church. He had known 16-year-old Becky Clark since she was six—a nice, but rather quiet and shy child. Her parents are both bright, well-educated, and very nice people. Becky's older brother, Greg, had just gone to college and was doing well. Judging by Becky's apparently normal vocabulary and conversational speech, Reverend Robertson was convinced that she did not have mental retardation.

Many youngsters of average or above average intelligence have academic problems for a host of reasons. Inadequate parental encouragement or adolescent "attitudes" are common contributors to less than stellar aca-

Pastoral Assessment

demic performance. And Reverend Robertson had seen many children slip in achievement if they or their families were going through a particularly stressful time. Many teens had struggled for a while in the wake of divorce, parental job losses, serious family illnesses, or the loss of a grandparent.

Yet in Becky's case, three factors stood out to suggest that her academic problems might be due to a *specific learning disability*. First, her problems were long-standing (most specific learning disabilities become apparent early—usually by second or third grade—and persist thereafter). Second, her parents valued education and provided appropriate models for learning as well as encouragement and help. Finally, Reverend Robertson knew the Clarks well enough to know that there were no serious recently occurring family stresses. These factors raise the strong possibility that Becky has a learning disability, and Reverend Robertson shared his impressions with Jill.

Diagnostic Criteria

As noted above, many factors may contribute to academic difficulties, including:

Intellectual deficiency such as below-average intelligence (IQ 70–85) or mental retardation (IQ below 70). These cognitive problems may be long-standing (for example, present since birth) or more recently acquired (such as in the case of children who have suffered serious head injuries or neurological diseases like encephalitis). Global intellectual impairment affects a wide array of abilities including notable weaknesses in: learning, memory, problem solving, judgment, verbal skills, and mathematical abilities. Often such conditions are accompanied by motor difficulties (such as poor handwriting, incoordination), speech problems, emotional immaturity, and social skill deficits. Children with significant global intellectual impairment are generally identified early in life and typically are offered special education services.

Learning problems in the context of completely adequate intellectual potential. Here, academic problems may be attributed to any or all of the following: poor models, such as parents who do not value education or encourage learning; inadequate parental involvement in school-related tasks (such as homework); emotional disturbances (such as depression, severe situation stress, major psychiatric disorders). These disorders frequently interfere with one's ability to concentrate and attend to the task and may take a toll on motivation as well (Kaslow and Cooper 1978).

In certain cultures or subcultures, education may be de-emphasized. An example may be seen in youth of the inner-city, where to take school seriously is "not cool." Here there may be incentives for avoiding academics and ridicule for those who are studious.

Lack of motivation or "laziness." There may be no more elegant way to say it. This may be influenced by a variety of factors such as emotional immaturity, a "laid-back" personality style, or being preoccupied with other interests such as dating, sports, or video games (Dweck 1986).

Substance abuse that interferes with motivation and/or cognitive functioning.

Adequate intellectual abilities, *per se*, but **difficulties with concentration and problems staying task-focused due to attention deficit disorder** (see Case 18). Please note: ADD may also be accompanied by "specific learning disabilities" as discussed below.

A final category exists, which has generally been referred to as **specific learning disabilities** (Rourke 1985). These problems are not primarily attributable to social, cultural, emotional, or motivational factors. Learning disabilities (LD) are defined as circumscribed cognitive problems in the context of an otherwise average to above-average intelligence (Smith 1985). These areas of impairment may include any or all of the following:

- *Alexia* (inability to read) or *dyslexia* (difficulties in reading)
- *Acalculia* or *dyscalculia*: A specific learning disability dealing with the ability to understand and carry out mathematical calculations
- *Spelling dyspraxia*: Notable problems in spelling (which may or may not go along with dyslexia)
- *Language/linguistic disabilities:* Here the children may be able to do math problems, excel in drawing, or solve complex nonverbal tasks (such as putting together puzzles or repairing a car engine) yet experience significant difficulties in one or all of the following areas: *verbal communication skills, verbal reasoning, verbal comprehension*
- *Handwriting disorders* manifested by poor fine-motor coordination and/or visual motor abilities (also may be revealed in difficulties reproducing geometric designs)
- *Memory disorders:* In such cases, general intelligence, reasoning, and verbal abilities are intact; however, the child exhibits marked difficulties in learning new information, and in general, is very forgetful.

Obviously such disabilities greatly interfere with a child's ability to succeed in school, and chronic school failure almost always leads to feelings of inadequacy and low self-esteem. Depression, demoralization, and simply "giving up" are not uncommon outcomes for teenagers with learning disabilities.

To make matters worse, often parents, friends, and teachers clearly recognize outward signs of the child's average or above-average intelligence. This may be seen at times when such youngsters readily grasp complex story lines in movies, exhibit the ability to solve some challenging problem, or use sophisticated vocabulary. Impressed by these manifestations of general intellectual competency, others naturally come to expect commensurate academic performance. When the adolescent does poorly in school, frequently the assumption is made that he or she is not trying hard enough, is unmotivated, or is "lazy." In cases of specific learning disabilities, these children experience considerable problems with academic performance even when motivation and effort are optimal. This set of circumstances sets the stage for incredible frustration and feelings of inadequacy, and it can become the focal point for heated parent-child conflicts. Teenagers with unrecognized and untreated learning disabilities are at high risk for academic failure, emotional disturbances, and often, substance abuse.

Relevant History

Becky showed absolutely no signs of significant developmental delays. By all outward appearances, she was a bright and normal child. However, in the first semester of second grade, her teacher contacted Mr. and Mrs. Clark to report that Becky seemed to be having trouble learning to read. Later in the year, she was evaluated by the school psychologist. Testing revealed that she was of above-average intelligence. However, she was below grade level in spelling and reading. Throughout elementary school and junior high school, her grades were marginal (Cs, Ds, and Fs). She maintained motivation to do homework, but as time went by she became more and more discouraged and frustrated. Despite the early recognition and psychological testing, Becky was never offered any special education services (unfortunately, this is not uncommon).

Indications for Referral

Any mention of academic problems in children and teenagers is reason enough to encourage parents to pursue an educational/psychological evaluation. It is not the pastor's job to pinpoint an exact diagnosis, but rather to direct parents to appropriate resources in the school system. Most states have a mandate to provide educational assessment for children with learning problems, and if learning disabilities are identified, to provide remedial services. However, with reduced funding for education, many states now only provide special remediation for children with very severe learning disabilities. In many instances, such resources are only available to those families where parents have been assertive and insistent that help be provided.

Parents can be helped to better understand their children by the explanation that there are a multitude of reasons for academic problems, and until a thorough assessment is done, it's best not to blame the child or to jump to conclusions. The bottom line is that with learning disabilities, simply encouraging a child to try harder rarely works—it may be somewhat analogous to insisting that blind persons should be able to see if they would only try harder.

Most remedial programs that work first determine a child's areas of strength and limitation, and then provide approaches to learning that utilize strengths.

In making a referral for an educational assessment, it may be helpful for the pastor to suggest that the most important goal is to help the teenager through adolescence with adequate feelings of self-worth. A secondary goal is to enhance or optimize school performance. Some moderate-to-severe learning disabilities are quite difficult to remediate, which is why the primary focus on the teen's emotional well-being may be important to underscore. Teens need to understand that a specific learning disability does not mean that they are "stupid." Many LD adolescents can find niches (academically and ultimately occupationally) where they can use their strengths and succeed.

Response to Vignette

Reverend Robertson shared three thoughts with Jill. First, he wanted her to know that learning disabilities are not a sign of general intellectual weakness and that they are quite common, affecting about 5 percent of schoolchildren in the United States (APA 1994). Second, he expressed his concern for Becky, in particular acknowledging how she apparently is developing feelings of inadequacy. "Finding ways to help her in school may be important, but possibly more urgent is the need to do something to help with her emotional pain." He suggested that Jill encourage Becky to meet with Laura Denning, the church's youth director and counselor. Finally, he urged Jill to approach Becky's school and request an educational assessment.

Jill took these recommendations and approached the school. She did, in fact, have to be rather insistent about having Becky receive the evaluation. At first the school was not too cooperative; however, within a few weeks she was seen by the school psychologist. The evaluation revealed that Becky had a moderately severe learning disability. She was subsequently offered remedial help.

Becky also met with Laura Denning for several counseling sessions. Within a few months, Becky was beginning to feel less tense, and her outer appearance showed that she was more calm and happy.

Treatment Within the Faith Community

One of the most embarrassing experiences for a learning-disabled child is to have the disability revealed publicly. In teenagers with LD problems, it is important for Sunday school teachers and other leaders to be sensitive to this issue. In classes, worship services, or other functions, the youngster should not be expected to do public speaking or read aloud, unless he or she volunteers. At the same time, these teens should not be treated with kid gloves, but as competent, capable adolescents (balanced with a sensitivity to specific limitations).

Often parents of LD children will need to face painful realities. It's hard to come to terms with the fact that a child may not do well in school, may not go to college, or may fall short of parental hopes. This may mean having to mourn the loss of some dreams, while learning to accept and appreciate the unique gifts that all of these youngsters do have.

Treatment by Mental Health Specialist

If learning disabilities are due primarily to emotional disorders (such as depression) then the treatment of choice is psychotherapy (and in some instances, medication). If the major cause is ADD, medical and psychological treatment are indicated.

Remediation of specific learning disabilities is generally done within the school system or by specially trained educational psychologists or tutors. However, specific learning disabilities that are generally due to subtle neurologic abnormalities are not "curable" in the ordinary sense of the word.

The most common approach to remediation is based on the assumption that areas of particular weakness will likely continue to be a problem. Forcing young people to do what they cannot do is an exercise in futility and may result in excessive frustration and a sense of defeat for the adolescent. Thus, remediation centers around two issues. First is a determination of the teen's strengths, helping him or her learn how to approach problem solving and learning using those strengths. The second element involves making specific accommodations for the youngster in the classroom. For example, a young person with dyslexia would not be asked to read aloud in front of the class and may be given tests orally (rather than having to read exam questions).

Central to successful outcomes for these teenagers are approaches designed to foster success and build self-confidence. If learning disabilities are not identified until the teenage years, it is very likely that the adolescents have experienced years of failure and will have developed low self-esteem and/or have given up. They need a tremendous amount of support and encouragement and may benefit from psychotherapy.

Cross-Cultural Issues

Parental attitudes regarding academic performance vary considerably and are greatly influenced by socioeconomic and cultural factors. Upper middle-class, white Americans generally place great emphasis on academic success (sometimes to a fault, putting unrealistic pressures on children).

Cultural factors also come into play regarding educational and psychological assessments, since many of the tests given to diagnose learning disabilities may not have been standardized using minority samples or may not be sensitive to cultural issues.

Resources

National Resources

Learning Disabilities Association of America, 4156 Library Rd., Pittsburgh, PA 15234; (412) 341-1515; www.ldanatl.org; ldanatl@usaor.net; is a national organization with 600 chapters founded in 1963. It is devoted to understanding and finding solutions for many types of learning problems. It has education information and a newsletter, and makes referrals.

International Dyslexia Association, 8600 LaSalle Road, Chester Building, Suite 382, Baltimore, MD 21286; (800) 222-3123; www.interdys.org; info@interdys.org.

National Center for Learning Disabilities, 381 Park Ave., South, Suite 1401, New York, NY 10016; (888) 575-7373; www.ncld.org.

National Information Center for Children and Youth with Disabilities (NICHY), P.O. Box 1492, Washington, DC 20013; (800) 695-0285; www.nichcy.org; nichcy@aed.org.

National Adult Literacy and Learning Disabilities Center, Academy for Educational Development, 1875 Connecticut Ave., NW, Washington, DC 20009; (800) 953-2553; www.nifl.gov/nalld/nalddesc.htm; info@nalldc.aed.org.

Council for Exceptional Children, 1920 Association Drive, Reston, VA 22091; (888) CEC-SPED; www.cec.sped.org.; service@cec.sped.org., provides information about learning disabilities to teachers and other service providers.

Council for Learning Disabilities, P.O. Box 40303, Overland Park, KS 66204; (913) 492-8755; www1.winthrop.edu/cld; eversr@winthrop.edu.

Self-Help Resources

The Gift of Dyslexia: Why Some of the Smartest People Can't Read and How They Can Learn, by Ronald D. Davis and Eldon M. Braun (NY: Perigree, 1997) and *In the Mind's Eye: Visual Thinkers, Gifted People with Dyslexia and Other Learning Difficulties, Computer Images and the Ironies of Creativity,* by Thomas G. West (NY: Prometheus Books, 1997) are highly recommended books.

Sixth Grade Can Really Kill You, by Barthe DeClements (NY: Puffin, 1995), a book for children about a youngster's struggle with learning to read.

How to Teach Your Dyslexic Child to Read: A Proven Method for Parents and Teachers, by Bernice M. Baumer and Melanie Trendelmann (NY: Birch Lane Press, 1996).

References

American Psychiatric Association. (1994). *Diagnostic and Statistical Manual of Mental Disorders, Fourth Edition.* Washington, DC: APA.

Adelman, H.S. and Taylor, L. (1986). Summary of the survey of fundamental concerns confronting the LD field. *Journal of Learning Disabilities, 19.* 391-393.

Amerikaner, M.J. and Omizo, M.M. (1984). Family interaction and learning disabilities. *Journal of Learning Disabilities, 17.* 540-543.

Brown, A.L. and Campione, J.C. (1985). Psychological theory and the study of learning disabilities. *American Psychologist, 41.* 1059-1068.

Deshler, D.D., Schumaker, J.B., Alley, G.R., Warner, M.M. and Clark, F.L. (1982). Learning disabilities in adolescent and young adult populations. *Focus on Exceptional Children, 15.* 1-12.

Dweck, C.S. (1986). Motivational processes affecting learning. *American Psychologist, 41.* 1040-1048.

Horn, W.F., O'Donnel, J.P. and Vitulano, L.A. (1983). Long-term follow-up studies of learning-disabled persons. *Journal of Learning Disabilities, 16.* 542-555.

Kaslow, F.W. and Cooper, B. (1978). Family therapy with the learning disabled child and his/her family. *Journal of Marriage and Family Counseling, 4.* 41-49.

Rourke, B.P., ed. (1985). *Neuropsychology of Learning Disabilities: Essential of Subtype Analysis.* NY: Guilford Press.

Smith C.R. (1985). Learning disabilities: Past and present. *Journal of Learning Disabilities, 18.* 513-517.

Taylor, H.G. (1989). Learning disabilities. In E.J. Mash and R.A. Barkley (eds.) *Treatment of Childhood Disorders* (pp. 347-380). NY: Guilford Press.

Schizophrenia

"Someone Was Controlling His Thoughts"

Ben's mother, Katherine, called Father Flannerly at the rectory and asked him to come to her house. Ben, a 17-year-old high school junior, had been acting strangely for the past several months. When the priest arrived, they found Ben sitting in a corner of his room writing in his notebook. Ben began to tell a confused story about how an alien spaceship had come into his room and implanted a device in his head and controlled his thoughts. He explained that the aliens were broadcasting thoughts to him via the televisions in the house. Ben rambled from one topic of conversation to another with little apparent connection between the ideas. He smiled broadly as he told the story, although he appeared to be anxious and agitated. Katherine said that Ben had been increasingly isolated and withdrawn from family and friends. Over the past several months, he had lost his usual drive and wanted to sleep a lot. His interest in being clean and neat was disappearing. He wrote notes to himself in his private notebook late into the night. Today he began to tell the family his secret story about the aliens controlling his mind.

Pastoral Assessment

Ben is showing active signs of the psychotic disorder schizophrenia, which is marked by "gross impairment in reality testing and the creation of a new reality" (APA 1994). Ben reports that aliens are talking to him (auditory hallucinations or hearing voices others do not hear) and that they are controlling and broadcasting his thoughts and placing devices in his body (delusions or fixed, false beliefs from which he cannot be dissuaded). He speaks without apparent connections between his thoughts (loosening of associations), and his emotional expression is inappropriate to the situation (smiling broadly as he tells his odd story). Ben's judgment is grossly impaired, and his state of mind lacks the usual anchors to ground reality. He is living in a world of distortions that are frightening and highly confusing. Ben needs immediate medical attention and hospitalization.

Relevant History

Often there is a period before the active stage of schizophrenia when early warning signs of the illness occur. Ben had several of these early warning signs, including noticeable social withdrawal, poor personal grooming and hygiene, significant change in sleep patterns, and loss of motivation.

Diagnostic Criteria

Schizophrenia is a severe, episodic condition caused by a chemical imbalance in the brain that frequently has serious impact on many aspects of an individual's life, as well as on the family. About half of males and one-fourth of females who develop this illness do so before they turn 19 (Loranger 1984). Schizophrenia clearly has a biological basis; there are numerous studies documenting changes in brain structure and function. Neurotransmitters—substances that allow communication between brain cells—are thought to be involved in the development of the disorder.

About 1 person in 100 develop schizophrenia. Individuals with a close relative who has this condition are at the greatest risk; 1 in 10 persons who have a parent with the disease will eventually develop it. Those without a family history of the illness are at a much lower risk. Schizophrenia carries a high risk of suicide (see Case 16). One in ten individuals with the illness end their life in suicide, especially in the first six years after the initial psychotic episode (Westermeyer et al. 1991).

The disorder's essential features consist of a mixture of symptoms that will have been present for a better part of a month, with some of the signs of the illness persisting for at least six months. The symptoms involve impairment of several psychological functions including: perception (hallucinations), reality testing (delusions), thought processes (loose associations), feeling (flat or inappropriate effect), behavior (disorganization), concentration, motivation, and judgment. This condition usually impairs occupational, educational, and social activities.

About 20 to 30 percent of those with schizophrenia recover to lead a normal life. Another 20 to 30 percent continue to suffer from moderate symptoms, while 40 to 60 percent continue to be seriously impaired from the disease. Approximately one-half of all mental hospital beds in the United States are occupied by people who have this illness (Keshaven, Valx-Smith and Andreson 1995).

Response to Vignette

Ben appears to be in the active stage of schizophrenia and requires immediate medical attention. He must be admitted to inpatient hospital care without delay. He needs a psychiatrist who can give him antipsychotic medications that will reduce, or possibly end, his confusion between reality and his psychotic symptoms. Antipsychotic medications are not a cure, but they offer the best treatment now available. Most people show substantial improvement within a few weeks. The medications will be especially helpful in reducing Ben's delusions, hallucinations, agitation, confusion, and distortions. The antipsychotic medications also reduce by half the risk of future episodes for Ben (Carpenter et al. 1990).

Antipsychotic medications may have side effects, including stiffness, tremors, restlessness, drowsiness, dry mouth, and occasionally, a chronic irreversible movement disorder (tardive dyskinesia). Newer antipsychotic medications appear to cause fewer side effects. The biggest problem in treating persons with schizophrenia is that they often stop taking their medications. Short-term hospitalization in a well-staffed facility can offer Ben needed stress relief in a protective environment while he is adjusting to medications, and it will reduce pressure on the family.

When Ben's symptoms have decreased, he can begin to function better and benefit more from other forms of treatment, such as individual, group, or family therapy and social and vocational training. Ben has become ill during his education-building, career-forming years, so it is critical that he continue to develop his vocational and social skills to ensure as normal a life as possible. Unfortunately, many individuals with schizophrenia suffer not only mental health problems, but lack social and work skills that can give them life-satisfaction and emotional stability.

Ben's parents may need help to accept the fact of the illness and to begin to learn how best to manage it. Research has shown that a good family environment can be a major factor in improving the chances of stabilizing the schizophrenia and preventing relapse. Families that are supportive and nonjudgmental can do much to foster a person's recovery, while chaotic or unstable families can increase the risk of relapse.

Treatment Within the Faith Community

The faith community can be of great value as a continuing source of contact and support for Ben and his family. Their church can offer acceptance and care often not found elsewhere. Families with any chronic illness undergo considerable strain, and this is no less true for mental illness. Since schizophrenia is a disease of the brain, it is important that pastors encourage blame-free acceptance of the disorder.

In a recent study, researchers discovered that 3 in 4 psychiatric patients identified religion to be an important source of comfort and support. Unfortunately, the same study found that psychiatric inpatients were less likely to have talked to a pastor than a comparable group in a general medical/surgical hospital. Moreover, while 80 percent of the psychiatric patients considered themselves spiritual or religious only 20 percent had a pastor or spiritual adviser to consult (Fitchett, Burton and Sivan 1997).

Some religious organizations (see Resources) have developed outreach programs to help clergy and congregations support and care for those with mental illnesses like schizophrenia. These groups can help combat the stigma that is often the "second wounding" of mental illness. Families report that societal stigma toward the mentally ill has a negative impact in the form of lowered self-worth, difficulty making and keeping friends, lack of success in getting a job or finding a place to live, and overall recovery. Popular movies about mentally ill killers and high-profile news coverage of tragedies involving the mentally ill contribute to the stigma (Wahl and Harman 1989). The families of the mentally ill believe that accurate, factual information about mental illness is the best remedy for the situation.

The truth is that people with schizophrenia are usually less violent than others. They are often very timid and emotionally vulnerable. Very few are dangerous. They do not have a "split personality" as portrayed in *Dr. Jekyll and Mr. Hyde*. Problems with violence and aggression may arise among a few individuals who do not continue their medications, especially if they abuse drugs or alcohol. Otherwise, people with schizophrenia are no more likely to commit crimes than the general population.

Indications for Referral

Sometimes people have psychotic symptoms due to undetected medical disorders. For this reason, a complete medical history and examination should be conducted to rule out other possible causes of Ben's symptoms before concluding he has schizophrenia.

Treatment by Mental Health Specialist

Since schizophrenia is usually a long-term illness, continuing medical care and medications will be needed. It is important to find a psychiatrist who is well qualified, interested in the illness, empathic with the sufferers, and who can work well with others on a treatment team. The treatment team may include family members, psychologists, nurses, social workers, and case managers.

Individual psychotherapy can be helpful (Coursey 1989). It involves regularly scheduled conversations between the client and the mental health specialist. These sessions focus on current or past problems, thoughts, feelings, or relationships. By sharing his experiences with a caring person, Ben may gradually come to a better understanding of himself and learn to more effectively sort the real from the unreal and distorted. A supportive, reality-oriented approach is generally of more benefit than probing insight-oriented psychotherapy. Offering Ben accurate, simple information about schizophrenia and his medications will be an important part of the process.

Family therapy can be very helpful, too, since the family is an important source of information and caregiving. Meeting as a group, Ben and his parents (in some cases siblings and other relatives are included) can be helped to gain a better understanding of one another's viewpoint. Therapy sessions can help with discharge planning from the hospital, as well as offering support for Ben's ongoing rehabilitation. Therapy sessions can provide families with support in a crisis and understanding of the emotional strain often associated with schizophrenia.

Self-help groups have become increasingly common and are often used by mental health professionals in addition to therapy. These groups, usually led by ex-patients or family members of people with schizophrenia, provide patients with mutual support as well as comfort in the awareness that they are not alone. Self-help groups also seek to promote accurate information about mental illness in order to dispel the stigma and to empower those affected by it.

Cross-Cultural Issues

Schizophrenia is found all over the world, in all races, in all cultures, and in all social classes. Women tend to have a later onset of schizophrenia and generally a better prognosis.

Resources

National Resources

National Alliance for the Mentally Ill (NAMI), 200 N. Glebe Rd., Suite 1015, Arlington, VA 22203; (800) 950-6264; www.nami.org; helpline@aol.com. Founded in 1979, NAMI is a network of self-help groups for relatives and friends affected by mental illness. It has a section devoted to giving support and information to siblings and children of persons with mental illness. NAMI has a bimonthly newsletter and runs an antidiscrimination campaign in behalf of persons with mental illness. It provides educational materials to clergy and religious organizations.

Schizophrenia Society of Canada, 75 The Donway West, Suite 814, Don Mills, Ontario M3C 2E9 Canada; (800) 809-HOPE; www.schizophrenia.ca; info@schizophrenia.ca. This is a national organization with 116 chapters. It was founded in 1979 to support and advocate for families and friends of those with schizophrenia. It has public awareness campaigns, referrals, phone assistance, and conferences.

Federation of Families for Children's Mental Health, 1021 Prince St., Alexandria, VA 22314; (703) 684-7710; ffcmh@crosslink.net; www.ffcmh.org. This national parent-run organization has 122 affiliated groups. It focuses on the needs of children and teens with mental health problems, providing information and advocacy. Web site is available in Spanish.

Schizophrenia Anonymous, c/o Mental Health Association in Michigan, 15920 West Twelve Mile Rd., Southfield, MI 48076; (810) 557-6777. This international group is organized and maintained by individuals with schizophrenia-related disorders. It offers fellowship, support, information, and professional assistance. It has weekly groups, guest speakers, and phone help.

Pathways to Promise: Interfaith ministries and prolonged mental illness, 5400 Arsenal St., St. Louis, MO 63139; (314) 644-8400, helps to develop outreach programs to the mentally ill through religious communities. It offers information, educational materials, and other resources for clergy.

Parents Involved Network, 1211 Chestnut St., Philadelphia, PA 19107; (800) 688-4226; www.libertynet.org/mha/pin.html; fine@libertynet.org; is a statewide program to give support to families with children/adolescents with emotional and behavioral problems.

Self-Help Resources

Surviving Schizophrenia: A Manual for Families, Consumers and Providers (3rd Ed.), by E. Fuller Torrey (NY: Harper, 1995); *The Broken Brain: The Biological Revolution Psychology*, by Nancy C. Andreasen (NY: Harper Collins, 1984); *Coping with Schizophrenia: A Guide for Families*, by Kim T. Mueser and Susan Gingerich (Oakland, CA: New Harbinger, 1994); *When Someone You Love Has a Mental Illness: A Handbook for Family, Friends, and Caregivers*, by Rebecca Woolis and Agnes Hatfield (NY: Putnam's Sons, 1992); and *Grieving Mental Illness: A Guide for Patients and Their Caregivers*, by Virginia Lafond (Toronto, Canada: University of Toronto Press, 1995) are high quality books on schizophrenia and how to cope with it.

A Stranger In Our Midst, by Ruth Fowler (St. Louis, MO: Pathways to Promise, 1987) is a congregational study guide on prolonged mental illness. It offers a continuing education curriculum and training manual designed for pastors and churches.

Clinical Psychopharmachology Made Ridiculously Simple, by John Preston & James Johnson (Miami, FL: MedMaster, 1997) offers the layperson a succinct, practical guide to medications used when treating mental health problems, including schizophrenia.

References

American Psychiatric Association. (1994). *Diagnostic and Statistical Manual of Mental Disorders, Fourth Edition*. Washington, DC: APA.

Carpenter, W.T., Hanlon, T.E., Henrichs, D.W., Summerfelt, A.T., Kirkpatrick, B., Levine, J. and Buchanan, R.W. (1990). Continuous versus targeted medication in schizophrenia outpatients: Outcome results. *American Journal of Psychiatry, 147*. 1138-1148.

Coursey, R.D. (1989). Psychotherapy with persons suffering from schizophrenia. *Schizophrenia Bulletin, 15(3)*. 349-353.

Fitchett, G., Burton, L.A. and Sivan, A.B. (1997). The religious needs and resources of psychiatric inpatients. *The Journal of Nervous and Mental Diseases, 185*. 320-326.

Keshavan, M.S., Vaulx-Smith, P. and Andreson, S. (1995). Schizophrenia. In V.B. Van Hasselt and M. Hersen (eds.) *Handbook of Adolescent Psychopathology* (pp. 465-496). NY: Lexington Books.

Glossary of Terms

Acquired Immunodeficiency Syndrome (AIDS) is caused by the human immunodeficiency virus (HIV), which destroys the body's capacity to fight infections. Transmission of the virus primarily occurs during sexual activity and by sharing needles used to inject intravenous drugs.

Acting out is the indirect expression of feelings through behavior that attracts the attention of others.

Active listening is alert listening with an attitude of wanting to hear what the person is saying.

Addiction: The condition that arises when a medication or drug causes physical tolerance (the need for an increasing amount to achieve the desired effect) and withdrawal symptoms (unpleasant symptoms) when its use is stopped. A person who is addicted to alcohol or drugs is also dependent on the substance.

Adolescence is the developmental transition between childhood and adulthood, generally considered to begin around age 12 or 13 and end in late teens or early twenties.

Affective disorder: A mental disorder involving mood.

Al-Anon: An organization dedicated to helping the families of alcoholics through a support group and twelve-step program.

Anorexia nervosa: An eating disorder marked by a refusal to eat and a fear of gaining weight. It can lead to serious health problems including: insomnia, fatigue, constipation, heart disease, susceptibility to infection, and death.

Anxiety: The state of feeling apprehension, agitation, uncertainty, and fear from an anticipated event.

Attention Deficit Disorder (ADD): A disorder that causes a person to have problems organizing work, easy distractibility, impulsivity, and short attention span.

Attention Deficit Hyperactivity Disorder (ADHD) is a form of ADD in which the person also exhibits hyperactive behavior. The individual with ADHD has a hard time being at rest.

Behavior disorders/emotional disturbance: These terms are used interchangeably to describe children who exhibit extreme and chronic behavior problems. These children lag behind their peers in social development. They are isolated from others either because they withdraw from social contact or because they have unsocial behaviors.

Bereavement: A normal emotional reaction to the loss of anyone who is very important to the person; this usually refers to the grief that follows the loss of a family member or other loved one.

PART THREE

Collaboration with Mental Health Specialists:

You
Are
Not
Alone

You Are Not Alone

Experience shows a need for greater collaboration and mutual learning between clergy and mental health professionals. Clergy and mental health professionals need to regard each other as valuable resources to increase the effectiveness of their care for teens and their families. Studies over three decades have demonstrated that tens of millions of Americans with mental health and family problems first seek the help of clergy. A National Institute of Mental Health survey found that clergy are more likely than psychologists or psychiatrists combined to be sought out for assistance by a person with a mental health diagnosis (Hohmann and Larson 1993). Yet research indicates that the linkage between mental health professionals and religious leaders is too often inadequate (Weaver, Samford, Kline, et al. 1997).

Frequent reliance on rabbis, priests, and ministers by the public should not be a surprise, given their availability, accessibility, and the high trust that Americans have in clergy. Over the past several decades, clergy have been ranked as the first or second most trusted professional group in the United States (Gallup 1996), while churches and organized religion rank near the top among institutions in which Americans have confidence (Hastings and Hastings 1994). Young adults view clergy higher than either psychologists or psychiatrists in interpersonal skills including warmth, caring, stability, and professionalism (Schindler et al. 1987).

Clergy often have long-term relationships with young people and their families, which enables these professionals to observe changes in behavior that may indicate early signs of distress. Furthermore, clergy are accessible helpers within faith communities that offer continuity with centuries of human history and an experience of being a part of something greater than oneself. Religious communities also have established patterns of responding to crises. Clergy can help mental health specialists gain access to teens and their families in crisis who would otherwise not receive psychological care. Clergy are also in a unique position of trust to assist families in connecting to support systems available through their faith communities and beyond (Koenig and Weaver 1997).

Unfortunately, clergy are frequently unprepared to assess the mental health problems of persons who seek their help. In a national study of almost 2,000 United Methodist pastors in which 95 percent of the sample supported having some counseling training in seminary, about 2 in 5 rated the overall quality of pastoral counseling as poor (Orthner 1986). Other studies indicate that diverse groups of Christian and Jewish clergy perceive themselves as inadequately trained to meet the mental health and family counseling needs of the persons who come to them for help (Weaver 1995). Unlike growth in other areas of pastoral ministry (such as administration, preaching, and teaching), pastors report that no matter how long they serve in a parish, they believe that their counseling skills do not increase without continuing education (Orthner 1986). Seventy to 90 percent of surveyed clergy recognize a need and indicate a desire to have additional training in mental health issues (Weaver 1995).

Referral skills are closely related to evaluation skills, since the clinical evaluation usually guides the course of action, particularly the treatment goals and objectives. Research has found that training clergy in diagnostic skills enhances their ability as pastoral counselors as well as their effectiveness in making referrals (Clemens, Corradi, and Wasman 1978). Clergy with the highest rates of referrals have attended a workshop or seminar in the area of mental health during the past year (Wright 1984). Clergy need to understand that a timely referral is an act of responsible pastoral care. They can serve most effectively in the mental health network as skilled facilitators, identifying the needs of the persons and connecting them to a larger circle of specialized helpers.

This section of the book makes several suggestions as to how clergy can become more effective partners within the mental health network.

1. Develop a collaborative relationship with several mental health specialists who have a comprehensive knowledge of the mental health services for teenagers in your community. Some psychologists and psychiatrists have specialized training in working with adolescents. A child/adolescent psychologist is a doctor with a research degree (Ph.D.) who is trained in evaluating teens and doing therapy with families. A child/adolescent psychiatrist (M.D.) is a medical doctor with special training in mental health issues who can administer medications. A social worker (M.S.W.) is a mental health professional trained in coordinating access to available community services. A marriage and family therapist is usually a person who has at least a master's degree in working with marital and family problems. Nurses can also obtain specialized training in counseling. There are more than 2,000 parish-based nurses in the United States, and the movement is growing rapidly (Miskelly 1995). The mental health specialists clergy most commonly work with are pastoral counselors who have seminary training (M.Div.) and frequently a license to practice in one of the other mental health disciplines (Orthner 1986).

Seek out mental health specialists who are open to people of faith and have some appreciation for the growing evidence that nonpunitive, nurturing religious commitment is a positive coping resource for teens and their families. About 30 to 40 percent of surveyed psychologists and psychiatrists report that religion is important in their lives. Higher percentages of social workers, marriage and family therapists, and mental health nurses indicate religion is important in their lives (Weaver, Koenig and Larson 1997). Interview mental health specialists before you make a referral. Ask them detailed questions about their experience, training, and education. What sorts of cases have they worked with in the past? What specialties do they have? How do they develop a treatment plan for various crisis situations and other mental health problems? How easily can they be located in a crisis? Are they willing to do some free or low-fee work for those who cannot afford to pay normal fees? Keep a record of available providers to whom you can refer in an emergency.

2. **Develop a list of professional and community resources before you are faced with a mental health emergency.** Where is the nearest hospital emergency room if a teenager becomes suicidal or overdoses? Where is the local mental health center located? How can you contact social service agencies, and what can they do in an emergency? Where is a local reproductive care center? To whom do you report child abuse in your area? Many jurisdictions mandate child abuse and neglect reporting by clergy: What are the procedures for reporting? Where can you take a runaway teenager for mental health care? Most areas publish listings of social services resources for teens in their region. Using these, develop appropriate plans of action with your mental health colleagues.

3. **Clergy need more training in mental health evaluative and referral skills, while mental health professionals often lack the knowledge and experience needed to sensitively address religious issues in their clients.** Studies indicate that few psychologists receive training in any aspect of religion or spirituality while in graduate school, and few seek postgraduate continuing education in those topics (Sheridan, Wilmer and Atcheson 1992). A survey of 409 clinical psychologists revealed that only 5 percent had religious or spiritual issues addressed in their professional training (Shafranske and Malony 1990). It would be of mutual benefit to the mental health and religious communities to learn from one another. Mental health professionals could be invited to take part in the training of clergy. By mixing these two groups in the same learning forum, clergy could learn more about approaches to mental health care and mental health specialists could begin reexamining their preconceived beliefs about religion and the role of clergy in mental health. In addition, this learning experience would allow mental health specialists and seminary students to formulate

ways to develop more effective working relationships in order to better serve those who come for help.

4. Significant increases in the numbers of women clergy and mental health specialists offer new opportunities for these historically under-represented groups to work together in the twenty-first century. The number of women in seminary has risen steadily over the past two decades. In 1995 one-third of the 66,000 seminary students in the United States and Canada were women, up from 10 percent in 1972 (Bedell 1997). Similar increases have been seen in the mental health professions. Forty-five percent of the members of the American Psychological Association were women in 1995, and this percentage will increase in the twenty-first century (APA 1995). Religious communities need be linked with mental health specialists who are trained to provide preventive interventions for "at risk" teenagers and their families and who are skilled in working collaboratively with rabbis, priests, and ministers. Sixty-three percent of surveyed Lutheran clergywomen reported counseling women more frequently than men and many of the problems brought by their parishioners were gender-related, such as eating disorders, unplanned pregnancies, spouse abuse, and being adult survivors of sexual abuse (Wood 1996). Development of more collaboration and training between female mental health professionals and their female counterparts among religious leaders offers creative opportunities for collegiality, while at the same time addressing important issues affecting teenage girls and women. The mental health and religious communities share many common values and goals. They need to work together more effectively for the best interest of those they are called to serve.

References

American Psychological Association. (1995). *Women in the American Psychological Association*. Washington, DC: APA.

Bedell, K.B. (1997). *Yearbook of American and Canadian churches*. Nashville: Abingdon Press.

Clemens, N.A., Corradi, R.B. and Wasman, M. (1978).The parish clergy as a mental health resource. *Journal of Religion and Health, 17(4).* 227-232.

Gallup, G.H. (1996). *Religion in America: 1996*. Princeton, NJ: The Gallup Organization, Inc.

Hastings, E. and Hastings, H. (eds.) (1994). *Index to International Public Opinion: 1993–1994*. Westport, CT: Greenwood Press.

Hohmann, A.A. and Larson, D.B. (1993). Psychiatric factors predicting use of clergy. In E.L. Worthington, Jr. (ed.) *Psychotherapy and Religious Values* (pp. 71-84). Grand Rapids, MI: Baker Book House.

Koenig, H.G. and Weaver, A.J. (1997). *Counseling Troubled Older Adults: A Handbook for Pastors and Religious Caregivers*. Nashville: Abingdon Press.

Miskelly, S. (1995). A parish nursing model: Applying the community health nursing process in the church community. *Journal of Community Health Nursing, 12(1).* 1-14.

Orthner, D.K. (1986). *Pastoral Counseling: Caring and Caregivers in the United Methodist Church.* Nashville: The General Board of Higher Education and Ministry of The United Methodist Church.

Shafranske, E.P. and Malony, H.N. (1990). Clinical psychologists' religious and spiritual orientation and their practice of psychotherapy. *Psychotherapy, 27(1).* 72-78.

Sheridan, M.J., Wilmer, C.M. and Atcheson, L. (1994). Inclusion of content on religion and spirituality in the social work curriculum: A study of faculty views. *Journal of Social Work Education, 30(3).* 363-376.

Schindler, F., Berren, M.R., Hannah, M.T., Beigel, A. and Santiago, J.M. (1987). How the public perceives psychiatrists, psychologists, nonpsychiatric physicians, and members of the clergy. *Professional Psychology: Research and Practice, 18(4).* 371-376.

Weaver, A.J. (1995). Has there been a failure to prepare and support parish-based clergy in their role as front-line community mental health workers? A review. *The Journal of Pastoral Care, 49(2).* 129-149.

Weaver, A.J., Koenig, H.G., and Larson, D.B. (1997). Marital and family therapists and the clergy: A need for collaboration, training and research. *Journal of Marital and Family Therapy, 23.* 13-25.

Weaver, A.J., Samford, J., Kline, A.E., Lucas, L.A., Larson, D.B. and Koenig, H.G. (1997). What do psychologists know about working with the clergy? An analysis of eight American Psychological Association journals: 1991–1994. *Professional Psychology: Research and Practice, 28(5).* 471-474.

Wood, N.S. (1996). An inquiry into pastoral counseling ministry done by women in the parish setting. *The Journal of Pastoral Care, 50(4).* 340-348.

Wright, P.G. (1984). The counseling activities and referral practices of Canadian clergy in British Columbia. *Journal of Psychology and Theology, 12.* 294-304.

Additional Resources

Resources

American Academy of Child and Adolescent Psychiatry, 3615 Wisconsin Ave., NW, Washington, DC 20016; www.aacap.org; communications@aacap.org; (202) 966-7300. Publishes a pamphlet series on child and adolescent mental health issues.

American Academy of Pediatrics, 141 Northwest Point Blvd., Elk Grove Village, IL 60000; www.aap.org; kidsdocs@aap.org; (847) 228-5005.

American Association for Marriage and Family Therapy, 1133 15th St., NW, Suite 300, Washington, DC 20005; www.aamft.org; (202) 452-0109; offers continuing education programs for those who work with families.

American Association of Pastoral Counselors, 9504A Lee Highway, Fairfax, VA 22031; www.metanoia.org/aapc; info@aapc.org; (703) 385-6967; provides information on qualified pastoral counselors and church-related counseling centers.

American Psychological Association, 750 First St., NE, Washington, DC 20002; www.apa.org; (202) 336-5500; publicinterest@apa.org.

Association of Mental Health Clergy, 12320 River Oaks Point, Knoxville, TN 37922; (615) 544-9704.

Canadian Association for Pastoral Practice and Education, 47 Queen's Park Crest, E., Toronto, Ontario M5S 2C3 Canada; (416) 977-3700; CAPPE@icon.net.

Interfaith Health Program, The Carter Center, One Copenhill, Atlanta, GA 30307; (404) 420-3846; www.interaccess.com/ihpnet.

International Parish Nurse Resource Center, 205 West Touhy Ave., Suite 104, Park Ridge, IL 60016; (800) 556-5368.

National Association of Social Workers, 750 First St., NE, Suite 700, Washington, DC 20002; www.socialworkers.org; info@naswdc,org; (202) 408-8600.

National Alliance for the Mentally Ill: Religious Outreach Network, 1900 NW 89th Street, Seattle, WA 98117; (206) 784-3789. It provides educational materials to clergy and religious groups, enabling them to dispel myths about mental illness and guide churches and synagogues into service to persons with mental illness.

National Organization for Continuing Education of Roman Catholic Clergy, 1337 West Ohio St., Chicago, IL 60622; (312) 226-1890.

Northwest Parish Nurses Ministries, Legacy Emanuel Hospital and Health Center, 2801 North Gantenbein, Room 2037, Portland, OR 97227; (503) 413-4920; www.cyberword.com/npnm; stixruda@iscn.com.

Samaritan Institute, 26965 South Colorado, Suite 380, Denver, CO 80222; (303) 691-0144, helps communities develop interfaith counseling centers.

Stephen Ministries, 8016 Dalke Ave., St. Louis, MO 63117; (314) 645-5511, offers training in counseling skills for local church members.

Glossary of Terms

Acquired Immunodeficiency Syndrome (AIDS) is caused by the human immunodeficiency virus (HIV), which destroys the body's capacity to fight infections. Transmission of the virus primarily occurs during sexual activity and by sharing needles used to inject intravenous drugs.

Acting out is the indirect expression of feelings through behavior that attracts the attention of others.

Active listening is alert listening with an attitude of wanting to hear what the person is saying.

Addiction: The condition that arises when a medication or drug causes physical tolerance (the need for an increasing amount to achieve the desired effect) and withdrawal symptoms (unpleasant symptoms) when its use is stopped. A person who is addicted to alcohol or drugs is also dependent on the substance.

Adolescence is the developmental transition between childhood and adulthood, generally considered to begin around age 12 or 13 and end in late teens or early twenties.

Affective disorder: A mental disorder involving mood.

Al-Anon: An organization dedicated to helping the families of alcoholics through a support group and twelve-step program.

Anorexia nervosa: An eating disorder marked by a refusal to eat and a fear of gaining weight. It can lead to serious health problems including: insomnia, fatigue, constipation, heart disease, susceptibility to infection, and death.

Anxiety: The state of feeling apprehension, agitation, uncertainty, and fear from an anticipated event.

Attention Deficit Disorder (ADD): A disorder that causes a person to have problems organizing work, easy distractibility, impulsivity, and short attention span.

Attention Deficit Hyperactivity Disorder (ADHD) is a form of ADD in which the person also exhibits hyperactive behavior. The individual with ADHD has a hard time being at rest.

Behavior disorders/emotional disturbance: These terms are used interchangeably to describe children who exhibit extreme and chronic behavior problems. These children lag behind their peers in social development. They are isolated from others either because they withdraw from social contact or because they have unsocial behaviors.

Bereavement: A normal emotional reaction to the loss of anyone who is very important to the person; this usually refers to the grief that follows the loss of a family member or other loved one.

Binge eating is the rapid consumption of a large amount of food in a short period of time.

Bipolar disorder/manic depression is a serious mood disorder that involves extreme mood swings and sometimes psychosis.

Blended family: A new family unit formed by the marriage of divorced persons, including their children from former marriages.

Bulimia nervosa: An eating disorder that is marked by binge eating followed by purging behavior and extreme preoccupation with body image. It can lead to serious health problems.

Child abuse: Maltreatment of a minor involving physical, sexual, and/or emotional injury.

Child/adolescent psychologist: A doctor with a research degree (Ph.D.) who is trained to use a variety of treatment modalities with children and teenagers including individual and group psychotherapy, cognitive therapy, behavior modification, psychodynamic psychotherapy, and family systems. She or he also does psychological testing.

Child/adolescent psychiatrist: A medical doctor who has special training (medical residence in psychiatry) to work with children and youth. A psychiatrist may treat with medications, psychotherapy, or both.

Child neglect is the withholding of adequate care from a minor. It usually refers to physical needs such as food, clothing, medical care, and supervision.

Cognitive: Having to do with the ability to think or reason; sometimes used to describe memory process; the operation of the mind, as distinct from emotions.

Cognitive Behavior Therapy (CBT) is a form of psychological therapy that focuses on directly modifying both thought processes and behavior.

Collaboration: The shared planning, decision making, problem solving, and goal setting by persons who work together.

Compulsion: An intrusive, repetitive, and unwanted urge to perform an act that is counter to a person's usual conduct.

Conduct disorder is a persistent pattern of behavior that involves violations of the rights of others such as disobedience, destructiveness, and boisterousness with little sense of guilt.

Coping: The process of using personal, spiritual, and social resources to manage stress.

Countertransference: Feelings that a counselor or therapist develops toward a client, such as overconcern, sexual attraction, or anger. Such feelings can interfere in the process of counseling if not recognized and addressed.

Crisis: A disturbance caused by a stressful event or a perceived threat to the self.

Crisis intervention: Emergency assistance that focuses on providing guidance and support to help mobilize the resources needed to resolve a crisis.

Culture: An ordered system of shared and socially transmitted symbols, values, and meanings that give a worldview and guide behavior.

Delusions are fixed, false beliefs from which an individual cannot be dissuaded.

Depression: Emotional disturbance in which a person feels unhappy and often has trouble sleeping, eating, or concentrating.

Diagnosis: The process of collecting data for the purpose of identifying a problem.

Diagnostic and Statistical Manual of Mental Disorders, Fourth Edition (DSM-IV): An official manual of mental health problems developed by the American Psychiatric Association. This reference book is used by mental health professionals to understand and diagnose psychological problems.

Disorder: A mental health problem that impairs an individual's social, educational, or mental functioning or significantly interferes with her or his quality of life.

Dysfunctional: Abnormal or impaired functioning.

Dyslexia: A common learning disability marked by impaired word recognition and reading comprehension problems.

Empathic listening: Listening that conveys genuine concern for the feelings of another.

Empathy: The ability to put oneself in another's place and feel what another person feels.

Family therapy: A therapeutic method that involves assessment and treatment with immediate family members present. This model of therapy emphasizes the family as a whole rather than a focus on one person.

Grandiosity: Overappraisal of one's value and ability.

Hallucinations: Abnormal perceptions that occur as symptoms in schizophrenia, mostly in the form of hearing voices or seeing objects.

Hospice care: Warm, personal patient- and family-oriented care for an individual with a terminal illness.

Hyperactivity: A condition in which activity is haphazard and not organized.

Hypervigilance: Increased watchfulness.

Learning disabilities: A specific set of problems that cause an individual to have difficulties understanding and may lower academic achievement.

Maladaptive behavior: Behavior that does not adjust to the environment.

Mania: A symptom of bipolar disorder marked by exaggerated excitement, physical overactivity, and rapid changes in ideas. A person in a manic state feels an emotional high and often follows his or her impulses.

Nicotine tolerance: This symptom occurs in the absence of nausea, dizziness, and other like symptoms despite using substantial amounts of nicotine-containing products.

Obsession: The mental state, occurring in obsessive-compulsive disorder, of having recurrent thoughts about something or someone. The recurrent thoughts are difficult to stop and difficult to control.

Oppositional defiance disorder: A condition marked by recurrent patterns of negative, defiant, disobedient stubbornness and hostile behavior.

Paranoid thinking: Exaggerated belief or suspicion that one is being persecuted, harassed, or unfairly treated.

Parish nurse: A nurse working in a congregation promoting all aspects of wellness. Parish nurses train and coordinate volunteers, develop support groups, liaison within the health care system, refer to community resources, and provide health education.

Pathological gambling: Persistent and recurrent gambling behavior that disrupts personal, educational, or occupational life.

Phobia: An intense, irrational fear of an object or situation that the individual seeks to avoid.

Post-Traumatic Stress Disorder (PTSD): An anxiety disorder in which symptoms develop following a psychological trauma. The essential features of PTSD include increased physical arousal, intrusive reexperiencing of the traumatic event, and avoidance.

Prognosis: A forecast about the outcome of a disorder, including an indication of its probable duration and course.

Projection: Attributing one's own thoughts or impulses to another.

Psychoanalysis: An approach to psychotherapy that emphasizes unconscious motives and conflicts. In this therapy the effort is to bring unconscious material to awareness to increase conscious choice.

Psychopharmacology: The management of mental illness using medications.

Psychosis: A mental condition that involves hallucinations or delusions or paranoia.

Psychosomatic: A physical disorder of the body caused or aggravated by chronic emotional stress.

Psychotherapy: A process in which an individual seeks to resolve problems or achieve psychological growth through verbal communication with a mental health professional.

Rape: Sexual intercourse or other sexual acts without a person's consent. Rape is an act of violence, not sexuality.

Reframing: Relabeling behavior by putting it into a new, more positive perspective, thus changing the context in which it is understood.

Regression: A process in which a person exhibits behavior that is more appropriate to an earlier stage of development.

Schizophrenia: A chronic mental disorder associated with a loss of contact with reality in the form of hallucinations and delusions.

Self-esteem: A person's positive self-evaluation or self-image.

Self-help groups: Therapeutic groups without the leadership of a health professional.

Social worker: A mental health professional (M.S.W.) who is trained to appreciate and emphasize the impact of environmental factors on mental problems. They often work with individuals and their families to access available community services.

Stepfamily: A linked family created by the marriage of two people, one or both of whom has been married before, in which children from the former marriage live with the remarried couple.

Substance abuse: Excessive, abnormal, or illegal use of drugs or alcohol.

Thought-stopping techniques: A self-taught method that a person can use each time he or she wishes to stop unwanted thoughts.

Summary and Conclusions

A growing number of families with teenagers will be asking clergy and the community of faith for counseling and guidance in the early decades of the twenty-first century. Teenagers and their families live in a society with epidemic levels of social problems that put adolescents "at risk" for emotional problems. These teens will have special mental and emotional issues that need to be addressed by pastors and their colleagues in ministry. For this reason, clergy and caregivers need to know about the most common mental disorders that occur in adolescents, including how to assess and diagnose them, what types of treatment can be initiated in the faith community, when referral is required, and to whom to make a referral. This text identifies twenty-two of the most common mental health conditions that occur among adolescents, provides illustrative cases, lists national resources available to help, and suggests when and from whom to seek additional professional help. There is an emphasis on self-help resources available on the Internet, a major source of information for teens.

Because of the important role that religion plays in the lives of many adolescents and their families, it is essential that pastors, youth workers, and chaplains be knowledgeable about preventive aspects of faith for teens "at risk" for emotional and mental problems. Studies link religious involvement to many positive social benefits. Youth who practice their faith have more prosocial values and caring behaviors and their families are more stable. Commitment to nonpunitive, nurturing religious beliefs and activities reduces alcohol and drug abuse, premature sexual behavior, depression, suicide, and antisocial behavior. The religious community is a powerful preventive and healing resource that will increasingly be relied upon to help meet the emotional needs of adolescents and their families.

Pastoral care is a responsibility of the entire faith community. Pastors can offer guidance and direction, but the task of caring for teens requires a larger group of helpers. Much emphasis has been given to preventive adolescent mental health care through education within the community of faith. This book offers concrete suggestions as to how the issues addressed in the case studies can be understood as forms of ministry for the congregation.

Index

abortion, 21, 125, 126

abuse, 31-32, 36, 73-80, 107, 108, 132, 133; child, 17, 18, 31, 34-35, 73-78; emotional 32, 34-41, 75, 76; physical, 26, 32, 75, 76, 78, 134; sexual, 32, 36, 37, 75, 76, 81-87, 90, 126, 134, 230; spouse, 18, 230; verbal, 35, 39, 73, 76, 105, 106

Achenbach, T.M., 208

Adelman, H.S., 215

addiction, 31, 44, 47-72

adolescents: and addiction, 50, 52, 55, 57, 60, 62, 68, 69, 70; and depression, 157, 163, 166, 172, 174; and disorders, 189, 196, 197, 202-3, 206, 212-13, 214; and family crises, 117, 121-22, 123, 124, 126, 131-34; and illness, 137, 138-39, 140, 147; and mental health, 17-44, 239; and violence, 74, 83-84, 90, 98-99, 109

African Americans, 18-19, 21, 52, 94, 98, 100, 110, 126, 134, 142, 174, 207

Ageton, S.S., 92

Aguilera, D.C., 138

AIDS, 18, 19, 21, 44, 60, 122, 137-45

Akman, D., 83

Alan Guttmacher Institute, 122

Albrecht, G.L., 22

alcohol, 44, 49, 60, 73, 76, 78, 83, 92, 93, 134, 137, 141, 164, 165, 172, 189. *See also* alcoholism

Alcoholics Anonymous for Teens, 51, 70

alcoholism, 34, 68, 106, 178. *See also* substance abuse

Allan, M.J., 23, 172

Alley, G.R., 216

Allison, K.W., 142

Allison, P.D., 106

Allman, C.J., 23, 172

Altman, D.G., 62

Amato, P.R., 110

American Academy of Child and Adolescent Psychiatry, 123

American Association for Marriage and Family Therapy, 119

American Humane Association, 74

American Psychiatric Association, 48, 59, 61, 68, 164, 179, 190, 194, 196, 208, 213, 217

American Psychological Association, 125, 230

American School Health Association, 99

Amerikaner, M.J., 215

Amick-McMullan, A., 103

amphetamine, 56-57

Andreson, S., 218

anorexia nervosa, 178, 180

antidepressants, 189, 206

antisocial behavior, 19, 22, 23, 76-77, 92, 138, 140, 149, 150, 164, 239

anxiety, 83, 98, 101, 138, 140, 141, 149, 157, 167, 178, 186

anxiety disorder, 30, 48, 69, 84, 201-8

Arcuri, A.F., 69

Asians, 181

Atcheson, L., 229

attention deficit disorder, 29, 185-91, 194, 195, 197, 211, 214

Bachman, J.G., 60, 61

Backus, C.J., 101

Backus, W., 101

Balach, L., 172

Ballenger, J.C., 178

Bamber, J.H., 208

Barber, B.L., 108

Barker, P., 208

Barkley, R.A., 190

Barrett, M.E., 20

Barrios, B.A., 208

Bass, E., 82

Baugher, M., 166, 172

Bavolek, S.J., 74

Bedell, K.B., 230

Behrens, B.C., 199

Beigel, A., 227

Beitchman, J.H., 83

Benner, D.G., 18

Bennett, T., 126
Benson, P.L., 19, 22
Bentler, P.M., 123
Berbaum, M., 50
bereavement, 155-61, 164
Berkowitz, A., 92
Berkowitz, I.H., 123
Berren, M.R., 227
Best, C.L., 98, 103
Bezilla, R., 18, 19, 20, 21, 50, 62, 173
Billingsley, A., 19, 100, 104
Bird, M.E., 78
Birmacher, B., 164, 165
Bland, R.C., 70
Blume, E.S., 82
Blumenthal, C., 121, 122, 125, 126
Bly, Robert, 35
Boutcher, F., 85
Boisvert, J., 70
Boldizar, J.P., 22
Bondurant, D.M., 78, 85
Boscarino, J., 77, 100
Bowser, B.P., 52
Boyer, D., 124
Bradshaw, John, 36
Brammer, L.M., 117
Braswell, L., 190, 199
Brent, D.A., 23, 164, 165, 166, 172, 174
Brewerton, T.D., 178
Broatman, A.W., 178
Brooks-Gunn, J., 178
Brown, A.L., 215
Brown, D.C., 101
Brown, S.A., 50
Bruvold, W.H., 63
Bryant, D., 50
Buchanan, R.W., 219
Bucholtz, G., 50
bulimia nervosa, 164, 166, 178-82
Bureau of Justice Statistics, 98
Burgess, A.W., 132
Burke, J.D., 20
Burke, K.E., 20
Burstein, O.G., 172
Burton, L.A., 219
Burton, V.S., 22
butane gas, 21, 55

Caldwell, C., 100
Caldwell, C.H., 19, 104
Camburn, 21
Campbell, S.B., 208
Campione, J.C., 215

Carpenter, W.T., 219
Catalano, R.F., 50
Causcasians, 20, 23, 94, 98, 110, 134, 142, 172, 174, 181, 214
Centers for Disease Control, 22, 60, 61, 62, 63, 122
Check, J.V.P., 93
Chesney, M.A., 140
child protection agencies, 31, 34, 75, 84, 85, 132
children, 11, 22, 82, 84, 106-7, 116, 134, 148-49, 189, 197, 202-3, 207, 210-12; development of, 27-42, 186-87. *See also* abuse, child; adolescents; neglect, child
chlamydia, 139, 144
Christopherson, C.R., 125
church, the. *See* religion
Clark, F.L., 216
Clarke, G.N., 167
Clemens, N.A., 18, 228
clergy, 159, 160, 166, 203; as counselors, 17, 18, 23, 31, 34, 42-44, 50, 61, 77, 78, 85, 101, 122, 140, 180, 197, 203, 219, 239; and mental health professionals, 51, 227-32; and referrals, 124, 174, 212-13
cocaine, 20-21, 49, 56, 60
Coeytano, R., 62
Cohen, C., 61
collaboration, 227-32
Collins, D., 50
conduct disorder, 84, 193-99
Conrad, N., 23
contraception, 21, 122, 124-25, 126, 139
Cooksey, E. C., 125
Cooper, B., 210
Corradi, R. B., 18, 228
Cotton, N. U., 101
Coursey, R. D., 220
Crawford, I., 142
crime, 19, 22, 69, 132, 134, 193-99, 220
Crumley, F. E., 48
Cullen, F. T., 22
cultural factors, 52, 63, 70, 78, 85, 94, 101-2, 113, 119, 134, 160, 167, 181-82, 189, 197-98, 207, 214, 221
Cundick, B., 21, 122

daCosta, G.A., 83
Dadds, M.R., 199
Dahl, R.E., 164, 165
Daro, D., 42, 76
date rape, 11, 89-96

Davantes, B., 141
Davidson, L., 171
Davis, L., 82
Davis, T.C., 91
death, 47, 49, 76, 98, 137, 138, 140, 155-60, 164, 210
DeBlassie, R.R., 21, 125
DeBruyn, L.M., 78
delinquency, 22, 193-99
depression, 23, 30, 36, 133, 155-76, 239; and addiction, 48, 68, 69, 70; and disorders, 178, 179, 181, 186, 195, 197, 211, 214; and illness, 51, 138, 141, 149; and trauma, 83, 84, 98, 101
Deshler, D.D., 216
Desmond, S.M., 93
Diagnostic and Statistical Manual of Mental Disorders (DSM), 48
discipline, 39, 73, 76
Dishion, T.J., 199
divorce, 18, 76, 105-13, 159, 210
Donahue, M.J., 19, 22
dopamine, 187
Douvan, E., 77
Dowd, T.J., 20, 50
drugs, 44, 49, 54-58, 60, 73, 76, 92, 133, 134, 137, 164, 165, 172, 189. *See also* medication; substance abuse
Dunaway, R.G., 22
Dweck, C.S., 211
dyslexia, 211, 214

eating disorders, 83, 166, 177-83, 230
Eccles, J.S., 108
Eckenrode, J., 75
education, 68, 77, 85, 108, 118, 141, 166, 173, 212-13, 214
Eggertson-Tacon, C., 133
Elders, M.J., 66
Elifson, K.W., 20
Elliott, D.S., 21
Ellis, G.M., 92
Eriksen, M.P., 66
ethnic factors, 30, 101, 119, 134, 142, 151, 178
Evans, T.D., 22

Fallon, B.A., 180
families, 34-44, 93, 132, 133-34; and faith, 18, 50, 227-28, 239; stability in, 22, 27, 33, 50, 157; and illness, 148, 149, 219; instability in, 17, 30, 31, 34-35, 76, 107, 131, 172, 202, 203, 227; and treatment, 51, 61, 68-69, 85, 99, 180, 188, 197; and violence, 77-78, 101, 174. *See also* parents; stepfamilies; therapy, family
Faulkenberry, J.R., 123
Federal Bureau of Investigation, 22
Field, B., 139
Field, J., 139
Fine, D., 124
Fisher, R.L., 169
Fisher, S., 169
Fitchett, G., 219
Fitzpatrick, K.M., 22
Fleming, J.E., 164
Foley, L.A., 93
Folkman, S., 140
Fortune, M.M., 78
Francis, L.J., 21
Franklin, K.M., 109
Freiberg, P., 67
Frost, C.J., 23
Furstenberg, F.F., 106

Gadow, K.D., 167
Gallop, R., 85
Gallup, G.H., 18, 19, 20, 21, 50, 62, 173, 227
Gallup Youth Survey, 20, 22, 23, 62
Gamblers Anonymous, 70
gambling, 67-72
gangs, 19, 22
Garbarino, James, 32, 34, 36
Garrison, C.Z., 172
gender factors, 23, 93, 172, 198, 230; females, 21, 68, 82, 84, 85, 89-96, 121-29, 167, 172, 178, 182, 196, 197, 218, 221, 230; males, 23, 55, 61, 63, 68, 70, 78, 82, 92, 93, 98, 121, 155, 167, 172, 174, 196, 197, 202, 218
Gershon, S., 191
Giaresso, R., 93
Giovino, G.O., 66
Ginther, D.W., 132
Glei, D.A., 121, 122, 125, 126
Glenn, N.D., 108
Glick, P.C., 116
Glod, C.A., 82
glue, 21, 55
Goldfarb, A.F., 139
Goldstein, C.E., 23, 172
Goltz, J.W., 108
gonorrhea, 139, 145
Goodchild, G., 93

Gordon, J.S., 131
Gorsuch, R.L., 21, 50
Gould, M., 174
grief, 48, 116-17, 138, 140, 149, 151, 155-76
Griffin, C.B., 137
Guild, P., 126
Guilkey, D.K., 125
Guttman, E., 34, 36
Gwinn, M., 142

Haggerty, K.P., 50
Hall, J., 93
Hall, M.N., 69
hallucinogens, 55-56
Hamilton, L.R., 74
Hammer, L.D., 182
Hannah, M.T., 227
Hanlon, T.E., 219
Hansen, D.J., 78
Hansen, G.L., 108
Haraway, C.K., 20
Hardert, R.A., 20, 50
Harkness, W.L., 90
Harman, C.R., 220
Harrow, M., 218
Hartmann, C.R., 132
Hartmann, D.P., 208
Harvey, M.R., 90, 91, 92, 94
Hastings, E., 227
Hastings, H., 227
Hawkins, J.D., 50
Haydel, F., 182
Hayward, C., 182
Heaton, T.B., 108
Hechtman, L., 191
Hegar, R.C., 78
Heishman, S.J., 62
Helton, J.R., 132
Henningfield, J.E., 61, 62
Henrichs, D.W., 219
hepatitis B, 139, 145
heroin, 21, 57
herpes, genital, 139, 144-45
Herzog, D.B., 178, 179
Hick, R., 174
Hicks, D., 94
Higgins, P.L., 22
Hinshaw, P., 199
Hinshaw, S., 199
Hispanics, 20, 94, 134, 181
HIV, 137-145

Hofferth, S.L., 124
Hohmann, A.A., 25, 227
Holderness, C.C., 178
Holttum, J., 191
Hood, J.E., 83
Hood, R.W., 21
Horn, W.F., 216
Horney, Karen, 33
Hughes, D., 142
Hughes, J.O., 90
human papilloma virus, 139, 145
hyperactivity, 185-91

illness, 210; physical, 29-30, 33, 36, 147-53, 159, 187, 188, 202, 203, 205, 218; mental, 30, 36, 51, 76, 133, 149, 166, 197, 220
incest, 81-87
Indian Gambling Regulatory Act of 1988, 70
Ingram, B.L., 18
inhalants, 49, 55

Jaffe, R., 62
Jaklitsch, B., 75
James, J.E., 199
James, M., 123
Janoff-Bulman, R., 109
Jarvis, S.V., 132
Jensen, J.M., 50
Jensen, L., 21, 122
Johnson, A., 19
Johnson, A.M., 139
Johnson, J., 189, 206
Johnson, J.M., 78, 85
Johnson, K., 50
Johnson, P., 93
Johnson, W., 123
Johnson, W.G., 178
Johnston, L.D., 60, 61

Kalichman, S.C., 141
Karon, J.M., 142
Kaslow, F.W., 210
Kaufman, J., 164, 165
Keith, B., 110
Keller, M.B., 179
Kendall, P.C., 190, 199
Kennedy, C.E., 118
Kennedy, G.E., 118
Keshavan, M.S., 218
Kethineni, S.R., 22
Khare, M., 142

Killen, J.D., 182
Kilpatrick, D.G., 98, 103
King, P.K., 125
Kirkpatrick, B., 219
Klerman, L.V., 126
Kline, A.E., 227
Klingaman, L.R., 90
Knowles, J., 123, 126
Koenig, H.G., 18, 23, 62, 100, 102, 113, 118, 173, 228, 229
Kolko, D.J., 23, 172
Koop, C.E., 98
Koopman, C., 134
Koss, M.P., 90, 91, 92, 94
Koyle, P., 21, 122
Kozlowski, L.T., 62
Kramer, T.L., 104
Kulka, R.A., 77
Kurtz, G.L., 132
Kurtz, P.D., 132

Ladouceur, R., 70
Langabeer, K., 134
Larson, D.B., 18, 113, 229
Larson, L.E., 108
Lavori, P.W., 179
learning disabilities, 30, 209-16
Lefley, H.P., 94
Lehman, W.E.K., 20
Leitenberg, H., 92
Lester, D., 23, 69
Levine, D.W., 62
Levine, J., 219
Lewinsohn, P.M., 167
Leyser, Y., 151
Litt, I.F., 182
Llabre, M., 94
Loda, F., 126
Loranger, A.W., 218
Lowe, D., 18
Lowe, D.W., 18
LSD, 49
Lucas, L.A., 229
Lucke, G.M., 93
Lujan, C., 78
Lukasik, V., 180
Lunderberg, G.D., 98
Lydiard, R.B., 178

Mahler, K.A., 134
Mahler, Margaret, 29
Malamuth, N.M., 93

Males, M.A., 17
Malinosky-Rummell, R., 78
Maloney, H.N., 229
manic/depressive illness, 30, 164, 196
Marengo, J.T., 218
marijuana, 21, 49, 54, 60
Markowitz, J., 138
Marmar, C.R., 156
Martin, S.L., 101
May, P.A., 78
McAuliffe, T., 141
McCarraher, D.R., 101
McClellan, J., 164
McCormack, A., 132
McKain, B., 166
McKenry, P.C., 107, 118
McKeown, R.E., 172
McLendon, K., 93
McMahon, R.J., 199
McQuillan, G., 142
MDMA, 58
medication, 63, 101, 159, 165, 166, 181, 187, 189, 205, 206, 214, 218-19
mental health, 17, 24, 50, 227
mental health professionals, 18, 27, 44, 227-32, 239; and abuse, 31, 75, 78, 85, 93; and addiction, 51-52, 63, 70; and disorders, 181, 189, 196, 197, 203, 206, 214; and family crises, 106, 107, 108-9, 118, 126, 134; and grief, 158, 159-60, 166-67; and illness, 141, 150-51, 166-67
mental illness. See illness, mental
methamphetamine, 57
Miler, B.C., 121, 122, 125, 126
Miller, A.T., 133
Miller, E.C., 125
Miller, L.F., 107, 110, 116
Miskelly, S., 228
Mollica, R.C., 77, 100
Moncher, F.J., 76
Monitoring the Future Study, 55-58
mood disorders, 30
Moore, K.A., 121, 122, 125, 126
Mor-Barak, M., 133
Morgan, S.P., 106
Moritz, G.M., 172
Morrison, R.R., 121, 122, 125, 126
Morse, B.J., 21
Mothers Against Drunk Driving, 50
Mullen, K., 21
Mullis, R., 123
Mulry, G., 141

Multhauf, K., 141
Murray, J.B., 68

National Association for Prevention of Child Abuse, 31
National Center for Child Abuse and Neglect, 132
National Center for Educational Statistics, 17
National Center for Health Statistics, 22, 23
National Clearinghouse on Child Abuse and Neglect Information Survey on Mandatory Reporting, 77
National Council of Welfare, 68
National Highway Traffic Safety Administration, 50
Native Americans, 70, 78
Neal, A.M., 207
neglect, child, 32, 34, 75, 76, 77, 132, 134, 229
Nelson, B., 164, 165
New Beginnings, 74
Newcomb, M.D., 123
Newman, B.M., 118
Newman, S.C., 70
Noe, T., 50
Norton, A.J., 107, 110, 116

obsessive-compulsive disorder, 30, 203, 206
Ochberg, F.M., 100, 102
O'Donnel, J.P., 216
O'Donnell, C.R., 22
Office of the Attorney General of California, 75
Offord, D.R., 164
O'Leary, K.D., 199
Olsen, J., 21, 122
Olweus, D., 199
O'Malley, P.M., 60, 61
Omizo, M.M., 215
O'Neil, P.M., 178
Orme, J.G., 78
Orn, H., 70
Orthner, D.K., 228, 229
Orton, J.D., 132

Page, D.I., 101
panic disorder, 69, 141, 202-3, 204, 206
parents, 115-20, 123, 134, 186, 189, 211, 212, 213-14; as child abusers, 35-42, 74, 76, 77, 82, 107; as substance abusers, 31, 34, 60, 61, 67, 73, 76, 106; and divorce,

107, 109; and illness, 30, 149, 172, 188; relations with teens, 19, 20, 27-29, 42-44, 91, 209
Pargament, K.I., 100, 118, 151
Parker, H.C., 190
Parrott, L., 50
pastoral counseling, 18, 205, 228. See also clergy, as counselors
pastors. See clergy
Patterson, G.R., 199
Patterson, V., 21
Payne, G.L., 22
PCP, 58
Peck, G.Q., 91
peer relations, 19, 20, 22, 43, 44, 93, 126, 141, 149, 151, 187
Perel, J., 164, 165
Perper, J.A., 23, 172, 174
Perry, C.L., 66
Perry, L., 93
Perry, S.W., 138
Petersen, D.M.M., 20
Petersen, L.R., 142
Peterson, K.C., 104
Pill, C.J., 117
Planned Parenthood Federation of America, 121
Poling, K., 166
Pollay, R.W., 66
pornography, 37, 75
Porter, B., 199
post-traumatic stress disorder, 84, 85, 90, 97-104
poverty, 17, 30, 36, 68, 132
Powers, J.L., 75
pregnancy, 17, 18, 19, 21, 121-29, 230
Preston, J., 189, 206
Preston, John, 32
Price, S.J., 107
Prout, M.F., 104
psychotherapy, 101, 109, 110, 159, 167, 181, 206, 214

Quigg, B., 133
Quinn, S.C., 100

racial factors, 30, 101, 119, 134, 142, 151, 178
rape, 11, 17, 75, 89-96, 124
Rando, T.A., 156
Rea, D.S., 20
Redlich, F.C., 77, 100
referrals, 44, 228, 229; for abuse, 77-78, 85, 93; for addiction, 51, 63; for depression,

166, 174; for disorders, 181, 188, 195, 205, 206, 212-13; for family crises, 109, 118, 126, 133, 134; for illness, 140, 141, 150, 220

Regier, D.A., 20

religion, in teen's lives, 17-26, 62, 67, 125, 173, 203, 227-28, 239. *See also* religious community

religious community: and abuse, 76-77, 84-85, 92-93, 99-101; and addiction, 50, 62, 69; and family crises, 108-9, 118, 125-26; and disorders, 180-81, 188, 196-97, 206; and grief, 159, 166 173-74; and illness, 140-41, 150, 151, 219-20; and mental health, 227-28, 229-30. *See also* religion

religious workers, 31, 44, 61, 77. *See also* clergy

Resnick, H.S., 98, 103

Resnick, J., 101

Reynolds, W.M., 166

Rindfuss, R.R., 125

Roberts, J.E., 109

Robinson, L.C., 118

Robinson, T.N., 182

Robinson, W.L., 142

Rohde, P., 167

Rosenberg, D.R., 191

Rosenberg, P.S., 142

Rossignol, A.M., 122

Roth, C., 172

Rotheram-Buros, M.J., 134

Rourke, B.P., 211

Rowatt, G.W., 50, 166

Rubin, R.H., 19, 104

runaways, 75, 131-36

Ryan, N.D., 164, 165

Sacks, N.R., 179

Sadik, C., 180

Samaryk, M., 142

Samford, J., 227

Sanborn, M.D., 20

Sanders, M.R., 199

Sandler, B.R., 90

Santello, M.D., 92

Santiago, J.M., 227

Sanders, G., 123

Saoud, J.C., 180

Saunders, B.E., 103

Sawyer, R.G., 93

Schaffer, D., 174

Schaffer, H.J., 69

Schindler, F., 227

schizophrenia, 29, 186, 196, 217-23

Schlegel, R.P., 20

Schlundt, D.G., 178

schools, 19, 20, 21, 22, 30, 36, 75, 78, 83, 187, 189, 194-95, 209-14

Schumaker, J.B., 216

Schwartz, S., 199

Schwarz, R.A., 104

Schweers, J., 172

Scott, C.S., 94

Scott, M.A.K., 139

Scott, R., 99

Seeley, J.R., 167

Seeley, J.W., 34, 36

Seitz, Frank, 42

Seligman, M.E.P., 166

sex, 19, 21, 23, 44, 121-26, 134, 139, 157, 194, 239

sexuality, 18, 37, 43, 126, 140, 164

Shafranske, E.P., 229

Sharlin, S.A., 133

Sheridan, M.J., 229

Shrum, W., 108

Shubiner, H., 99

Sikkema, K.J., 141

Silitsky, D., 109

Simpson, D.D., 20

Sivan, A.B., 219

Skatrud, J., 126

Skopin, A.R., 118

Slade, J., 62

Slade, J.D., 61

Sloan, L., 93

Smart, R.G., 133

Smith, C.R., 211

Smith, F.O., 69

smoking. *See* tobacco

Somlai, A.M., 141

Soll, S.K., 132

Spek, N.B., 132

Spilka, B., 21

Stark, R., 22

STDs, 122, 126, 137-45

Stebelsky, G., 70

stepfamilies, 18, 115-20

stimulants, 189

Storment, J.M., 91

Strader, T., 50

Streets, F.J., 77, 100

stress: in families, 31, 37, 74, 76, 109, 118,

132, 151, 196, 202; on teens, 33, 62, 98, 141,172, 179, 186, 205, 210

Studer, M., 21, 125

substance abuse, 17, 18, 19-21, 27, 30, 47-58, 123, 132, 149, 157; and trauma, 76, 78, 84, 98; and disorders, 178, 204, 205, 211; and gambling, 68, 69, 70; and suicide, 171, 174, 229; by parents, 37, 76, 202; and religious belief, 23, 239

suicide, 17, 19, 23, 68, 69, 124, 126, 133, 171-76, 229, 239; and abuse, 78, 83; and depression, 164, 165, 166, 178, 181; and illness, 150, 218; and grief, 156, 157, 159, 160

Summerfelt, A.T., 219

Sylvain, C., 70

syphilis, 139, 145

Taylor, C.B., 182

Taylor, H.G., 216

Taylor, L., 215

teenagers. *See* adolescents

Teicher, M.H., 82

Tittle, C.R., 22

therapy, 85, 94, 181, 187, 205, 206; cognitive, 51-52, 70, 166, 167; family, 85, 101, 119, 133, 166, 167, 181, 206, 220-21; group, 85, 94, 100, 141, 159, 181, 221. *See also* psychotherapy

Thomas, S.B., 100

Thornton, A., 21, 125

Thorton, 21

trauma, 22, 32-34, 48, 73, 78, 84, 85, 90, 91, 94, 97-104, 124, 134, 159

treatment, 228, 230; for addiction, 50-51, 62-63, 69-70; for disorders, 180-82, 187, 188-89, 196-97, 206; for family crises, 108-10, 118-19, 125-26, 133-34; for grief, 159-60, 166-67, 173-74; for illness, 138, 141, 150-51, 218-21; for trauma, 76-78, 92-94, 100-101

trichomoniasis, 139, 145

truancy, 51, 132, 195

Turner, S.M., 207

Tzelepis, A., 99

U.S. Bureau of the Census, 17, 106-07

U.S. Department of Health and Human Services, 50

Valois, R.F., 172

Vaulx-Smith, P., 218

Veroff, J., 77

Veronen, L.J., 103

Vicary, J.R., 90

Vincent, M., 123

Vincent, M.L., 172

violence, 17, 22, 27, 30, 33, 37, 60, 69, 73-104, 156, 220

Virkler, H.A., 18

Vitulano, L.A., 216

Vogel, J., 69

Wadsworth, J., 139

Wahl, O.F., 220

Walsh, B.T., 180

Walsh, G.W., 133

Wang, C.T., 76

Warner, M.M., 216

Warren, M.P., 178

Wartella, M.E., 176

Wasman, M., 18, 228

Weaver, A.J., 18, 23, 77, 100, 102, 113, 118, 166, 173, 227, 228, 229

Weaver, C.N., 108

Weinbender, M.L.M., 122

Weiss, G., 191

Welch, M.R., 2

Wellings, K., 139

Wells, E. A., 50

Wender, P., 191

Werry, J., 164

Wesley, A., 93

Westermeyer, J. F., 218

Whitaker, A. H., 179

Whitaker, L., 139

White, S. D., 21, 125

Williams, D., 19

Williamson, D. E., 164, 165

Wilmer, C. M., 229

Wilson, D. M., 182

Wineberg, H., 116

Winnicott, D. W., 27

Wisecarver, S. J., 23

Wood, N. S., 230

Woodside, M., 76

Word, C. O., 52

Wright, L. S., 23

Wright, P. G., 228

Yarnold, B. M., 21

Young, Jeffrey, 40

Zelenak, J. P., 23, 172

Zellman, G., 93

Zitlow, D., 70

Zucker, K. J., 83

Zuravin, S. J., 78

Printed in the United States
78134LV00006B/4